To Christopher Wilson and Steven Graham, with Love

wykked wyves
and the
woes of marriage

❖

Misogamous Literature from Juvenal to Chaucer

❖

KATHARINA M. WILSON
and
ELIZABETH M. MAKOWSKI

❖

State University of New York Press

Published by
State University of New York Press, Albany

©1990   State University of New York

Printed in the United States of America

For information, address State University of New York
Press, State University Plaza, Albany, NY   12246

Library of Congress Cataloging-in-Publication Data

Wilson, Katharina M.
    Wykked wyves and the woes of marriage : misogamous literature from
Juvenal to Chaucer / by Katharina M. Wilson, Elizabeth M. Makowski.
        p.   cm.—(SUNY series in medieval studies)
    Bibliography: p.
    Includes index.
    ISBN 0–7914–0062–X.   ISBN 0–7914–0063–8 (pbk.)
    1. Literature, Medieval—History and criticism.   2. Satire.
Medieval—History and criticism.   3. Marriage customs and rites,
Medieval.   4. Marriage in literature.   5. Misogyny in literature.
6. Wives in literature.   7. Women in literature.   8. Juvenal-
-Influence.   I. Makowski, Elizabeth M., 1951–   .   II. Title.
III. Series.
PN682.L68W55   1990
809'.93354—dc19   88–29156
                                                                  CIP

10 9 8 7 6 5 4 3 2 1

CONTENTS

ACKNOWLEDGMENTS

This book was born in conversation en route to Kalamazoo. One of us, we discovered, was a historian with a keen interest in literature; the other a literary scholar with a keen interest in history. With work that we both enjoyed, what began as a dissertation on the literature ended up as a book on the history of ideas.

This book would not have been possible without the help and support of many people. We gratefully acknowledge our special debts to Jean Wirth, Robert Nelson, A. Owen Aldridge, James Márchand, and James A. Brundage, for excellent advice and guidance; to Paul Pascal for a most helpful and kind reading of the penultimate version of the manuscript. To our anonymous readers, whose criticism was very beneficial, added thanks.

INTRODUCTION

A decision to remain unmarried, freely made, and in epochs hostile to such an "unnatural" course often valiantly adhered to, could have important economic and social consequences. In antiquity, women who were traditionally subordinate as wives could advance beyond the biologically determined life if they remained virgins or if they resisted pressure to remarry when widowed. Throughout the early Middle Ages, men and women vowed to chastity and living in monastic communities made major cultural contributions, while in late medieval Europe, only those young men who remained celibate could expect to attain the choicest positions of wealth, learning, and status that were at the bequest of the dominant corporate employer, the Church.[1]

In spite of a recently revived scholarly interest in "single blessedness," the persuasive literature that has traditionally recommended the celibate state remains inadequately studied.[2] Because misogamous (antimarriage) tracts in antiquity and throughout the Middle Ages were written almost exclusively by and for male readers, both literary critics and historians have dealt with them only incidentally—as a subspecies of, or as corollaries to, the broader category of literary misogyny.[3] The conflation of the two types is particularly understandable when dealing with the many medieval compilations addressed to the young man for the purpose of dissuading him from matrimony. Because woman was commonly associated in medieval theology and law with gross corporeality, sexual temptation, and lust, it is logical to assume that any polemic against carnal union necessarily included, or assumed, rejection of the gender that symbolized the lower appetites; that a caution against marriage, in short, necessarily involved a hatred or distrust of women.

I

Yet misogamy, far from being a category of misogyny, is by definition quite distinct: misogamy is the hatred of (opposition to) marriage; misogyny, the hatred of women. Misogamous ideals or those opposed to the rearing of children do not necessarily preclude the glorification of women, nor does the exaltation of marriage and childrearing necessarily entail the exaltation of women. Thus, for example, all dualistic heresies have historically rejected marriage and procreation because coition perpetuates the imprisonment of the divine spirit in evil flesh, yet some dualistic sects have granted women important positions in their religious hierarchies.[4] Similarly, the antigamous (or at least adulterous) tenets of courtly love ushered in a literary convention placing women on a pedestal. Conversely, while the Jews of antiquity glorified the marital ideal and imposed strict penalties on those evading their duty to marry, they also proposed stringent restrictions on the religious, social, and political involvement of [their] women and when the fifteenth-century Italian humanist argues from classical models that marriage is good, he does not, *ipso facto*, extol women as anything but, to use Diane Hughes' term, *invisible madonnas*.[5]

Some misogamous texts, then, are clearly misogynistic and some misogynistic texts are also misogamous, but some celibate propaganda is not misogynistic at all; on the contrary, some are panegyrics of chaste womanhood. Methodius' *Symposium*, for example, while deprecating marriage and exalting the chaste ideal, presents the misogamous arguments in erudite speeches by and about clearly admirable women.[6] Similarly, Heloise's argument against marriage contained in the twelfth-century *Historia Calamitatum* of Abelard, is misogamous but not misogynistic.[7] Granted, when that argument is delivered by a male persona, the likelihood of the occurrence of misogynistic topoi in support of antimarriage arguments increases rapidly, yet even in these instances, misogynistic topoi are often used only as supporting evidence (i.e., not as major arguments) for the misogamous polemic. When Theophrastus, John of Salisbury, and Peter of Blois, to name just a few, assert that marriage and philosophy do not mix because marital responsibilities and the resulting material needs prevent the scholar from dedicating all his energies to the pursuit of philosophy, then they are clearly misogamous but not necessarily misogynistic.[8] Moreover, when Jerome, Tertullian, and Augustine propose that virginity is more perfect than the married state, they do not (at least in this course of argumentation) deprecate women.[9] One of the most significant ideological ramifications of the bilateral chaste ideal promoted by the patristic writers, in fact, was the spiritual equality of the two sexes. When, on the other hand, the *persona* of Juvenal's *Sixth Satire* asserts that no woman could be found worthy to wed even a notorious adulterer, and that therefore the wish to marry is a clear indication of insanity, then he is not only misogamous but also misogynistic.[10]

Rhetorically, two clearly discernible branches of the topos of misogamy in ancient and medieval literature exist: first, limited misogamy, which advocates the celibate ideal of a select group; and second, unlimited misogamy, which promotes it for all.[11] This rhetorical distinction is clearly drawn by Quintilian (first century A.D.) and Boethius (sixth century A.D.). When discussing particular and general subject matters for deliberation, Quintilian distinguishes between the indefinite topos (*propositum*) *an vir ducat uxorem* (should a man marry?) and the limited topos (*causa*) *an vir sapiens* [Cato] *ducat uxorem* (would the wise man [or Cato] marry?). Boethius later maintains that a thesis (i.e., *an vir ducat uxorem*) belongs in the realm of dialectic and of philosophy, while the more specific questions of hypothesis are the domain of rhetoricians. Not limited to the schoolrooms of antiquity, these two misogamous topoi of rhetoric continued to be debated in medieval schools.[12]

Aside from the dual rhetorical grouping of works of misogamy, there is also a clear tripartite division of the topos (according to the dissuasive argument and methods it employs) into ascetic, philosophic, and general works of misogamy, all advocating celibacy in one or the other extreme of its application: promiscuity or inviolate chastity. Ascetic misogamy was initially eschatological, linking the avoidance of marriage to the expectation of an imminent cataclysm and the hope for heavenly reward, thereby emphasizing the importance of preparedness for the second coming of Christ.[13] Eschatological ascetic misogamy was the product of the Christian subculture in the Roman Empire. As such, it reflected ultimate dissatisfaction with the social and cultural institutions of the dominant Roman culture. The eschatological celibate and chaste ideal was preached to all Christians, male and female, who could anticipate eternal joy in heaven but only pain, suffering, and persecutions on earth.

Gradually, following its recognition as the state religion, the Church accepted marriage as a valuable and important institution for most of its members and championed the celibate ideal only for an elite, set apart by presumed sanctity.[14] Even in this its more pragmatic manifestation however, Christian ascetic misogamy differed fundamentally from pagan misogamy. Its preoccupation was with the genuinely chaste and/or virginal as opposed to the merely celibate ideal. It promoted antigamy on a much grander scale than did antique misogamous literature and, significantly, Christian ascetic misogamy addressed itself to both men and women. Emphasizing self-transcendence and a distrust of *all* appetites, it encouraged the mortification of the flesh as Christ-like conditioning for a life devoted to prayer and contemplation. The works of Jerome, notably his polemical treatise *Adversus Jovinianum,* established the tone and format of that genre for centuries to come.[15] Here the topos of misogamy becomes subordinate to the upholding of the chaste ideal, the speaker posing as a teacher of morality who praises the ideal of virginity—*propter regnum coelorum*—while denigrating marriage as an imperfect and impure state. In works of ascetic misogamy, as in most proposals for a hierarchical system of values, the ideals proposed for a select group are expected to be espoused but not practiced by all. It is this branch of misogamy that characterizes monastic propaganda in subsequent centuries.[16]

Second, philosophic misogamy advocates celibacy (not necessarily chastity) for a select group of philosophers and scholars because care for a family entails distractions from the more important concerns of philosophy, religion, and learning. The philosophical branch of misogamy usually traces its beginning from Theophrastus' *liber aureolus* preserved only in Jerome's *Adversus Jovinianum*, even though similar ideas were proposed by Plato, Epicurus, and proponents of the Neopythagorean and Stoic schools of philosophy. This type of misogamy is particularly characterized by its elitist exclusiveness; in the Middle Ages it is addressed to career men and propounds a moral applicable to and promoted for a select group of the clergy, learned *men* for whom promotion in a competitive setting was made adjunct to celibacy which guaranteed not only the dedication of all of their energies but also their absolute loyalty to their employers.[17] In this group of misogamous works, marriage is regarded not as sinful or insane, not as *morally* dangerous, but as unwise because it impedes the philosopher's freedom to think and to study. The narrative setting is usually moral-social; an experienced man feels compelled to instruct his friend concerning the burdens of married life and to remind him of the privileged status of celibacy.[18] Both ascetic and philosophic works of misogamy advocate pseudofamilial ties in place of actual families: Mary, the Church, and Christ as parents and spouses; disciples as children; Athena or Philosophy as wives.[19] Just as the burgeoning canon law treated lust as sin but the advocating of clerical marriage as heresy, philosophic misogamy considers multiple extramarital affairs far preferable to marriage.

Finally, general misogamy takes the incipient worldliness, secularism, and careerism of philosophical misogamy to its logical rhetorical roots. Juvenalian misogyny, farce, and a strikingly nonascetic blasphemy become commonplace. General misogamy carries misogyny to a *reductio ad absurdum* and advocates wifelessness on the grounds that no woman is worth marrying. Often, promiscuous celibacy is advocated as the desired form of wifelessness.[20] Intended for a mixed (lay and clerical) audience, works of general misogamy are often cast in vernacular verse.[21] The denunciation is usually not spoken *in propria persona*, and a stated purgative and medical purpose is found in the work which is reflected in the method of argumentation by inversion. In most cases, the inversions concern both contemporary marital ethics and contemporary desiderata of ideal female behavior; the Christian purposes of marriage—*proles, fides, sacramentum*—are presented as antivalues and woman is depicted as the embodiment and source of all of man's sufferings. Almost invariably there is a surrounding narrative setting justifying the attack, and the accusations, although absurdly exaggerated, cater to contemporary prejudices. A persistent undercurrent of irony exists, however, in this general branch of misogamy, which often serves to undercut the attacks on wives and marriage.[22] The irony pervading the texts prompts the observation that exploitation of misogynistic stereotypes serves not only to cater to contemporary prejudice but also to show how women are irrationally maligned. Tracts of general misogamy are invariably addressed to Everyman, thus claiming to answer the "infinite" universally applicable question *an vir ducat uxorem* always in the negative.

Misogamy as a topos is exploited in early Western literature for two fundamental purposes: propaganda and entertainment. Propagandistic works are substitutional, while entertaining texts are ironic. As propaganda, works of misogamy draw on a wide range of social, philosophic, and religious sentiments supporting the view that for a select group of people, usually men, especially those who distinguish themselves not so much by birth as by intellectual or religious achievements, celibacy is not only a viable alternative to marriage, but a wiser alternative at that. The men to whom philosophic misogamous propaganda is addressed and by whom it is composed are members of an intellectual elite who generate ideas, not children. Thus, the surrogate familial patterns offered to them are spiritual marriage with philosophy or the Church and spiritual parenthood by teaching.

As entertainment, on the other hand, the topos capitalizes on contemporary and perennial prejudices by presenting stereotypic accusations intended for a varied audience, thus catering to, and sometimes ridiculing, misogamous and misogynistic prejudices. The stereotypes of wifely misbehavior in works of general misogamy are funny because their stock characters are predictable, and, through obvious exaggeration, sufficiently removed from reality to appear comic rather than tragic. At the same time, the exaggerated episodes are based on clearly recognizable and observable behavioral traits, so that works of misogamy are a source of entertainment not only for generations of wife-beaters and henpecked husbands but also for the general audience. As in most comedy, so in comic and satiric misogamy, the humor derives from a clear incongruity between what is and what should be; between legal and social models and situational ethics, on the one hand, and actual human behavior, on the other; between institutionalized male superiority and occurrences of marital *mundus inversus*.

Both as propaganda and as entertainment, the topos of misogamy is the product and the reflection of a complex cultural matrix. Misogamy occurs in literature only when there is a certain level of civilization, order, and urbanization in a society and when women attain a certain level of economic or legal independence. When, conversely, a society struggles for survival and against anarchy, famine, and destruction, there is usually neither time for, nor interest in, marital casuistry: nomadic tribes and small agricultural communities do not seem to produce works of secular misogamy. Similarly, when women are in complete dependence on men, marital *dissuasiones*, particularly of the general kind, are ludicrous. Thus, the age of Trajan and Hadrian gave rise to Juvenal's Sixth Satire; the Christian controversy regarding marriage and celibacy occurred not during the early years of the persecutions but in the fourth century of legitimization and expansion; the reemergence of works of misogamy in the Middle Ages is concurrent with the rise of civilization, order, urbanization, and learning in the twelfth century.

Overtly misogynistic misogamy seems to surface at periods when the dichotomy between the legal inequality and *de facto* equality of women is quite pronounced and when there is some (often begrudged) improvement in the status of women—real or imagined. Thus, for example, the persona of Juvenal's Sixth Satire indignantly exploits an imperial Roman's dissatisfaction with the freedom, power, influence, education, and economic independence of Roman matrons. Correspondingly, the twelfth-century tracts of philosophic misogamy and the later

works of general misogamy embody clear and concerned pre-
occupations with the courtly love ideal and with the apparent
de facto equality of wives among the lower social classes respectively.

The marital ethics of the respective periods act as *matrices*
for the specific works of misogamy, particularly of general misogamy. Juvenal's Sixth Satire, for example, shows a pronounced preoccupation with the "marital evils" of Imperial
Rome: declining birthrate, easy and frequent divorces, erotic
fascination with social inferiors, and unprocreative sexual intercourse. Medieval works of general misogamy, on the other
hand, show an overriding preoccupation with the indissoluble
nature of Christian marriage, the economic and the physically
destructive effects of matrimony, and concern with social
mobility.

While all three branches of literary misogamy oppose marriage, they differ considerably in their reasons for promoting
the celibate ideal. These reasons are contingent both upon their
chosen audiences and the professed limits of their moral application. Ascetic misogamy, originally directed to a wide Christian readership, came to be restricted to a monastic audience in
the Middle Ages. Consequently, its proposed hierarchical value
system concerned all Christians, but in the Middle Ages its
practice was restricted to men and women living under a rule
and to the clergy. Ascetic misogamy propounds that the virginal state is superior to marriage because the unmarried can
better devote themselves to the service of the Lord than the
married, but that procreative marital state is best-suited for laymen. When Jerome, for example, sarcastically remarks that he
does not condemn marriage (which he equates with barley in
comparison to the wheat of virginity) but permits it to those
who are frightened to sleep alone at night, then he is clearly
proposing a universal hierarchy of values.[23]

Philosophic misogamy, on the other hand, is written by and
addressed to the learned, without any claim to universal applicability. The promoted moral, that wife and family are a burden
to the philosopher-scholar who should devote his time and energies to the more important concerns of philosophy rather

than to the care for a family, concerns only and pronouncedly the professional clerical elite. When Peter of Blois, for example, resignedly observes that marriage is one thing but the marriage of a philosopher is another, he restricts the field of application of his *dissuasio* to learned men.[24]

Finally, general misogamy is written for Everyman: its topology is all-inclusive and its moral applicable to all. Writers of general misogamy argue that marriage is madness; that, because it lasts longer, it is a worse kind of self-destruction than suicide; and that marriage is hell for the poor, victimized husband whose goods and energies are drained by almighty Woman. The addressee of the very popular fourteenth century anonymous *De conjuge non ducenda,* for example, is presented a glimpse of marital life by angelic messengers that entails his total—physical, mental, and moral—destruction by his future wife who is painted as the representative of all women.

Methodologically, the three branches of misogamy—ascetic, philosophic, and general—differ in their use of documentation, language, and style. Works of ascetic misogamy dissuade by exemplification. Addressed to men and, less frequently, women, they rely heavily on an ornate florilegian structure, authoritative tone, and contrastive catalogues of *exempla in malo* (of evil and destructive women) and *exempla in bono* (of chaste and virtuous women) predominantly from biblical but also from pagan sources. They almost invariably refer to the Pauline epistles as their source of inspiration and systematically discredit the Old Testament procreative ideal by glossing the Old Covenant with the New. Tracts of philosophic misogamy, on the other hand, dissuade by theorization. They are preceptual and authoritative and contain catalogues only of *exempla in malo* concerning marital tribulations gathered predominantly from pagan and mythological sources. The tone is still authoritative and the documentation is learned, but because their audience is entirely male, the upholding of the virginal ideal for women (manifested in the *exempla in bono* catalogues of ascetic misogamy), the *exempla in bono* (of chastity and faithfulness) are omitted as are panegyrics of virginity. Finally, works of general misogamy dissuade by inversion;

characterized by everyday specificity, they claim to rely on experience rather than authority. The *personae* of general *dissuasiones* almost invariably express a regressive view of history. Thus, the *ubi sunt* theme (where are all the good wives of yesteryear?) is frequent.

On the whole, works of ascetic and philosophic misogamy (i.e., elitist misogamy) are written in Latin, while tracts of general misogamy are either written in the vernacular or become popularized through vernacular translations. Most works of ascetic and philosophic misogamy are written in prose but most works of general misogamy are in verse. Both ascetic and general misogamous works use frequent obscenities, usage once again reflecting their respective social matrices: polymorphous-scatological versus lustful-sexual.[25]

This book surveys the most commonly compiled and most frequently cited works of medieval misogamous literature written for a secular (that is, nonmonastic) audience. It combines a literary-critical with a historical perspective. Consequently, the analysis of Juvenal's Sixth Satire is preceded by an overview of Roman marriage law and custom; Walter Map's *Valerius* is examined in the context of the high medieval scholasticism that gave it purpose.

When looked at in this way, the easy identification of anti-matrimonial with misogynistic literature proves decidedly unwarranted. In terms of repeated imagery, continuous themes, and rhetorical devices, misogamous writings closely parallel and reflect economic and demographic shifts, theological and legal innovation. Anything but monolithic, misogamy varies in tone, style, and intent and encompasses celibate options ranging from the virtuous to the vicious. Paradox abounds—ascetic misogamy, for instance, written in what has been called an "extravagantly misogynistic" era, created the justification for centuries of the unintended yet institutionalized sex equity called monasticism.

Finally, a careful analysis of the constituent literary devices in each branch of the literature strongly suggests a link between the growing secularism and careerism of the late Middle Ages and the reduction in women's social status and public options.

An increased tendency to treat women first and foremost as wives and mothers, to confine them to an ever-more restrictive version of the household, corresponds to a rediscovery of the classics. Just as twelfth-century lawyers and schoolmen used the ancients as models, so the writers and compilers of late medieval antigamous tracts reveal a reliance on characteristic Juvenalian misogamy. Filled with attacks on aggressive, lustful, and competitive women, this literature might have amused a Roman audience; at the same time, its deployment of ancient prejudices was relevant (and useful) to a society in transition to the early modern era.

❖ I ❖

Classical Antecedents

Marriage law and custom in Imperial Rome

The evolution of Roman marriage

In Republican Rome, marriage was a relatively stable institution chiefly because of the power of the *patria potestas*.[1] Marriage during the Republic signified the passing of a young woman from one *manus* (that of her father or eldest male relative) into another (that of her husband). The basis of Roman legal theory that mandated all women to be under the custody of males was the supposed weakness and light-mindedness (*infirmitas sexus, levitas animi*) of the female sex. In her unmarried state, a girl was in full dependence on the *pater familias*, the eldest male member in her family whose power extended to matters of life and death for all male and female members of the household. Sons were automatically emancipated after the *pater familias* died if they had by then reached adulthood, but girls only if they became Vestal Virgins.

Girls were married at an early age, and even though the father arranged their children's marriages, the consent of both partners was necessary for the betrothal and the wedding. The bride, however, was allowed to refuse only if she could prove that her prospective husband was morally unfit for the marriage (*Dig.* 1.12 [Ulpian]). This legal provision was probably without much consequence, for as Pomeroy observes, "it is unlikely that girls of twelve ... were in fact able to resist a proposed marriage."[2]

Frequently, there was a great discrepancy of ages between the spouses, for even though fourteen-year-old boys were legally entitled to marry, they very rarely did so before age twenty-five or thirty, and then they married very young girls. Pierre Grimal comments on some of the reasons for this custom:

The husband's intention was naturally to form the character of
the person who was to be the lady of the house, in accordance
with his own desires. For him it was not enough to have her
come into his home innocent and undefiled. He wanted someone
who had not been exposed to any moral influence before his.
Was this a precaution stemming from jealousy, from a conscious
wish to establish his supremacy as a husband more easily? Or
simply the inevitable effect of ancestral tradition?[3]

The reasons proposed by Grimal are, of course, similar to those
advocated by Hesiod in the *Works and Days*. Hesiod recommends that a man marry, at age thirty, a girl of about fourteen
so that he can teach her good working habits. There seem to
be several reasons for the prolonged celibate life of men. In
Rome, as in any slave society, concubinage was widely practiced and, unlike the wife, the concubine or mistress could be
chosen by the young Roman himself. Moreover, society condoned a young man's premarital sexual liberty, as Cato's often
quoted remarks on the subject indicate. One day, returning
from the forum, Cato saw a young man leaving a courtesan's
house and hiding his face. The stern censor is reputed to have
said: "Courage, child, it is right that you should frequent harlots instead of going after honest women." The next day, the
young man greeted Cato in the same spot, this time without
trying to cover his face. Cato remarked, "I told you to frequent
the house, not to live there."

The double morality continued after marriage and *de facto*
polygamy was practiced widely. Adultery was a stain (*stuprum*)
for the wife only, punishable by death and, in a later period, by
banishment. According to Cato (*Au. Gellius* X, 23), a husband
might kill his wife without fear of punishment, but if he was
the one committing adultery, she must not dare to touch him
with a finger, and, what is more, she would not have the right
to punish him. The condoning of the double standard among
the aristocracy seems to have been based chiefly on pragmatic
reasons: having legitimate heirs was the husband's main concern. In addition, the concept of bloodtaint, as Grimal has ad-
mirably argued, lay at the heart of Roman sexual morality.[4] A
man could not contract this taint in any heterosexual affair. He

could, however, be tainted in a homosexual relationship if he was the "passive" (i.e., receiving) partner. Thus, there was no practical reason for restricting the heterosexual affairs of men and the relationships of women who were not considered worthy to be mothers: slaves, dancers, freedwomen, registered prostitutes, or any woman who happened to have contracted the *stuprum*. In fact, as Mommsen points out, Romans originally had no statutory prohibition of sexual relationships and of immoral behavior. Only women of the aristocracy were liable to punishment for prostitution (*Liv.* X, 31; XXV, 2) and in the official registers kept by the aediles only prostitutes were included but not dancers, fluteplayers, or actresses (*Tac. Ann.*, ii, 85). Consequently, any woman who did not belong to the upper classes of the indigenous population could conduct her sexual life with as much freedom as she wished.

Few spinsters were found in Roman upper-class society because most women married at least once. One reason for this occurrence is demographic: according to Cassius Dio, there were fewer women than men within the upper classes; some estimates place the difference as high as 17 percent.[5] Pomeroy observes:

> As in Greece, this disproportion was the result of the shorter lifespan of females, whose number fell off sharply once the childbearing years were reached. There were the additional factors of the selective infanticide and exposure of female infants, and, probably more important, a subtle but pervasive attitude that gave preferential treatment to boys.[6]

Moreover, girls were expensive: dowries among the rich were recorded at a million sesterces. Cicero, for example, when forced to pay the third installment on his daughter Tullia's dowry, contemplated arranging for her divorce.[7] The demographic imbalance of men and women is also attested by some archaeological studies. Lawrence Angel's study of skeletal remains in Greece under Roman dominion shows the adult longevity as 34.3 years for women and 40.2 years for men, and Keith Hopkins' tombstone findings show an even greater discrepancy in longevity: he places the median age of wives at 34 but of husbands at 46.5.[8]

The divorce rate was very low in Republican times and given the fact that the father's and subsequently the husband's power over the wife was almost unrestricted, and that they could kill her for certain crimes without fear of punishment, there was probably little opportunity or incentive for divorce.

Sterility, the reason for the first reported Roman divorce, was probably the chief practical reason for repudiation, for the Romans, as J. P. Wilkinson argues, were anxious about population: "Traditions about measures designed to increase the population . . . were [still] current in the late Republic."[9]

The cumulative implication from ancient writers regarding marriage in early Republican times is that marriage was a stable institution chiefly because of the unshakable and unquestioned power of the *patria potestas*. Consequently, the role and status of women were also stable, and their duties and responsibilities clearly defined.

A great change in the attitude toward women and marriage commenced with the political and economic upheavals in the second century B.C. and reached its height during the Empire. The change had many facets.

The military ideal was altered by the relatively unbroken peace; the religious climate changed because of the introduction into Rome of several almost omnipotent Oriental goddesses. The first century A.D. saw the growing worship of Cybele Magna Mater, the Bona Dea, and above all, the mysteries of the universal goddess from the Nile.[10] The cult of Cybele was the antipole of the limited and restricted native cults of female deities, of the cults of the Pudicitia Patricia, the Fortuna Muliebris, and the Fortuna Virilis, for example, because Cybele was the goddess of wives, mothers, virgins, and prostitutes alike. While the cults of these female deities coexisted with the militant and masculine cult of Mithras, their growing popularity not only undermined the religious importance of the indigenous Latin gods and of the male hierarchy of the Olympians, it also counteracted the image of the often-defeminized and highly specialized Olympic and native goddesses. As Jerome Carcopino observes, "One great spiritual fact dominated the history of the Empire: the advent of personal religions which followed on the conquest of Rome by the mysticism of the East."[11]

The economic status of women was greatly improved by the first century because of their ability to hold, accumulate, and inherit wealth. The economic change was fundamental to women's relative emancipation, for, as Verena Zinserling observes in her study on Greek and Roman women, "the key to the relation to power between men and women is, as in all other things, private ownership. The greater the economic independence of woman becomes, the more emancipated she is in all spheres of life."[12]

The legal emancipation of the Roman matron paralleled her economic freedom and was manifested in the growth of the number of marriages without *manus,* the abolition of automatic agnateship over women by Claudius, and in the increased divorce rate. By Hadrian's reign, for example, a married woman did not need a guardian even to draft her will, and she was the mistress of her own property because of her *sine manu* status. The juridicial doctrine of the moral weakness of the female was also impaired by Augustus' legislation, for according to the *ius trium liberorum,* a freeborn woman who bore three children and a freedwoman who bore four children were exempt from any guardianship, because as Augustus argued, those women had demonstrated responsible behavior by bearing the children Rome needed. That the change in attitude regarding woman's legal status was completed in the second century A.D. is clear from the remarks of Gaius: "There is no serious reason whatsoever why persons of the female sex who are of full age should remain under guardianship" (*Gaius,* 190, 191).

There is also some evidence for the limited political emancipation of Roman women. Otto Kiefer points out that during and after the reign of Tiberius, authors speak of an *ordo matronarum* (*Val. Max.* 2, 1), of *mulierum conventus* (Suet., Galba, 5), of a *conventus matronalis,* and *mulierum senatus.*[13] Lampridius calls the women's decrees "ridiculous" and says that they were concerned chiefly with etiquette. On the more serious side, we have Livy's account of the repeal of the Lex Oppia due to pressure from women. In addition, contemporary evidence from Pompeii attests to the fact that women there (*vicinae*) backed and endorsed local candidates for municipal elections. Moreover, women like Catullus' mistress Clodia (Lesbia) and Sempronia supported Catiline, using their wealth and influence for his promotion. Sallust gives us a vivid, if somewhat biased picture of one of these emancipated ladies:

> Now among these women was Sempronia, who had often committed many crimes of masculine daring. This woman was quite fortunate in her family and looks, and especially in her husband and children; she was well read in Greek and Latin literature, able to play the lyre and dance more aptly than any respectable woman would have needed to, and talented in many other activities which are part of over-indulgent living. But she cherished everything else more than propriety and morality; you would have a hard time determining which she squandered more of, her money or her reputation; her sexual desires were so ardent that she took the initiative with men far more often than they did with her.... Yet she possessed intellectual strengths which are by no means laughable: The skill of writing verses, cracking jokes, speaking either modestly or tenderly or saucily—in a word, she had much wit and charm. (*Cat. Con.*, 25)

From Sallust's portrait of Sempronia one may infer the change in the intellectual status of Roman women that resulted from the increasing number of upper-class women receiving more and better education. The intellectual and cultural emancipation is reflected in their growing participation in the life of letters; several literary salons were known to have been organized and frequented by women, notably the two Sulpicias and the Empress Julia Domna. The young Agrippina wrote her memoirs, which were used as a reference by Tacitus, and Sulpicia composed passable poertry that was still read in fifth-century Gaul. Diodorus even mentions a female orator, Hortensia, whose speech was praised by as stern a critic as Quintilian (*Inst.*, i, 6), and some women gained vocational recognition; there is even record of a woman engineer.

Women's intellectual emancipation had vast implications: it made friendship between men and women possible. Previously, because women were assumed to have weak minds and, therefore, did not receive the same education as men, men thought that friendship between members of the two sexes was unusual if not impossible, as Aristotle's statement in the *Nicomachean Ethics* testifies: "Since most husbands and wives are not equals, the wife cannot be a true friend to her spouse." Modestinus' definition of marriage in the *Corpus iuris,* however, reflects the changed conception of marriage and of women in the late Empire: "Marriage is a union of man and woman for the establishment of a community of their whole life and for the conferment upon one another of all rights whatsoever, whether connected with things human or divine."

By the second century A.D., the two essential ingredients of the *patria potestas* were gradually disappearing; the *pater familias* had been deprived of the right of life and death over his children, and the husband had lost his absolute power over his wife. The popularity of prolonged celibacy, as well as the widespread and socially condoned practice of concubinage and other extramarital affairs, and the bisexuality of some Roman men also combined to make marriage appear less desirable. From an economic point of view, the advantages of childlessness (notably the practice of "legacy hunting") outweighed the rewards of the Augustan pro-marriage legislation.[14] In addition, the nature of the slave culture in ancient Rome occasioned that many of the functions usually performed by a wife were automatically done by slaves.[15] Unlike the hardworking Hesiod, who recommended the acquisition of a ploughing ox and a wife to help with the farm chores, the young Roman had all of his personal and economic needs administered to by a multitude of specialized slaves. Moreover, the increased ease of divorce and woman's relative emancipation probably also acted as an impediment to childbearing. Finally, celibacy and childlessness were by no means unanimously considered immoral. The Epicureans, Cynics, and Neoplatonists—all minority philosophies—advocated celibacy in one form or another, while the younger Stoa strongly recommended marriage only as the civic and moral duty of the individual, and the Neopythagoreans advocated for women the traditional roles of mother and wife.[16]

The Epicureans, the most influential of the minority philosophies in Rome, discouraged the political and civic involvement of the wise man and were in general averse to public life. Family life shared the same fate as civic life with them, for Epicurus propounded that it is better for the wise man to forego marriage and the rearing of children because he would thereby save himself from major disturbances. Jerome quotes Seneca as saying: "Epicurus asserts that the wise man ought not marry because there are many inconveniences that come from married life" (*Adv. Jov.* 1, 49). Epicurus' marital views are a direct consequence of his materialism that would cause him to value connections freely entered upon and sustained over those held involuntarily.

The second minority philosophy in Rome, the Cynic School, was also opposed to the marriage of the wise man. Diogenes praised those who were about to marry but refrained (*Diog. Lives* 6, 29), and when asked about the right time to marry, he replied, "For young men, not yet, for old men, never." The Cynics advocated that a select order of philosophers devote themselves entirely to the welfare of humanity. These wise men, therefore, would have no time for wife and children.

The Roman Neoplatonists, however, came closest to advocating complete asceticism. This is naturally reflected in their views of marriage, because abstinence from pleasures also implies abstinence from sexual intercourse. Their greatest thinker, Plotinus, although somewhat removed from our present chronological field of inquiry, summarizes Neoplatonic dogma by suggesting that the truly human life is the *vita contemplativa* and, further, that ". . . to lapse into carnal love is sin" (*Enn.* iii, 5.1).

Thus, by Juvenal's time, we see Rome's upper class disconcertingly reduced in size in a city whose slave population had just reached one million and whose freedmen often held important administrative positions and possessed enormous wealth.[17] In the face of this situation, officials of the Roman aristocracy were becoming increasingly concerned with the decline in numbers of the indigenous upper class and the growth of celibacy. They were seconded in their attempts to increase the marriage and birthrates and in their advocacy of the familiar roles of wife and mother for women by the most popular philosophic school of the period, the younger Stoa. Evidently, however, both propagandas were without much consequence. Women were freer, ostensibly richer, better educated, more influential, and more visible than in Republican times; cosmopolitan men placed personal preferment over civic obligation. The stolid virtues born in a largely rural society were inverted. The situation contained everything, in short, that a satirist could ask for in his model.

Misogyny and mirth: Juvenal's *Sixth Satire* as prototype

Juvenal's sixth and longest satire variously termed "satire on the female sex," a "legend of bad women," the "most horrifying of all catalogues of female vices," and a "formless, chaotic invective"[18] might be best described by the Chinese pictogram for satire, "laughter with knives." Juvenal is appealing to traditional prejudices for comic effect while safely undercutting the validity of his misogynistic remarks by the paradoxicality and ambiguity of his arguments. The tone of the poem is sustained irony and the method of argumentation is the systematic inversion of two sets of commonly accepted moral ideals: the Stoic marital ethic and the concept of the sacred or archetypal role of women. The satire's persona presents these direct inversions as the organizing principles of the poem and, documented by exaggerated instances of contemporary female misbehavior, they constitute the subject matter of his exempla.

By far the most violent and one of the most influential of the pagan misogamous works, Juvenal's Sixth Satire is the first extant text of general misogamy, and, as such, its audience is not limited to a select group of philosophers and religious enthusiasts. Rather, the poem is designed for the amusement of Everyman, its long-lasting popularity reflecting both a broad-based sentiment and a masterful execution. The Sixth Satire is also preeminently a social barometer reflecting the recurring

relationship between misogamous literature and social/
demographic trends because it responds to the tremendous al-
terations that had taken place in Roman law and custom from
the late Republican to the Imperial period.

The topography of the poem

The prologue begins with a humorous and ambiguous eulogy
of the commonplace chaste Golden Age of man.[19] During the
Golden Age, wild-looking husbands and their even more
ferocious-looking spouses shared simple cave dwellings with
their livestock. Wives breast-fed their numerous and healthy ba-
bies and were kept constantly occupied by having to fight for
the bare necessities of life. People were virtuous then, Juvenal
seems to suggest, because they had no leisure time for luxurious and, thus, potentially corrupting practices.

The equation of virtue with full occupation and a hardened
way of life in savage circumstances establishes the moral index
of the poem and the link is reiterated by the persona's answer
to Postumus' question regarding the origin of present-day
monstrosities later in the poem: "Unde haec monstra tamen vel
quo de fonte requiris?" (line 286). In the old days of the Hannibalic wars, the adviser says, humble fortunes, toil, brief slum-
bers, hard work, and the threat of war kept Roman wives
chaste; but now, luxury avenges a conquered world: "Nunc pa-
timur longae pacis mala; saevior armis, luxuria incubuit vic-
tumque ulciscitur orbem" (lines 292–293). The linkage of
desidia, longa pax, and luxuria with libido as the reason for
Rome's decline is traditional: it occurs in the writings of Sallust, Livy, Seneca, and in the fierce attacks of Cato on declining morals and their cause: imported luxury.[20] The date for the
onset of declining morals given in the Sixth Satire is also traditional, for virtually all ancient writers agree that Roman morals
deteriorated in the second century B.C. They disagree only as to
when the decline began to accelerate noticeably.

Juvenal exploits the traditional topos by taking the argument ad absurdum without, however, idealizing Golden Age
man. He implies that virtue is an act not of moral decision but
of necessity and lack of temptation: Golden Age wives were

chaste not because of an innate, primeval, moral rectitude, but because they had little opportunity for vice.[21]

The chastity topos introduced in the prologue is followed by the establishment of beauty as an antivalue. The virtuous wives of the Golden Age were unkempt, unclean, and ferocious looking; their uncouthness, linked to their natural way of life, is initially established as a positive quality. The antibeauty topos recurs in direct and modified echoes throughout the poem; beautiful wives are either actually or potentially unfaithful, beauty is associated with artificiality, and the results of the beautification process are seen only by the adulterer: "interea foeda aspectu ridendaque multo/pane tumet facies aut pinguia Poppaena/spirat, et hinc miseri viscantur labra mariti:/ad moechum lota veniunt cute./Quando videri vult formosa domi?" (lines 461–65). On the linguistic level, the illusory nature of beauty is emphasized by the use of verbs of appearance such as *videri* (appear) and also by the extensive use of the passive voice in the context of the description of beauty rather than verbs of fact.

The persona completes the discussion of beauty as an antivalue by using the example of Bibula to show that physical beauty can only inspire short-lived passion: Sertorius loves Bibula's beautiful face now and fulfills her every desire, but he will repudiate her as soon as a few wrinkles appear. He loves the face, not the woman: "Cur desiderio Bibulae Sertorius ardet? Si verum excutias, facies, non uxor amatur" (lines 142–43).

Neither beauty as an antivalue nor its opposite, the appearance of the *montana uxor*, are presented by the persona as absolutes.[22] To introduce an ambiguity of values, Juvenal has his persona evoke the elegiac ideals of Cynthia and Lesbia in contrast to the crude Golden Age wives. As W. Anderson observes, Lesbia does not only function as a symbol of "the vapidity of her type," but both women also serve as visual contrasts to the "uncouthness, the physical grossness of the aboriginal woman."[23]

A direct address by the poem's persona to Postumus follows the prologue. Postumus, like the persona, is sketched with consistency, and everything we learn about him is incriminating: he finds marriage attractive because it will assure his eligibility as an heir according to Augustus' marital legislation. He once used to be the most notorious of Rome's lechers: "moechorum notissimus olim" (line 42) and also an occasional homosexual. Although the prologue condemns adultery as the root of all subsequent corruption, the persona sees it as madness for Postumus to surrender his former way of life in favor of marriage. This is the first link in the subsequent chain of paradoxes serving to develop the unreliable character of the persona.

The persona of the poem is outraged at Postumus' plans for marriage when there are ropes to be had, windows and bridges to jump from: "Ferre potes dominam salvis tot restibus ullam,/ cum pateant altae caligantesque fenestrae,/cum tibi vicinum se praebeat Aemilius pons?" (line 30–32). The adviser suggests that suicide is better than marriage, pederasty is even better, but remaining in his present state (i.e., as the greatest of adulterers) is the best choice of all for Postumus. He warns Postumus that if he refuses to listen to the persuasive "arguments of sanity," he, the once successful cuckolder, shall become the cuckolded, subjugated, tormented husband himself, and what's worse, to "bring up a dear little heir," he will have to forego the pleasures of all the legacy-hunting delicacies of the meat-market: the fine turtle doves, and the bearded mulletts (lines 39–40).

As if the generalities of the madness hyperbole were not sufficient to dissuade Postumus, the adviser plunges into a diatribe against the contemporary state of marriage, highlighting the special vices of Rome's matrons. In the best satiric manner, the persona does this by employing concrete examples. Foremost on his list is adultery, especially the erotic attractiveness of social and intellectual degradation, documented by examples from contemporary and near-contemporary life: Eppia, the senator's wife, ran away with a gladiator. The reason for her doting is a thinly veiled but brutally obscene double entendre: she is attracted not by the man, but by his "sword" (lines 110–12). The ironic mockery of the Eppia passage is clear from the almost epic tone of the denunciation which concludes on an anticlimactic note introduced by a suspenseful interpolation by the persona: "She had no thought of her home, her sister, husband or country,/Wickedly left her children in tears, and—this will astound you!—/Even forsook the games and that marvelous Thespian, Paris" (lines 85–87). The last line probably contains a topical reference when it mockingly praises Eppia's rejection of even imperial pleasures, for the handsome pantomime Paris was Domitian's reason for separating from his wife (*Suet*. Domitian, 3).[24]

The adviser alludes to many instances in which the fibulae of comedians, tragedians, musicians, and gladiators were endangered by the voracious appetites of upperclass matrons (lines 73–75). While in this passage women are reproached for not caring a bean for Quintilian, later in the poem (lines 267–85) the eloquent rhetor is shown to be cared for too much. Again, the context is *impudicitia,* for the wife caught in *flagrante delicto,* will outspeak Quintilian. Here, as in the Eppia passage, the language of obscenity is handled ambiguously. The persona uses expressions with clear double entendre such as, for example, "cantare vetent," "solvitur fibula," which, in the narrative context, clearly refer to intercourse with inferiors.

Parallel to this example of the attractiveness of social degradation runs the suggestion that the higher the woman's status, the more corrupt she is and the worse example she sets. Thus, the adviser culminates his examples of base attractions with a recounting of Messalina's nightly escapades. The characterization of Claudius' wife may be more vivid and memorable than in some other contemporary accounts, but it is in accordance with Tacitus' and Suetonius' account of her. The visual and sensual impact of the Messalina passage shows the satirist at his best. The Empress appears exposing her gilded breasts and the belly that bore "noble Britannicus" to her crude customers; the nauseating odor of the filthy *lupanar* pervades every line of the description.

The gallery of concrete examples demonstrating the depravity and stupidity of wives also includes instances of insane fashions and cosmetics, of foreign and foolish superstitions, and of religious misuse. (These themes will become traditional to the misogamous canon.) The religious misuse topos is coupled

with the *impudicitia* topos in the episode concerning the Bona
Dea, whose festivities disintegrate into orgiastic revels. The absurd and sensational treatment of the passage not only makes
the reader wonder about the way Juvenal may have collected
his information, but it also calls to mind details revealed during
the famous Senate investigation of the Bacchanalia in 186 B.C.
The passage, as Anderson points out, should invite skepticism,
because the repeated use of terms like *omnis* and *nullus* openly
call attention to the persona's tendency to exaggerate.[25]

The all-pervasive theme of *impudicitia* underlies the "musical joys" passage (lines 379–84) as well. In consistently ambiguous vocabulary, the persona describes the joys of a musical
wife who is so devoted to the talents and instruments of her
tutor that his voice will not survive her attention:

> If she delights in song, she will make the professional singers
> Come at her bidding; she holds their instruments in her hands,
> While her sardonyx rings flash as her fingers are moving
> Up and down the scale, and she holds the pick, and it quivers
> As it used to do in the hand of the soft Hedymeles.
> So she fondles it, finds it a joy and a consolation,
> Gives it more than one kiss by way of endearing indulgence.
>
> (lines 379–84)

The list of female vices in the Sixth Satire continues with
examples of wives engaging in inappropriate (i.e., manly) behavior such as sports and court litigations. While the frequency
of such instances is absurdly exaggerated (the persona uses the
terms *all* and *never* with suspicious ease), we have other contemporary evidence for the details: Suetonius says that Domitian gave performances not only between gladiators and beasts
but between women as well, and that in the stadium there were
races between girls.

The persona also describes wives as always cruel toward
their husbands, servants, and neighbors and attacks the prevailing female lust for dominance. The matrons of the Sixth Satire
always win the fight for the breeches. Consequently, Juvenal's
persona is remarkably reminiscent of the older Cato's fearful
assessment of the disaster that would result should wives receive more rights. Cato had said: "Review the laws with which
our forefathers restrained their licence and made them subject

to their husbands; even with all these bonds, you can scarcely control them. What of this? . . . . do you think you will be able to endure them: the moment they become your equals they will be your superiors" (*Liv.* XXXIV, iii).

The misogynist persona of the Sixth Satire is consistent; even the perfect wife comes under attack. The absurdity of the *rara avis* passage scarcely needs comment: "Sit formosa decens dives fecunda, vetustos/porticibus disponat avos, intactior omni/crinibus effusis bellum dirimente Sabina,/rara avis in terris nigroque simillima cycno;/quis feret uxorem cui constant omnia?" (lines 162–66) The very existence of the good wife is questioned; she is described in the subjunctive mood and probably presents the general idea of the respectable Roman matron: beautiful, decent, rich, fecund, of old ancestry, and chaste. These are all qualities whose existence the persona either denies or whose inherent value he questions: beauty and riches in a wife have previously been established as antivalues; old and glorious ancestry is criticized in connection with Cornelia; fecundity and chastity, the adviser claims, have disappeared from Rome.

That Juvenal's persona meant to draw attention to the existence of the plague of assertive, intellectual, and thus inappropriately "unfeminine" women is clear from the structural punctuation of the poem, for one of the few narrative breaks in the Sixth Satire occurs in the context of the description of a bluestocking. In lines 451–56, the persona steps out of his quasi-altruistic role as friendly adviser when he describes what appears to be the most disconcerting type of wife:

> How I hate them,
> Women who always go back to the pages of Palaemon's grammar,
> Keeping all of the rules, and are pedants enough to be quoting
> Verses I never heard. If she has some friend from the country
> Let her correct her speech! Is this a business for men?
> Husbands should be allowed their solecisms in comfort!
>
> (lines 451–56)

In this passage, the misogyny of the persona is coupled with a strong anti-intellectual tendency and the link is further emphasized by the jealousy exclamatory nature of the intrusion.

After an attack on mothers-in-law, gossips, and spend-thrifts, the catalogue of *exempla* concludes with the climactic section on murderesses using poison. Thus, Roman wives are shown to be not only immoral and worthless but also menacing and dangerous—of no value when poor, and more pain than they are worth when rich.

The accusations by Juvenal's persona are all-inclusive and categorical. Every type of rich Roman matron is under attack. The categorical denunciation immediately suggests a comparison with the categorical and ambiguous eulogy in the prologue: as structural parallels to the evocation of the elegiac ideal in contrast to the *montana uxor,* the supposed victims of the Sixth Satire's monstrous women, the husbands, are worthy neither of respect nor sympathy. Sertorius is a selfish man whose lust (*desiderio ardet*) for Bibula's beauty is scarcely more noble than Eppia's love for her gladiator, and his repudiation of her on account of three wrinkles and the impending loss of beauty in favor of a younger wife parallels Eppia's desertion of her husband. Similarly, Censennia's husband, judged by the persona's own dictum, is worse than all the lusty ladies, for he prostitutes himself for money (644–52). While the persona is obviously condemning Censennia, his criticism backfires once again, for her husband is even more incriminated. Monstrosities committed in passion are much less miraculous and wicked than those calculated or done for mercenary reasons, as are the husband's crimes (in blatant contrast to the preceding gallery of passion-ridden matrons). The ridiculousness of prophylactic-gulping Pontus has already been noted by Anderson, and Postumus' sordid character makes him a worthy member of the group.[26]

The method of dissuasion

There is one discernible pattern in the catalogue of vices that seems to be compatible with the major themes of the satire (i.e., the general corruption of the times) and the tone of the poem (i.e., sophistic irony). Juvenal seems to be using the Ovidian *Remedia* technique of dissuading by inverting two generally accepted value systems. Just as Juvenal's Rome is corrupt because of the inversion of ancient ideals (generous patron/stingy upstart; sacred ceremonies/drunken revels), so the ideals of marriage and of womanhood are shown to have been destroyed by inversion, and the Stoic commonplace "marriage and procreation are natural" is denied by the persona's *exempla*.

This technique of inversion corresponds to the persona's quasi-medical purpose in the poem—to cure his protégé who has gone mad—for the concept of remedy by inversion is fundamentally a medical one. While Hippocrates advocated that in most cases illnesses be cured by the repeated application of their symptoms (*similia similibus*), Themison of Laodicena (fl. in Rome ca. 50 B.C.) and later Soranus of Ephesus (fl. in Rome second century A.D.) proposed that contraries be cured by contraries (*contraria contrariis*). Consequently because Postumus' madness manifests itself in his wish to marry, presumably because he has such a positive view of marriage, he has to be shown the opposite view of marriage in order to be cured. The gallery of examples consolidating the repugnant picture of marriage serves precisely that function.

Even though Juvenal subscribes to no orthodoxy, it has long been recognized that his philosophic sympathies are Stoic.[27] The Stoics distrusted emotion, viewed dependence on others with scorn, and asserted that there was a natural law by which acts unworthy of human beings might be judged.[28]

Even though the older Stoa was relatively indifferent to marriage, and Zeno, their founder, even advocated a community of wives for the wise men, the younger Stoa, with the possible exception of Seneca, was unequivocally in favor of marriage and the rearing of children as the civic and moral responsibility of the Roman citizen.[29]

Adherence to the Stoic ideal in general and the Stoic ideal of marriage in particular, however, is precisely what Juvenal's persona is unable to find in Rome, and he makes the categorical inversion of this ideal the subject of the bulk of his exempla against marriage. The wives in the Sixth Satire epitomize reason subordinated to passion, lack prudence, are slaves to excess, and defy virtue and decorum. In fact, the previously mentioned burlesque on the sacred mysteries of Bona Dea (lines 315–48) typifies this paradigmatic devotion to excess and disregard for virtue and decorum. Although the goddess frowns on any male presence in her sanctuary (even images depicting human and animal males must be veiled), her devotees celebrate orgiastic revels there. Similarly, the defilement of the statue of Chastity by women (lines 306–14), their irrational cruelty (lines 219–30; 413–18; 474–95), and their passion for the *spectacula* and the performers (lines 60–115), their foolish superstition (lines 511–91), as well as their homicidal practices (lines 627–661) are all clear inversions of the Stoic ideal. More specifically, the matrons of the Sixth Satire exemplify the inversion of the marital values of Stoic teaching.

Furthermore, the adviser's first and often repeated dissuasive arguments against marriage concern the offspring. He insists that heirs are either illegitimate or are aborted before birth because all wives are adulteresses. When introducing the topos, the persona links adultery, lust, and *spectacula*. This linkage, so well known from the early Christian Apologists, is indicative of rich matrons' erotic fascination with social and intellectual inferiority.[30] Incidentally, the illegitimate offspring is described as having "the lineaments of Euryalus or of a murmillo" (81) because all wives are attracted to lowerclass types, especially gladiators whose race, not that of the husband, shall be propagated. In fact, Postumus is urged to assist in the abortion of his wife's child, for his heir is likely to be an Ethiopian:

> Rejoice, unfortunate husband,
> Give her the dose yourself, whatever it is; never let her
> Carry till quickening time, or go on to full term and deliver
> Something whose hue would seem to prove you a blackamoor father,
> Sire of an off-color heir you'd prefer not to meet in the daylight.
>
> (lines 597–601)

Here, as previously, condemnation of adultery is not made on moral but on pragmatic grounds: obvious illegitimacy is far more inconvenient than abortion.

In having his persona depict women as sex fiends, Juvenal once more follows traditional wisdom, for in ancient medical and natural treatises, women were held to be much more libidinous than men.[31] In addition, complaints about women's proclivity for *impudicitia* were accelerated during the Empire. Thus, for example, Seneca says that the only chaste woman is an ugly one, and that no woman is satisfied with one man (*De ben.* 111, 2–4).

Concern for offspring is Postumus' chief reason for wishing to marry. He does not want children, however, in order to fulfill his civic or moral duty but for entirely selfish reasons: the famous adulterer now wants to be eligible "as an heir." But as the persona makes clear, even that purpose will be frustrated.

In his attacks on marriage in the Sixth Satire, Juvenal's persona only mentions one mother of a large family, while he provides abundant examples of women engaging in unprocreative intercourse employing castrati, abortifacients, and contraceptives. Even the example of the virtuous mother of a large family is a negative one, for "it is hell being married to Cornelia." Cornelia's terrible vice is that she is, justifiably, proud of her accomplishments:

I would rather, much rather, have a Venusian girl
Than the noble Cornelia, mother of heroes, those Gracchi,
Bringing, with all her virtues, those upraised and haughty eyebrows,
Counting as part of her dowry parades and processions of triumph.
Spare me your Hannibals, please, and your Syphaxes, conquered
    in camp;
Get to hell out of here with your Carthage, whole kit and caboodle!
                      (lines 286–92)

Paradoxically, Cornelia's fecundity is also presented as an anti-value: she is compared to Niobe and condemned by analogy. This reference to Scipio's daughter is especially paradoxical in light of lines 286–92, where the adviser nostalgically recalls the time of the Hannibalic wars as the virtuous epoch of Roman history and serves, once more, as an indicator of the absurdity of the persona's logic.

Interestingly, the persona of the Sixth Satire underplays the obvious arguments in favor of celibacy mentioned by contemporary writers: he does not dwell on the "rewards of childlessness" and the "opportunity for licentiousness and varied pleasures" (only alluding to them once in the prologue). Neither does he promote celibacy by subscribing to any of the cur-

rent philosophic schools advocating the unmarried state: the
adviser avoids making use of the Epicurean argument against
marriage (that a wife and child are major impediments to
the pursuit of happiness), and of the Neoplatonic ascetic
ideal which proscribes a contemplative life free of any carnal
pleasure. Rather, he describes wives as such monstrosities
and in such exaggerated terms, that no man in his sane
mind would marry them—and no sane reader could believe in
their existence.

As wives, the matrons of the Sixth Satire are formidable
tyrants, lively examples of the topos *mundus inversus*: they in-
vade spheres traditionally reserved for men. The persona implies that by abandoning their traditional roles, wives also
abandon the very essence of their sex (252–53). In this context, Seneca's remarks on the physical and medical repercussions of inappropriate behavior are relevant: Seneca says that
by practicing male vices women also fall heir to masculine diseases: "Beneficium sexus sui vitiis perdiderunt et quia feminam
exuerant, damnatae sunt morbis virilibus." In addition, wives
are adulteresses; as the adviser warns, they do not stay long
with any one husband: one wife had eight marriages in five
years (lines 229–30), and another Eppia, left home, husband,
sister, and country, abandoning her weeping children for the
love of a gladiator. The only pleasure wives are willing to give
is to their lovers but never to their husbands. They are superstitious, prodigal, luxurious, and spiteful to their husbands.

Clearly, the wifely practices of the women in the Sixth Satire stand in direct contrast to the Roman conjugal ideal as reflected, for example, by surviving epitaphs from the Imperial
period. Balsdon lists these inscriptions of traditional commonplaces praising the deceased wife's virtue of old-fashioned
(*antiqua vita*), content to stay at home (*domiseda*), chaste
(*pudicitia*), dutifully obedient (*obsequium*), friendly and amusing (*comitas, sermone lepido*), careful with money (*frugi*), not
overly dressed (*ornatus non conspiciendi*), religious without being fanatic (*religionis sine superstitione*), and commended for
spinning and weaving (*lanifica, lanam fecit*).[32]

In the climactic conclusion of the poem, the persona even
inverts women's sacred role as the layer out of the corpse by

describing wives as murdering their husbands and children. The mourning for the corpse becomes the joyful and proud revel over the accomplished deed: "tune duos una, saevissima vipera, cena?/tune duos? septem, si septem forte fuissent" (lines 641–42). Wives now sneer at Alcestis' example, the adviser says, and they would let their husbands die to save a pet: "spectant subeuntem fata mariti/Alcestim, et similis si permutatio detur,/morte viri cupiant animam servare catellae" (652–54). The return to the initial hyperbole (marriage is madness, suicide is better) seals the equation of death and marriage: woman is no longer the sympathetic performer of the last rites but the angel of death.

Intended as a cure for Postumus' insane wish to marry, Juvenal's Sixth Satire is *Remedia Uxorationis*.[33] Ovid teaches that if one can fall in love one can also fall out of it—all one needs to do is reverse the process. If, for instance, one was attracted to a woman because of her slender beauty, one ought to consider her emaciated. Or, in other words, one should turn the value into an antivalue. In fact, Ovid encourages the lover to invent shortcomings in his mistress, to have other affairs in order to weaken his desire for her, and force her to reveal her blemishes by flattering her into believing that they are actually wonderful ornaments.

The Sixth Satire is similar in argumentation. The adviser exaggerates or invents vices for his matrons in order to save his protégé, and he turns the valuable reasons for marriage into anti-values: if Postumus wants to marry because he wishes to have children, then he foolishly hopes for bastards; if he yearns for a virtuous wife, then he is insane, because virtuous wives are the hardest to put up with; if he hopes for a happy marriage like Censennia's, then he must realize that all happy marriages entail the subjugation of the husband.

Conclusion

Seen as a *Remedia Uxorationis* prescribed by a misogynist for a famous adulterer, Satire Six becomes the farcical platform for both celibate and anti-celibate propaganda, because the categorical nature of the accusations and the paradoxical treatment for the arguments undercut, and thus ridicule, the misogynistic arguments. For, how can the reader trust the observations and reflections of a person who repeatedly exposes himself as absurd, sensational, petty, and fanatical, whose stated purpose in the poem is to save his debauched protégé from the perils of marriage, and whose advice is based on transparently pragmatic rather than moral considerations?

The poem's persona claims that the perils of marriage he presents exemplify contemporary wifely practices. They are exaggerated to absurdity and demonstrate the inversion of accepted sets of values. Here, as in his other satires, Juvenal plays a safe game; by inverting such commonly accepted and traditional ideals as the Stoic marital ethic and the concept of the archetypal role of woman and making these inversions his targets for attack, he almost certainly assures the poem of considerable appeal to a predominantly male Roman audience.[34] As Spengler observes in his *Decline of the West*, "The true Roman is more strictly Stoic than any Greek could be—even the Roman who would have opposed Stoicism most resolutely"; by exaggerating and universalizing instances of existing and generally condemned female misbehavior, the satirist was sure to raise laughter.

Beginning in the twelfth century, in some cases even earlier, echoes of that laughter would be heard again—Juvenal's urbane secular Everyman finding his voice at a time of economic and demographic shifts and the renewed "threat" of female emancipation. For centuries, however, chic satires would not be a viable literature. The low level of learning, the sheer rustic bleakness of early medieval cultural life militated against its production and even threatened its transmission in the form of antique manuscripts.

Inimical on practical grounds, the early Middle Ages were also ideologically unsuited to the ephemera of satiric wit. On the brink of the millennium, early Christians sought transcendence, not double-edged wit. The somber asceticism that characterized so much of patristic writing was best expressed in didactic and propagandistic rather than amusing literature.

❖ II ❖

Ascetic Misogamy

Eschatology, dualism, and virginity
in the patristic period

Marginal, enthusiastic, and less involved in world-hating than in the simple refusal to credit the status quo, Christianity was at its outset a thoroughly radical movement. For the socially disadvantaged, a great part of its appeal involved a revolutionary teaching of spiritual equivalence that provided for a spiritual communion with the divine at a level previously reserved exclusively for men—and free men of substance at that.[1] Perfect communion, in turn, necessitated a revolutionary turning away from the traditional contexts of the home and family, theretofore the only viable context for most women, the procreative one. Christian perfection involved the application of a hierarchy of values that saw marriage not as a blessing but as a concession to human frailty, and hence an inferior state incompatible with holy devotion; a hierarchy of values, at the pinnacle of which was not merely celibacy, but chastity and abstinence.

At once the hallmark of early Christian communities and a rationale for such nearly antinomian teaching, apocalyptic eschatology colored the life and thought of Christians for centuries:

> A messiah who suffered and died, a kingdom which was purely spiritual—such ideas, which were later regarded as the very core of Christian doctrine, were far from being accepted by all the early Christians. . . . The celebrated prophecy recorded by Matthew is certainly of great significance and remains significant whether Christ really uttered it or was merely believed to have done so: "For the Son of Man shall come in the glory of his Father with his angels; and then he shall reward every man according to his works. Verily I say unto you, there be some stand-

35

ing here, which shall not taste of death, till they see the Son of
Man coming in his kingdom." It is not surprising that many of
the early Christians interpreted these things in terms of apocalyptic eschatology with which they were already familiar. Like so
many generations of Jews before them they say history as divided
into two eras, one preceding and the other following the trium-
phant advent of the Messiah . . . for a long time great numbers of
Christians were convinced not only that Christ would soon return in power and majesty but also that when he did return it
would be to establish a messianic kingdom on earth.[2]

The earliest influential spokesman for a Christian view of
marriage and sexuality, the Apostle Paul was obviously committed to such an imminent second coming. Paul's often derog-
atory statements on the married state reflect his belief that the
end was near and that human history would end within his
own lifetime (1 Thess. 4:17; 1 Cor. 15:51). Paul's eschatology
incorporates his marital views: "I mean, brethren, the ap-
pointed time has grown short; from now on, let those who
have wives live as though they had none, and those who mourn
as though they were not mourning . . . for the form of this
world is passing away" (1 Cor. 7:29–31). In the first letter to
the Corinthians, Paul asserts that marriage is permitted and
sometimes even necessary in order to prevent something worse
(i.e., fornication), but he does not seem to attribute any inherent value to the married state. He emphasizes that the chaste
state is more perfect because the celibate can devote themselves
better than the married to the service of the Lord. Paul's eschatological concern is summed up in 1 Cor. 7:32–34.

> I would have you free from care. He who is unmarried is con-
> cerned about the things of the Lord, how he may please God.
> Whereas he who is married is concerned about the things of the
> world: and he is divided. And the unmarried woman and the
> virgin thinks about the things of the Lord that she may be holy
> in body and spirit. Whereas she who is married thinks about the
> things of the world and how she may please her husband.

The passage in 1 Corinthians 7 is often quoted as the
canonic text of Paul's marital theory, and some of the long-
lasting interpretations of the Apostle's views are exemplified by

the exegetical tradition of the first lines of Chapter 7. First Corinthians 7 begins: "Now concerning the matters upon which you wrote: it is good for a man not to touch a woman." John Chrysostom, Tertullian, Jerome and countless numbers of their successors interpreted the second sentence to be the Apostle's dictum and used it accordingly in support of the celibate ideal.[3]

John Chrysostom, for example, emphasizes that the chaste ideal proposed by the Apostle is not only for priests, but for all Christians:

> Some indeed say that this discourse was addressed by him to priests. But, I, judging from what follows, could not affirm that it was so, since he would not have given his advice in general terms. For if he were writing these things only for the priests he would have said, "It is good for the teacher not to touch a woman." But now he had made it of universal application saying "It is good for a man"; not for priests only. . . . And the whole of his speech is in the same tone. And in saying "Because of fornications, let every man have his own wife, " by the very cause alleged for the concession he guides men to continence. (Homile XIV ad 1 Corinthians Vil 1, 2, pg. 62)

Some of the Pauline eschatologic misogamy is felt in the Gospels as well. In Matt. 19:12, Jesus speaks of those who have "made themselves eunuchs for the sake of the kingdom of heaven." The Matthew passage is usually interpreted as suggesting that virginity (like poverty and childlikeness) is a sign proclaiming the advent of the kingdom. From the third century onward, these lines have been the chief scriptural authority for showing Jesus' advocacy of celibacy. This interpretation of the eunuch reference originated with Basilides in the early second century, and was also championed by Tertullian who suggested that the Lord himself opened the kingdom of heaven to eunuchs and He himself lived as a virgin. Methodius, Jerome, and Augustine later adopted similar positions, thus making this interpretation dogmatic for the centuries to come.[4]

The eschatological emphasis is even stronger in Luke. His Gospel, more than the other synoptic Gospels, urges the anticipation and limitation of the life after the resurrection. In the text containing the promise that one shall receive a hundred-fold in the next life, Luke alone mentions him who abandons not only his house, brothers, and parents for the sake of the Kingdom (as the corresponding passages in Matt. 19:27–30 and Mark 10:29–30 do) but also his wife. As C. Travard observes, "Luke certainly believes that a new way of life which would include abstention from marriage is possible and desirable being in harmony with the coming Kingdom."[5] Luke also expands on Matt. 22:30: "The children of this world marry and are given in marriage. But those who shall be accounted worthy of that age and to the resurrection from the dead neither marry nor take wives" (Luke 20:23–26). This passage has also been used both for providing authority for the celibate ideal and for the noncarnal interpretation of resurrection. While the majority of writers provide a celibate interpretation of the passage, Clement of Alexandria, for instance, explained the passage without any antigamous tint: he claimed that ". . . anyone examining the passage carefully would realize that Jesus was not being critical of marriage but of a carnal interpretation for human resurrection."[6]

Proponents of the celibate ideal (especially Tertullian, Cyprian, Jerome, and Augustine) also utilized John's Revelation (19:7; 21:2; 22:17) both in regard to the image of the eschatological marriage between Christ and his Church and by the reference to the "144,000 who had been redeemed from the earth . . . it is these who had not defiled themselves with women" (14:3–4).

One of the staunchest and most influential upholders of the chaste ideal was the third century African teacher Tertullian. Later in life he joined the Montanist sect because their eschatological beliefs and ascetic practices appealed to him. His works provided much fuel for subsequent misogamous and misogynistic texts. Tertullian's three treatises on marriage, or, more specifically, on monogamy, the *Ad uxorem*, *De exhortatione castitatis*, and *De monogamia*, show a gradual change toward Montanism. The first treatise, *Ad uxorem*, written as Harnack argues, between 200 and 206, is his earliest extant work on the subject. In it, Tertullian urges his wife not to remarry after his death. Like Paul, he embeds his reasons in a future-oriented setting: "We have been taught by the Lord and God of salvation that continence is a means of attaining eternal life ... a pledge of the glory of that body which will be ours when we put on the garb of immortality" (*Ad uxorem*, 1.7 CCL 1). He uses John's Gospel to attack the procreative idea:

> We are so sure of our salvation that we have time for children! We must hunt up burdens for ourselves with which, for the most part, even pagans refuse to be encumbered—burdens which are forced upon people by the law, but of which they rid themselves by resorting to murder of their own flesh and blood. . . . Why did our Lord prophesy "Woe to them that are with child and that give suck," if he did not mean that on the day of our great exodus children will be a handicap to those who bear them? This is what comes of marriage. . . . At the first sound of the angel's trumpet, the widows will leap forth lightly, easily able to endure any distress or persecution with none of the heaving baggage of marriage in their wombs or at their breasts. . . . Are we to have weddings every day and, in the midst of nuptials, to be overtaken by the day of dread even as were Sodom and Gomorrah?

Commenting on the words of Paul (it is better to marry than to burn), Tertullian observes that what is better is not necessarily good. It is better, he explains, to lose one eye rather than both, but neither is actually good (*Ad uxorem* 1.3, CCL 1; *De monog.*, 3, CCL 1). Thus, Tertullian introduces into orthodoxy the interpretation of Revelation (14:4) as a Scriptural authority upholding the bilateral celibate ideal. In doing so, he emphasizes the burdensome encumbrances of children to their mothers.

Tertullian's catalogue of wicked women in the *Ad uxorem* is similar to Semonidas' but different from Juvenal's canon:

> Their loquaciousness leads to the use of words offensive to modesty; their slothfulness engenders disloyalty to the austere life; their trifling issues in every sort of evil and their prurient gossip is responsible for inciting others to engage in the lustful conduct which such talk exemplifies ... their god is their belly, as the apostle says; and so also is that which lies adjacent to it. (*Ad uxorem* 1.8, CCL 1)

The stratification of vices is reminiscent of Semonidas of Amorgos' fragment: lust, idleness, gossip, and loquaciousness are all qualities that occur in the Greek iambic poem under the similarly harsh indictment. Neither Semonidas nor Tertullian is particularly elegant in his use of obscenity and both equate excessive dependence on the appetites with bad women. Tertullian, like Semonidas, links gluttony and fornication as related vices. This junction of the two vices as inextricably linked offenses (i.e., indulgences of the flesh) remained the standard interpretation for centuries to come.

Tertullian's second work on marriage, the *De exhortatione castitatis,* was written between 204 and 212 when Tertullian had Montanist sympathies but was not as yet a member of the sect. Again, it is a treatise discouraging digamy and while Tertullian does not condemn marriage outright, he does relegate it to an inferior state. He feels that there is something essentially unclean and degrading about sex: "Even monogamy," he says, "in the shameful act which constitutes its essence, is the same as fornication. Therefore, it is best for a man not to touch a woman." In this treatise, in a passage which foreshadows Methodius' evolutionary theory of the ages of mankind as reflected in sexual mores, Tertullian repeats the eschatological reasons for the chaste ideal:

> The blessed patriarchs contracted multiple marriages. Is it, then, not lawful for us to marry repeatedly? Certainly, it is lawful, if your nuptials are types or symbols prefiguring something yet to come, or if the ancient command "increase and multiply" is still valid in our own day and not superseded by the warning that "the time is short," that "it remaineth that they who have wives act as if they had none." Actually, the precept of continence in this text and the restriction based on intercourse, which is the seeding of the race, have abolished the ancient command to increase and multiply. (*De exhort.,* 6, *CCL* 1)

Like Theophrastus, Tertullian sees children as troublesome burdens, and, like Juvenal (but for different reasons), he comments on the madness of wishing to have a family:

> The fact that children are troublesome burdens, especially in our times, should be a sufficient argument for widows and widowers

to remain unmarried. Men have to be forced by law to father a family because no man in his right senses would ever care to have a family. (*De exhort.*, 7, CCL 1)

Tertullian's Montanist treatise on marriage, *De monogamia,* while using the same arguments in favor of chastity as the preceding two works, goes even further in its pitiless condemnation of human frailty. Composed between 212 and 222, the author denounces his opponents as "sensualists" who are "given over to wantonness" and who find "their joy in things of the flesh." Similarly, the *De pudicitia,* possibly the last of his extant works, is also a passionate attack on the doctrine of the Church. The *De pudicitia* was occasioned by a decree which stated that members of the church who committed adultery were not to be permanently excluded from the community. Tertullian is outraged at this "permissive" policy. He argues that adultery, like fornication, is an irremissible sin and, therefore, the Church cannot pardon it. It is an unnatural vice and, thus, a Christian who committed it should be not only refused absolution, but excluded from the church as well:

> All other frenzied lust, vicious and unnatural uses of the body and of sex we banish not only from the threshold of the Church but also from any shelter within it, since they are not sins but rather monstrosities.... And so adultery, since it is the next thing to idolatry—for idolatry is often made a matter of reproach to the people under the name of adultery and fornication—will share its fate as it does its rank, and be joined with it in punishment as it is in position. (*De pud.* 4, 5 CCL 1)

Because of the Decalogue sequence (God prohibits idolatry, adultery, and murder in that order), apostasy, adultery, and murder were considered unpardonable offenses in the first Christian centuries and Tertullian's bitter attack on the decree advocating forgiveness for adultery attests to the sensitivity of the issue. The *De pudicitia* is perhaps Tertullian's most violent antigamous work. The treatise begins on a Juvenalian note:[7]

> Purity is the flower of virtue. It does honor the body and is an ornament of both sexes. It preserves blood untainted and guarantees parentage.... Although it is found but infrequently and is

with difficulty brought to perfection, and hardly ever permanently maintained, yet it will, in some measure, remain in the
world. . . . But as evil more and more prevails—and this is a characteristic sign of the latter days—good is no longer even permitted to be born, so corrupt is the race. (*De pud.*, 1, CCL 1)

As usual, Tertullian musters the testimony of Paul. Paul's per-
mission to marry, he says, is a mere toleration. It is a remedy
for something worse. Tertullian quotes Paul: "Now concerning
the things whereof you wrote: It is good for a man not to
touch a woman. Yet for fear of fornication let each man have
his own wife. Let the husband render to the wife her due, and
the wife to the husband!" (1 Corinthians) Then in one of the
rare instances in patristic literature where infibulation is used
as a symbol of the chaste ideal, he comments: "Who does not
see that it was in order to prevent fornication that he, all un-
willingly, removed the pin which held this pleasure in check."
(*De pud.* 1, CCL 1)

Tertullian and the other Montanists and a very large proportion of the earliest Christians in general continued to expect
the Second Coming to happen "shortly." By the middle of the
second century, however, such an eschatology had to be modified in view of reality. The tone of the Second Epistle of Peter
which was written about A.D. 150 is hesitant: out of compas-
sion, Christ may tarry "until all should have come to repentance." At the same time a process began by which Christian
apocalypses which had hitherto enjoyed canonical authority
were deprived of it, until only Revelation survived—and only
because it was mistakenly attributed to John.[8]

The Pauline formulation of marital purpose continued,
however, to be rigorously upheld. Paul's statement, "It is better
to marry than to burn," had numerous echoes in subsequent
writings and his exaltation of virginity and of celibacy, which
would have been regarded as sinful by the Jews and irresponsi-
ble by most Greek and Romans of antiquity, continued to pre-
vail. Paul's reasons for upholding the chaste ideal were
eschatological but they were dangerously similar to some of the
contemporary heretical views which arrived at the same chaste,
or at least celibate, ideal and were based on Gnostic professions

of the inherently evil nature of all matter. The encratic justification of antigamy and sexual abstinence was based on the belief that marriage and coitus entrapped more souls (or sparks of light) into the prison of matter. Thus, Apelles, Marcion, Tatian, Saturninus, and Mani, for example, condemned marriage and the procreation of children as the work of Satan.[9]

In a fictitious dialogue between Mani and Archelaos by Hegemonius, Mani's views on marriage and procreation are recorded:

> If you truly consider how the sons of man are generated, you will not find the Lord the creator of man but the creator is another who is of that nature of which there is no builder nor creator nor maker for only his own wickedness bore him. The intercourse of you men with your wives comes from this kind of happening. When you are satiated with fleshly food your concupiscence is excited. The fruits of generation are in this way multiplied—not virtuously nor philosophically nor rationally, but from a mere satiety of food and from lust and fornication.[10]

Or, to quote Augustine, Manichees condemn procreation as evil because "it infects a particle of God with the foulness of their flesh" (*Contra. Faustum*, 15.7; *PL* 42). At the same time, the antinomian tendency in Gnosticism also rejected marriage and children. It, too, was a result of the contempt of the body because venereal licentiousness reflected the freedom of the true gnostic from all bondage (including moral law), which was ordained by the Demiurge.

By the fourth century, then, when Christianity became the official religion of the state under Constantine, the Church fathers were faced with a quandary, and they attempted to sustain orthodox teaching in the face of obvious contradictory intellectual and religious currents as well as their own ambiguity about the flesh.

Although condemning the encratic heresies, many of the Fathers, especially, Jerome, shared the general attitude toward marriage and sex with the dualists.[11] Because they had to affirm the essential validity of God's injunction in Genesis to "increase and multiply," and because they could no longer advocate the imminent termination of the now gradually Christianized society, they wholeheartedly embraced the Pauline hierarchy of values: virginity is best, widowhood is next, marriage is the least perfect state. They argued that the New Testament precept of chastity superseded the Old Testament commandment. Moreover, the Fathers asserted on eschatological grounds that marriage was no longer necessary simply for the propogation of the race but that it served to provide sinful mankind with a remedy against concupiscence (John Chrysostom, *De virg.*, 19, *PG* 48; Jerome, *Adv. Jov.*, I, *PL* 23; Tertullian, *De exhort.*, 6, *CCL* 2).

The essentially ambiguous nature of the Church's position on marriage is even reflected in the edicts of the fourth century. The Council of Gangra, for instance, condemned anyone who maintained that marriage prevented a Christian from entering Heaven, but councils of the same century anathematized Jovinian for maintaining that—all other things being equal— virgins and married persons have equal chance of salvation.[12]

The most vigorous defense of the new virginity against opponents such as Jovinian was levelled not by conciliar decree but by the pen of one of the most renowned Western Fathers. At the end of the fourth century (i.e., after Emperor Constantine's conversion to Christianity) three now lost treatises were all more or less violently attacked by Jerome, the unequalled champion of chastity in the West. They were the works of Helvidius, Vigilantius, and Jovinianus. Jerome's refutation of these works, especially his vitriolic attack on Jovinian, subsequently became the richest and most often used storehouse of misogynistic and misogamous sentiments in the Middle Ages.

St. Jerome's *Adversus Jovinianum* as radical critique

The polemical treatise against Jovinian can be dated with considerable accuracy to 393, during Jerome's self-imposed exile in Bethlehem. The tract was occasioned by the request of Jerome's Roman friends, notably Pammachius, to refute the "Christian Epicurus" Jovinian. Jovinian's views had already been condemned by Pope Siricius and by Ambrose and the monk had been excommunicated twice (389 in Rome; 390 in Milan).

Nevertheless, Jerome took the opportunity to use the polemical platform for his championship of virginity.

Jerome's Catholic biographer, Cavallera, has a very high estimate of this work and calls it "the most brilliant of Jerome's works." To the Protestant Grutzmacher, on the other hand, the tract appears low and malicious. At least one scholar, David S. Wiesen, sees this vituperative work as a masterful satire in the Roman tradition. Wiesen argues that Jerome refers to himself as a satirist on four occasions "in the larger sense of a penetrating, vituperative critic of human behavior."[13] He even calls Jerome an *anima naturaliter satirica*. Most convincing is the evidence Wiesen summarizes in his comments on *Adversus Jovinianum* and Letters 22, 54:

> Thus in three works separated by many years, Jerome's desire to ridicule the natural lasciviousness of women evokes satiric descriptions containing similar details. These similarities suggest that in none of these passages was Jerome simply expressing spontaneous moral anger, for it is unlikely that the unhampered overflow of *saeva indignatio* would have produced three such similar descriptions on three separate occasions.[14]

Furthermore, Wiesen comments on the passages of domestic trouble in *Adversus Helvidium:* "Plainly this extended satire of domestic life is not the spontaneous expression of moral indignation but a highly artificial caricature." He also suggests that "in his mordant attacks on women more than in any other aspect of his satire, Jerome was heir to an age-old literary tradition."[15] Wiesen's observation is accurate, but it also raises a question: why did Jerome, so eager to condemn marriage and so conversant with the Latin pagan writers, especially the satirists, avoid extensive use of Juvenal's Sixth Satire? Lübeck lists only three occurrences of a single quotation from Juvenal (*Sat.* I, 15) in the whole of Jerome's corpus, and even though Bickel attributes the *rara avis* dictum in *Adversus Jovinianum* to Juvenal's Sixth Satire,[16] it could just as well have been borrowed from Persius. According to Hagendahl, "it may have been even proverbial."[17]

The possibility always exists that Jerome was not familiar with the Sixth Satire, even though that would be unlikely in view of Juvenal's popularity in the late fourth and early fifth centuries. Gilbert Highet points out that between 350 and 420 A.D. a pagan scholar compiled a commentary on Juvenal's Satires and that Servius quotes Juvenal more than seventy times in his notes on Virgil.[18] Moreover, both Prudentius and Lactantius admired the satirist and, as Highet observes, with Lactantius, Juvenal appears ". . . in the guise which he was to keep for the thousand years or more—as a thinker with standards higher than most pagans, and as a coiner of pithy and memorable epigrams." It seems more likely, then, that Jerome was consciously avoiding the use of the Sixth Satire simply because the Roman satire did not suit his immediate purpose. Juvenal's Sixth Satire is a dissuasion from marriage purporting to depict the current evils of the married state. *Adversus Jovinianum,* on the other hand, is a polemical treatise aiming to uphold the value of the chaste ideal. Jerome's treatise is primarily concerned with delivering an unconditional panegyric on virginity. Only by extension, as a secondary purpose, is the marital state denigrated. Furthermore, when attacking marriage, Jerome is less concerned with specifics (unless, of course, they are either biblical or upholding the chaste ideal) than with broad generalizations or *praecepta,* conveniently available from a florilegium of pagan philosophers, but not contained in the Sixth Satire, which specializes in mordant and vivid accounts of wifely misbehavior. Most of Jerome's non-biblical illustrative examples are *exempla in bono;* for the non-biblical *exempla in malo,* he substitutes extracts from pagan philosophers and writers. Juvenal's Sixth Satire, on the other hand, contains almost exclusively *exempla in malo* and even his very rare *exempla in bono* are treated ironically.

The topography of the treatise

The *libri adversus Jovinianum duo* opens with a paragraph maliciously attacking the style of Jovinian. As Hagendahl observes, "Nothing in this paragraph reveals that it was written by a Christian or against a Christian. We listen to an antique rhetor, proud of his own ability, mocking superciliously at the shortcomings of his adversary."[19] After attacking the barbarous style and diction of Jovinian, Jerome summarizes Jovinian's propositions in Chapters 3 and 4 and defends himself against potential accusations of encraticism.[20] He says he is no Manichee nor a Marcionite; he only wishes to reestablish a true hierarchy of values. Jerome's fears were justified, to judge from the violent reaction to his treatise. He was accused of Manichaenism and even his Roman friends felt that he had unduly exalted virginity at the expense of marriage. Pammachius tried to buy up as many copies of the work as possible in order to withdraw it from circulation, and both Pammachius and Domnio asked Jerome to write an apology for this tract. The fact that Jerome felt compelled to justify his orthodoxy regarding marital matters, and that the reaction to his treatise was violently adverse, reflects clearly the improved social status of the Church—eschatology and the extinction of the race were no longer such viable alternatives.

Chapters 5 through 40 offer proof from the Bible of the superiority of virginity to the married state, Chapters 6 through 15 dealing with Paul's letter to the Corinthians, and Chapters 16 through 27 providing examples of virginity from the Old and New Testaments, while Chapters 28 through 40 concern the "misunderstood" (that is, used by Jovinian) passages from the Bible. The final nine chapters muster evidence for the chaste ideal from pagan history, literature, and philosophy.

Chapter 5 is the actual beginning of the treatise and here Jerome sets out to reinterpret the biblical examples and dicta that Jovinian used to support his view of the inherent value of marriage, such as Seth, Enos, Cain, Malelech, Enoch, Methuselah, Lamech, and Noah, Abraham, Isaac, and Jacob, all of whom had wives and children. The dicta that were apparently used by Jovinia and therefore deserve Jerome's reinterpretation are Gen. 1:28: "Increase and multiply," Gen. 2:24: "Therefore man will leave father and mother and follow his wife and they will be one flesh," and Matt. 19:5: "What God hath joined, let no man tear asunder."[21] Jerome attacks the Old Testament evidence by New Testament authority: he argues that, according to Paul (I Cor. 7:1–9), marriage is merely a concession to fornication. Paul does not advise marriage, Jerome argues, he merely tolerates it: "it is better to marry than to burn" is a relegation from an absolute to a relative good. To illustrate his point, Jerome, with his characteristic indelicacy, turns to an analogy: It is good to eat wheaten bread, he says, but in order to avoid having to eat cow dung, one may eat barley bread. Obviously, wheat is better than barley, Jerome continues, just as chastity is better than marriage. That leaves the eating of cow dung to be equated with fornication. Moreover, the champion of chastity does not fail to note that the Apostle recommends one should always pray. But how can one pray while performing the marital act? It is better, Jerome concludes, to be like Christ who, himself a virgin, was born of a virgin.

In order to undermine the importance of Jovinian's biblical examples, Jerome reinterprets these examples and musters a catalogue of his own of chaste Old and New Testament figures: Adam and Eve only married after the fall (i.e., not in Paradise); only unclean animals are taken in pairs by Noah; Jacob's four wives are meant allegorically; David and Solomon are bad examples of the value of marriage because David shed blood and Solomon became an apostate. With his characteristic fervor, Jerome next turns the testimony of Solomon into proof of his own thesis. Good rhetorician that he was, Jerome introduced the Solomonic corpus by a topos of objectivity, as Ilona Opelt observes. He says that he will treat of Solomon, "So that he [Jovinian] may not claim that his [Solomon's] or other patriarch's case is feared by us. . . ."[22] "Like a worm in wood, so a wicked woman destroyeth her husband," Solomon observes, and Jerome comments (Ch. 28):

> But if you assert that this was spoken of bad wives, I shall briefly answer: What necessity rests upon me to run the risk of the wife I marry being bad? . . . "It is better," he [Solomon] says, "to dwell in a desert land, than with a contentious and passionate woman in a wide house." How seldom we find a wife without these faults, he knows who is married. . . . A continual dripping on a wintry day turns a man out of doors and so will a contentious woman drive a man from his own house. She floods the house with her constant nagging and chatter.

Once again, Jerome anticipates the possible objection of speaking only of odious women:

> The mere possibility of such a danger (i.e., marrying a bad wife) is in itself no light matter. For he who marries a wife is uncertain whether he is marrying an odious woman or one worthy of his love. If she be odious, she is intolerable. If worthy of love, her love is compared to the grave, to the parched earth, and to fire.

Jerome's discussion of the sufferings of the often-wed Solomon became important and often repeated *exempla in malo* of the canon of both misogynistic and misogamous writings in subsequent centuries. Here Jerome, like Juvenal and other misogynistic and misogamous writers, follows an ironic syllogism: Women either are odious or too passionate. The possibility that there might be something in between seems to have escaped the polemicist. Concluding his discussion of the Old Testament, Jerome remarks that while the Old Testament exemplifies the commandment to "increase and multiply" (and, after all, Abraham and the other Old Testament figures had the obligation of founding a race), the New Testament gives the commandment of virginity. Jerome remarks on Christ's and the apostles' celibacy and asserts that Christ's love for the virginal John exemplifies his preference of the chaste state. Even the Song of Songs is interpreted as a praise of virginity by Jerome. Like Methodius, he sees the *hortus conclusus* (Song of Songs, 4:12), as the symbol of the beloved, as a symbol of the virginity of Mary. In Chapter 36, Jerome deals with Jovinian's objection to the excessive ascetical ideal that the exaltation of virginity will result in the extinction of the race and says that only a few are chosen to the privilege of chastity. Therefore, there is no need to fear suigenocide.

Most enduring and most influential is Jerome's exhortatory catalogue of pagan chastity, celibacy, and philosophic misogamy, contained in Chapters 41 through 49 of *Adversus Jovinianum*. The canonic catalogue of *exempla in bono* exalts Atalanta, Harpalyce, Camilla, Iphigenia, and the Sibyl; Cassandra, Chryseis, the virgin priestesses of Diana of Aturus, and the Vestal virgins in Chapter 42. Jerome lists as manifestations of virgin births Buddha, Minerva, Plato, and Romulus and Remus, and as examples of chaste pagan widows (of marital and even extramarital fidelity) Alcestis, Penelope, Laodamia, Lucretia, Bibia, Cato's daughter Marcia, Porcia, Annia, Porcia minor, Marcella, Valeria. He adds the example of the Indian custom of having the favorite wife burnt together with her deceased husband, the example of Alcibiades' mistress who chose to die with him, and the exemplary devotion of Pantha from Xenophon's *Xyropaedia*.

The method of dissuasion

Jerome's use of examples from secular literature in support of his contention that the chaste ideal was upheld even in antiquity is much more elaborate than Tertullian's and includes some little-known and bizarre instances of female behavior. As Hagendahl observes: "It stands to reason that Jerome did not himself take pains to bring together all these often far-fetched *exempla* some of which contain information inaccessible elsewhere."[23] According to Ernst Bickel, whose scholarly study *Diatribe in Senecae philosophi fragmenta* still remains the most complete study of Jerome's sources for the *Adversus Jovinianum*, Jerome's chief sources were Seneca and Porphyry.[24] Seneca is mentioned several times by name but the Neoplatonic archenemy of Christianity not once. In agreement with Bickel, Hagendahl concludes that Porphyry is likely to have been the ultimate source for the Theophrastus fragment and most of the pagan exempla, for "who is more likely to have communicated information about the Greek philosophers than the Neoplatonic philosopher? Who else was in possession of the exquisite knowledge of Greek antiquity of which so many exempla give evidence?"[25]

Chapter 47 of this catalogue begins with a reproach to Christian women:

> What am I to do when the women of our time press me with apostolic authority and before the first husband is buried, repeat from morning to night the precepts which allow a second marriage? Seeing they despise the fidelity which Christian purity dictates, let them at least learn chastity from the heathens.

Paradoxically, Jerome's exclamation is followed by the famous fragment of Theophrastus' *aureolus liber de nuptiis*, which is the philosophic treatment of the standard question: "Is the wise man to marry or not?" The rhetorical structure of the chapter (exhortatory statement to widows not to marry followed by a demonstrative quotation from ancient authority) demonstrates a remarkable leap of logic.[26] Why Theophrastus' fragment, rather than an excerpt from an ascetical or second-marriage oriented work (like the still orthodox *ad uxorem* of Tertullian), is used to persuade the marriage-lusty ladies of the virtue of widowhood, is baffling.

Theophrastus' fragment is the advice to the philosopher not to marry because wife and children entail a burden to the philosopher. The fragment became the canonical work on philosophic misogamy throughout the Middle Ages and is found in several misogamistic compilations alone or in conjunction with the *Adversus Jovinianum* and Walter Map's *Valerius*. Pratt cites seven instances in the twelfth century alone of such compilations.[27] The work is also quoted as an authoritative text on marriage in such divergent works as John of Salisbury's *Policraticus*, Chaucer's wife of Bath's *Prologue*, and Deschamps' *Miroir de mariage*. Moreover, Jean de Meun in the thirteenth century cites Theophrastus and says that he was read in schools. A wise man should not take a wife, Theophrastus argues, because marriage will hinder the study of philosophy. In a sentence strongly reminiscent of Cicero ("It is not possible to serve both books and a wife"), Theophrastus says, "It is impossible for anyone to attend to his books and his wife." The usual catalogue of bad wifely qualities follows: matrons want possessions, are jealous and suspicious; they give "curtain lectures" and prevent the philosopher from attending on the lectures of wise men. Furthermore, Theophrastus argues, when a man marries, he buys an unexamined product. All other things of lesser value and importance are carefully examined before purchase, but ". . . a wife is the only thing that is not shown before she is married for fear that she may not give satisfaction." A wife is vain, lascivious, adulterous, dominating, and she may even resort to poison to have her way. Theophrastus culminates the bad wives catalogue with a chain of antithesis: if she is fair, she will soon have a lover; if ugly, she will turn wanton. "It is difficult to guard what many long for. It is annoying to have what no one thinks worth possessing." If she has the management of the house, the husband is her slave; if he keeps some authority to himself, he is considered disloyal. If he lets in soothsayers, prophets, old women, and vendors, her chastity shall be endangered; if he does not, she will be upset. This carefully balanced string of antitheses creates the impression of universal applicability. Neither extreme is particularly desirable—so, marriage is to be avoided. Moreover, Theophrastus continues, a wife is of no practical value whatsoever: "A faithful slave is a far better manager, more submissive to the master, more observant of his ways than a wife who thinks herself mistress if she acts in opposition to the wishes of her husband, that is, if she does what pleases her, not what she is commanded." While a wife is usually a poor nurse and of little help to her sick husband, the husband, in turn, must stay at her bedside when she is sick. If she be a good wife (and this concession is prefaced by the obligatory *rara avis* exclamation), the poor husband suffers with her even when she "groans in childbirth." Moreover, to marry in order to avoid loneliness does not apply as far as the wise man is concerned: "A wise man can never be alone. He has with him the good men of all time. . . . He is never less alone than when alone." With this statement Theophrastus, like Hesiod, but unlike Juvenal, addresses the possible value of marriage as providing companionship. He vitiates this potential value, however, by rendering it nonapplicable to the wise man. Finally, Theophrastus concludes, to marry for the sake of children is sheer stupidity: "Friends and relatives whom you can judiciously love are better and safer heirs than those whom you must make your heirs whether you like it or not." These are words of wisdom after Jerome's own heart and the champion of chastity apostrophizes Theophrastus' pagan wisdom that puts Christians to shame: "Shall a joint heir to Christ really long for human heirs?"

But the Theophrastian fragment and Jerome's own hyperbole are not enough; Jerome is determined to give the *consensus omnium.* Many "fonts of pagan wisdom," he asserts, reject marriage: Cicero said that he could not possibly devote himself to both a wife and philosophy; Socrates, the wisest of men, was mistreated by both of his wives; Sulla, Pompey, Mithridates, and Cato all had unchaste and haughty wives. Terentia, Cicero's wife, married his enemy, Sallust; Xanthippe as a disagreeable and bantering wife; Metella and Mucia were openly unchaste; Cato's wife Actoria Paula was of low birth and of haughty disposition. What is more, Herodotus says that "a woman puts off her modesty with her clothes," and Terence thinks a man happy who is unmarried. Like Juvenal, Jerome maintains that women are the cause of war, murder, and other atrocities: Pasiphae, Clytemnestra, Eriphyle, and Helen of Troy all committed or caused monstrous deeds. Jerome concludes the catalogue of bad wives by citing the *consensus omnium* of philosophers. His mustering of authorities is impressive—even though he does not name his chief source anywhere in the tract. Plato and Lysias, Jerome says, show the drawbacks of love; Seneca tells of unreasonable passionate marital love, and the Neopythagorean Sextus says that "he who too ardently loves his own wife is an adulterer." Jerome concludes the first part of the treatise with his observations on Seneca's stance that chastity is the flower of all womanly virtue:

> This [chastity] holds the primacy of all virtues in a woman. This it is that makes up for a wife's poverty, enhances her riches, redeems her deformity, gives grace to her beauty; it makes her act in a way worthy of her forefathers whose blood it does not taint with bastard offspring; of her children who through it have no need to blush—blush for their mother, or to be in doubt about their father. . . . The consulship sheds lustre upon men; eloquence gives eternal renown; military glory and triumph immortalize an obscure family. Many are the spheres ennobled by splendid ability. The virtue of a woman is in a special sense, purity. It was this that made Lucretia the equal of Brutus, if it did not make her his superior.

Thus, Jerome restates his position: woman is a sexual being; only by her chastity can she become the equal of man in fame and virtue; a woman's *pudicitia* is the moral equivalent of a man's *virtus*.[28]

In spite of his hiding behind a mass of authorities,[29] Jerome was still accused of going overboard in defending virginity at the expense of marriage. In 393 when asked to write an apology for his tract against Jovinian (because most Romans, even his friends, felt that he had unduly deprecated marriage), his response was indignant: "While I close with Jovinian in hand-to-hand combat, Manichaeus stabs me in the back" (*Epist.* 48, 2; *CSEL* 54). In his letter to Pammachius, Jerome relies on Paul's authority when he reaffirms his position: virginity is gold and the perfect state (symbolized by the number *100*; marriage is silver and a refuge of the morally weak (symbolized by thirty). Similarly, in a letter to Domnio, Jerome emphatically restates his opinion on marriage. He does this in a masterfully satirical manner: "He [a Roman who was attacking Jerome] must hear at least the echo of my cry 'I do not condemn marriage.' Indeed—and this I say to make my meaning quite clear to him—I should like every one to take a wife who, because he gets frightened at night, cannot manage to sleep alone" (*Epist.* 50, 5; *CSEL* 54). This is Jerome's burlesque on the companionship value in marriage.

Letter to Eustochium

Jerome's second major attack on marriage is his letter to Eustochium (*Epist.* 22; *CSEL* 54). Virginity, as the great antithesis to Paganism, is singled out by Jerome as the index of a virtuous life. The letter became very influential in the Middle Ages not, however, in the philosophic and satiric traditions of the topos, but in the didactic and exhortatory treatises addressed to nuns, such as the works of Adlhelm, Boniface, Aelfric, and the Venerable Bede.

The letter begins with a fine use of *praeteritio*, that is, the refusal to mention a subject, followed by in-depth treatment (usually with considerable gusto):

> I wrote to you thus ... to show you by my opening words that my object is not to praise the virginity which you follow ... or yet to recount the drawbacks of marriage, such as pregnancy, the crying of infants, the torture caused by a rival, the cares of house-

hold management, and all those fancied blessings which death at last cuts short. (*Epist.* 22.2; *CSEL* 54)

Jerome then lists his catalogues of wicked or at least disrespectable wives: worldly women who "plume themselves . . . because of their husband's high position," are "puffed up by their husbands' honors," and are "hedged in with troops of eunuchs." They wear golden robes and are gluttonous, and, as Jerome does not fail to note, gluttony breeds lust: "First the belly is crammed, then the other members are roused." Jerome explains to Eustochium that while God is the fountainhead of chastity and modesty, the Devil is the author of love and lechery (*Epist.* 22.11; *CSEL* 54).

The *exempla in malo* contain diverse types of self-indulgence, and the already-familiar linking of gluttony and lust. The Church father's favorite writer, Terence, among others, had already coined a pithy phrase on the subject and Jerome quotes it in *Adversus Jovinianum:* "Sine Cerere et Baccho, amor moritur" (without food and wine, love dies).

When commenting on the Old Testament precept of procreation, Jerome resorts to his familiar argumentation:

> The command to increase and multiply first finds fulfillment after the expulsion from paradise, after the nakedness and the fig leaves which speak of sexual passion. Let them marry and be given in marriage who eat their bread in the sweat of their brow; whose land brings forth to them thorns and thistles and whose crops are choked with briars. My seed produces fruit a hundred-fold. . . . In paradise Eve was a virgin, and it was only after the coats of skins that she began her married life . . . to show that virginity is natural while wedlock only follows guilt. What is born of wedlock is virgin flesh and it gives back in fruit what in root it has lost. . . . Christ is born a virgin of a virgin. (*Epist.* 22.19; *CSEL* 54)

After grudgingly admitting that marriage does have some value as a provider of new virgins ("I gather the rose from the thorn, the pearl from the shell"), Jerome distinguishes the Old Testament procreative ideal from the new precept:

> In those days the world was still unpeopled. . . . But gradually the crop grew and then the reaper was sent forth with his sickle. . . . What is this distress which does away with the joys of wedlock?

> The apostle tells us in a later verse: The time is short; it re-
> maineth that those who have wives be as if they had none. Neb-
> uchadnezzar is hard at hand. (*Epist*. 22.22; *CSEL* 54)

Later in the treatise, Jerome presents Eustochium with another
catalogue of *exempla in malo*. Like Juvenal, Jerome also disapproves of women and wives with literary and musical ambi-
tions and draws a vignette worthy of his great predecessor:

> Do not seek to appear over-eloquent, nor trifle with verse, nor
> make yourself gay with lyric songs. And do not out of affectation
> follow the sickly taste of married ladies who, pressing their teeth
> together, now keeping their lips apart, speak with a lisp and pur-
> posely clip their words, because they fancy that to pronounce
> them naturally is a mark of country breeding. Accordingly, they
> find pleasure in what I may call an adultery of the tongue. (*Epist*.
> 22.29; *CSEL* 54)

Jerome instructs Eustochium to shun other wifely qualities as
covetousness, and love of finery.

One of Jerome's most repugnant scatological metaphors for
marriage, however, is not contained in his two major works on
chastity, but is included in the "consolatory" letter to the recently widowed Furia. Here Jerome with his accustomed indelicacy compares the death of Furia's husband to the relieving of
an overstuffed stomach. Therefore, the church father explains,
to remarry would be to return, like a dog, to its vomit or a
pig to its mud (*Epist*. 54.4; *CSEL* 54). The same letter also
contains a food metaphor for marriage, thus further linking the
vices of gluttony and lust to marriage; Jerome compares
marriage to the flesh of quails on which Israelites glutted
themselves.

Throughout his works, Jerome is consistent in his view of
marriage. He maintains that virginity is the ideal state and that
marriage, although permitted, is a less perfect and, therefore, a
less desirable state. There is no contradiction between the high
estimate in which Jerome held some women and his violent
attacks on marriage and on secular women. All women that he
respected were either virgins or widows, and they all led ascetic
lives either according to Jerome's instruction or under his di-

rect supervision. The champion of chastity wrote this very revealing statement about women:

> As long as woman is for birth and children, she is different from man as body is from soul. But when she wishes to serve Christ more than the world, then she will cease to be a woman and will be called man (*vir*). (*Comm. in epist. ad Ephes.* III. 5; *CSEL* 54)

What better expression of both the traditional view of the lower (sensitive) nature of woman and of the ascetic conception of male-female equality by means of transcending the traditional sex roles in pursuit of the chaste ideal!

Like Juvenal's Sixth Satire, Jerome's *Adversus Jovinianum* exhibits a perfect form-content bond. Juvenal's persona proposes what civic and moral authorities decried but which many of his contemporaries practiced. He advises against matrimony, saying that no woman can be found worthy to be a wife. He illustrates his assertion by means of the *reductio ad absurdum* of the inversions of generally accepted values. Consequently, his satire is a string of concrete examples with a few indignant interpolations. Jerome, on the other hand, is arguing for a way of life which was apparently not widely practiced and which was not unanimously upheld by civic and moral authorities. In fact, the more rigorous manifestations of the celibate life were condemned as heresies. Consequently, Jerome gathers a mass of authorities. He presents the *consensus omnium* regarding the wisdom of celibacy by parading authorities (both scriptural and worldly) on the subject. Juvenal's documentation is concentrated on everyday wifely atrocities which are augmented by a few parallel examples from history and literature. Jerome, of course, cannot claim any firsthand knowledge of wicked wives. He, too, has his examples of wicked wives, but they are almost invariably either biblical, historical, mythological, or admittedly based on secondhand information. Juvenal "entertains"; Jerome wants to convince. The *Adversus Jovinianum* or at least the most influential part of it is a florilegium on the subject of celibacy, while Juvenal's Sixth Satire is the indignant review of observation. The authoritative form characteristic of Jerome was adopted by most medieval writers of philosophic misogamy, while the Juvenalian personal form was reserved for works of general misogamy.

In their use of obscenity, the two writers differ markedly: Juvenal is voyeuristic and employs elegant innuendoes and double entendres while Jerome is basically indignant and scatological. Juvenal's use of obscenity is either visually direct or linguistically ambiguous; Jerome's is metaphorical. Juvenal gives a detailed description of female sexual perversity; Jerome presents the scatological metaphors of excrement and vomit as the physical and moral equivalents of fornication and marriage. Juvenal's use of sexual obscenity serves to show the inversion or perversion of a natural (and hypothetically good) function; Jerome's indignant attacks on sex equate it with a yet lower (more exclusively physical) level of materialism, the level of excremental discharge—a reflection of his undifferentiated distrust of all carnality.

Regarding children, the attitudes of the two writers reflect a similar discrepancy. Juvenal argues that Roman matrons thwart the husband's desire for legitimate heirs by either bearing bastards or by not bearing at all. In other words, he presents the inversion of a value as a dissuasive argument. Jerome, on the other hand, simply denies the inherent value of childbearing, and, in addition, he emphasizes (via Theophrastus) that children are a troublesome burden—again, an attitude thoroughly in keeping with the apocalyptic world view and Jerome's dualist disdain for anything except spiritual generation.

Conclusion

The patristic age was the cradle of ascetic misogamy, characterized chiefly by a disinterest in the procreative ideal and in the careful delineation of heirarchical values, the highest of which is chastity. Ascetic misogamy stressed not so much the advantages and virtues of celibacy as those of chastity and abstinence. Writers like Tertullian, Methodius, and, above all, Jerome helped to solidify the relatively low estimation of marriage by regarding it as a concession to human frailty and as an inferior state incompatible with holy devotion.

Upheld bilaterally, the chaste ideal denied the necessity of the traditional sex roles and thus continued the revolutionary New Testament emphasis on the baptismal equality of all: "There is neither male nor female; for you are all one in Christ Jesus" (Gal. 3:28). Although woman was less perfect and more libidinous than man and her reason for existence more closely tied to procreation, the patristic view was that she could rise above her subordination by becoming like a man, that is by denying her sexuality. Thus, Jerome writes to Demetrias:

> You must act against nature or rather above nature if you are to forswear your natural functions, to cut off your own root, to cull no fruit but that of virginity, to abjure the marriage bed, to shun intercourse with men and, while in the body, to live as though out of it.

Yet, clearly, the powerful influences of asceticism, if applied to the whole body of believers, would have resulted only in their "gradual extinction or in lawless licentiousness."[30] Thus, while it had arguably stimulated early conversions among the disenfranchised (hence the widely circulated Roman wisdom that Christianity was a religion for women and slaves), Christianity moved away from its marginal cult status only by disavowing its manifestly revolutionary ascetic ethos.

Early Christian eschatology and its correlative, thoroughgoing asceticism that rivaled competing dualist heresies, were two things that the Christian leadership needed to jettison, or at least to recast, in order to assure the Church's advance toward institutionalization.

In spite of their strict asceticism, the Fathers had to confirm the relative good of marriage as a divinely ordained and socially necessary institution. With the Church's rise to power, Christianity became not only a religious, but also a social and political force. As such, certain compromises had to be made: the Church abandoned (declared heretical) categorical antinomianism and misogamy and upheld the celibate ideal only for a select elite. The State, on the other hand, compromised by accepting the Church's hierarchical system of values that placed virginity at the pinnacle of excellence. Thus, for example, after

his conversion to Christianity Constantine encouraged the prevailing tendency by not only repealing the Augustan marital
legislation that imposed penalties on the unmarried, but he
even extended the power of making wills to minors who
wished to become celibate. In the next centuries, the full ramifications of this compromise would begin to be appreciated—
the fusion of ascetic chastity with celibacy would gradually lose
its broad appeal and the promise of gains in this world would
again provide the inducement for choosing single blessedness.

❖ III ❖

Philosophic Misogamy

The great and lesser silence:
the reemergence of antimarriage
literature in the twelfth century

St. Augustine, the great synthesizer of patristic thought on marriage and the spokesman whose systematic treatment of the subject would make all preceding comments seem like asides, was not immune to the appeal of eschatology. Declaring, in fine Jeromian style, that thanks to pagan fecundity there are already enough souls to fill heaven, Augustine counseled all men to refrain from the obsolete Old Testament command to increase and multiply. By rising to the angelic life where there is no more "marrying and giving in marriage," the end of the world would be hastened and the time of blessedness, when the physical cosmos would be transformed into the spiritual New Creation, would dawn the sooner.

In viewing virginity "as the shortest route to heaven not only for man but for the cosmos," Augustine clearly shows his continuity with early Christian apocalypticism and a "fin de siècle" mentality of late antiquity at the time of the fall of a civilization.[1] Yet even as he wrote, a new "frontier" civilization was taking shape in Western Europe, one in which scarcity and pragmatism would make arguments against "marrying and giving in marriage" unthinkable in a secular sphere. While men and women from the sixth to the eleventh centuries continued to be exhorted to chastity and ascetic manuals were repeatedly composed for the benefit of monks and nuns, marriage as an institution was not attacked in separate tracts.[2]

The extent to which early medieval secular society was inimical to antigamy can be gleaned from a glance at the prevailing barbaric customary laws and their ecclesiastic equivalent, the Penitentials. Germanic custom, not Roman law, provided the basic models for marriage in this primitive period and the incorporation of Germanic marital customs into religious practice is most apparent in the system of composition which is based on the Celtic and Germanic custom of paying compensation as a satisfaction to the injured party's relatives.

Among the Germanic tribes, polygamy and concubinage were common. Wives, as Frances and Joseph Gies point out, were bought and sold; rape was treated as theft, and husbands could easily repudiate their wives.[3] Thus, it is not surprising that compensation is offered for many marriage or sex-related offenses in the penitentials, our best sources of evidence for medieval ecclesiastical, marital, and sexual ethics before their codification in the twelfth century.[4] The *dos* or bride-price, for example, is required by the *Book of David* for the seduction or rape of virgins and the *Columban Penitential* requires a certain *pretium* (comparable to that paid for theft) to be paid to the girl's parents for her misuse or humiliation by any man.[5] Of particular interest, the penalties imposed for sex not involving a woman and for manifest sexual crimes are often substantially more severe than the penalties for abortive or heterosexual practices.[6] The penitentials show a marked pragmatism as regards sexual mores. As Flandrin observes, the separate punishment assigned to either contraception or adultery is consistently more severe than the penalty for the two sins combined. If, for example, a child illegitimately fathered by a clerk is aborted, the penalty is generally only one-half of what it is when the child is born and the sin is manifest (*manifestum peccatum*) (*Penitentialis Vinniani* 21; *Penitentialis Columbani* 2).

The implication arising from this inequality of penitential prescriptions is that protection of life (in the foetus or the born child) is less of a motive for the authors than is the control of lust and the upholding of discipline. Similarly, the pragmatism underlying the discrimination in assigning penitence for those clerks whose crime is evident to all (i.e., cases where the child is born), and for those whose crime is not, suggests that the writers of penitentials were more concerned with the social repercussions of obvious clerical misbehavior than with the misbehavior itself. In an age as chaotic and anarchic as the early

Middle Ages, it is hardly surprising that penitential writers are more concerned with upholding a semblance of order, and with castigating violent sexual crimes and crimes of bestiality, than with marital casuistry.

From the middle of the eighth century sources for studying early medieval society became more varied and abundant.[7] Like the Germanic law codes and the Penitentials, these sources too, whether charters or manorial surveys, attest to a society in which barbarian rather than classical Roman models of marriage hold sway. The Germanic reverse dowry or bridewealth, for instance, becomes the universal rule. The chief beneficiary of payment and gifts remains the bride—a situation reflecting continued scarcity of females and the essential character of their services in the manorial (rural) household.

It is not until the great ecclesiastical reform movement and the correlative aristocratic retrenchment of the eleventh and twelfth centuries that classical models, regarding marriage, as well as the market place, begin to reassert themselves.[8] In the new milieu of continuing population expansion and finite resources, both nobles and clergy had to find new ways of managing and conserving their resources. For the noble household, this would increasingly mean limiting the acquisition of property and public power of aristocratic women. For the Church, it meant a clear enforcement of its authority over lay marriages and insistence on celibacy for its own elite.

Shifting patterns of marriage among the nobility

From the eleventh century on, greater peace and stability in Western Europe brought with it an irony for the aristocracy. Not only were there fewer opportunities to enhance family fortunes through war and plunder, but the reformers in the Church strove diligently to deprive the laity of control over profitable ecclesiastical lands and benefices.

Faced with a population surge that would not crest until the 1300s, the nobility was forced to find new ways to shore up and increase their existing, and relatively scarce, proprietary holdings. Primogeniture was one common expedient that began to be employed. Except in unusual circumstances, daughters and younger sons were barred from a claim on patrimony. In addition to favoring male descendants over females, the twelfth century nobility also began once again to shift the "burdens of matrimony" to the bride and her family, resurrecting for the first time since antiquity the dowry in its classical sense.[9]

The goal of both of these trends, which would accelerate in the late Middle Ages, seems to be to preserve scarce resources and opportunities for the exercise of public power by limiting their acquisition by women, via marriage gifts or other means:

> With the power of their women thus severely reduced, the aristocratic family was in better condition to face the ensuing period of struggle with the resurgent monarchies—a struggle that continued well into modern times. But by the twelfth century, public power was gradually being recaptured from the great aristocratic families by kings and princes. Institutions outside the household were being created to administer public affairs. The success of the aristocracy as a class in adjusting itself to this broad political change was accomplished largely at the expense of the aristocratic women.[10]

Jurisdiction over marriage

Until the later Middle Ages, neither the Church nor the aristocracy held unchallenged, exclusive jurisdiction over marital matters. In the eleventh and twelfth centuries as the struggle between Church and feudal aristocracy greatly intensified, it began to involve questions of the form for a valid, and so binding, marital contract—another in the Church's attempts to direct the course of secular affairs.

Lay and Church models of marriage differed considerably. The lay model of marriage, as Georges Duby observes, had three basic features: First, it regulated sexual impulses in the interest of a patrimony (as long as no inheritance was involved, society permitted extramarital sex for the unmarried people and husbands, even though the wife's fidelity was upheld as the most important safeguard against the intrusion of the heir of another man's blood).[11] Second, this moral code encouraged widowers to remarry, and recognized the validity of the practice of repudiation as long as both houses agreed. Third, the lay model showed a strong tendency toward endogamy as a means of reuniting the family estate.

The Church, on the other hand, emphasized the importance of the consent of both parties (not only their parents'), it condemned extramarital sex as fornication, disapproved of second marriages and of repudiation, and it insisted on strict exogamy extending prohibitions to the seventh degree of consanguinity. The Church model, although modified, prevailed. The reforming Lateran Councils and the works of the twelfth century decretists are characterized by an increased juridical interest in marital affairs. Both this evolving law and the Church's interest in clerical celibacy, was influenced by the reemergence of heretical sects opposed to marrying and procreation.

Heresies

Although several dualist heresies survived in the Balkan countries and in Asia Minor throughout the Middle Ages, it was in the eleventh and twelfth centuries in France and Italy that they surfaced with great vigor.[12] Dualist teachings, like the early Christian eschatological and heretic beliefs, were antisocial, antimarriage, and antiprocreation, and whatever the reason for the resurgence of the dualistic heresies, the problem was severe enough in 1028 to prompt the Duke of Aquitaine, William V, to summon a council of bishops to discuss plans for crushing the heresy. Noonan points out that a "Manichaeism is reported in Aquitaine in 1018 and in 1025 and that a certain Gandulph was preaching the rejection of marriage in Arras."[13] At the same time, there was a religious community in Moneforte that discouraged marriage, and, in 1045, heretics appeared in Châlons that opposed marriage. Almost 100 years later in 1119 Pope Calixtus II held a council to anathematize certain heretics "who denied the sacraments of Holy Communion, baptism and marriage." In 1157, Archbishop Samson of Reims complained that Manichaeism was disseminated throughout his diocese by itinerant weavers who "condemned marriage."[14] There was a burning of Cathars in Cologne in 1163, but in Languedoc the heresy triumphed for over half a century.

All of the twelfth century heresies were opposed to marriage and procreation not because it meant sexual indulgence but because the creation of new life somehow entrapped the divine spirit further into matter. An anonymous *Summa* against heretics from the late twelfth century states that according to Cathar teaching no one can be saved who exercises the "rights of marriage." And Rainer Sacconi, a reconverted Cathar, alleged that "to Cathars carnal marriage is mortal sin." By 1139, the danger of the heresy was felt to be strong enough to warrant the attention of an ecumenical council. The second Lateran condemned those heretics who opposed marriage and "the carnal works of marriage." Lateran III and IV as well as II were concerned with the Cathars and instituted the Dominican inquisition in 1217 with the specific purpose of converting the Cathars.

Given this situation, the reforming Lateran councils were faced with a difficult problem. They wished to promote and enforce the celibate ideal for the clergy while, at the same time, combatting antinomian heresies. Conversely, while emphasizing the Pauline hierarchy of values (chastity is best, widowhood is next and marital state last), justifying, thus, the celibate ideal for the clergy (at a time when nepotism and nicholaism were a very real problem and concubinous clergy frequently advocated marriage for all), the Church also had to reaffirm the divine right of marriage. As Gilchrist observes, the "corporate nature" of the Church had to be safeguarded against clerical individualism. Clerics had to be prevented from treating their benefices as private property—disposable at will: the concept of the inalienability of ecclesiastical lands was connected with the moral imperative of eliminating priest-marriage and abolishing simony. As with the aristocracy, the Church began to hold on to its lands.[15]

From the sixth to the eleventh centuries, councils and synods repeatedly passed sanctions against the marriage and concubinage of the clergy which testifies both to the widespread custom of clerical marriage and the impossibility (or disinclination) to enforce celibacy. Some popes were severe enough: Nicholas II reaffirmed the ascetic reformatory efforts of the Cluniac movement and forbade the attendance of Mass celebrated by a priest who was either married or kept a concubine. However, the resistance to the celibate ideal was strong. The conflict between married and celibate clergy even produced an antipope, the Milanese Honorius II. Nevertheless, the celibate program gradually prevailed due not least to Gregory VII's efforts at enforcing and propagating clerical celibacy, and, most of all, to the latter efforts of Innocent III. Church authorities tried to resolve the problem by proposing two sets of codes of behavior. To quote Bishop Gerard of Cambrai, ecclesiastical men were encouraged to avoid "the servitude to the marriage bed," while for laymen "neither the Gospels nor Paul prohibited marriage."[16] Laymen could marry, provided that they knew how to avoid lust (*voluptas*) and had desire to beget children. The professed superiority of the celibate ideal as well as the Church's legal and corporate personality, and her omnipresent influence are reflected in the enormous surrogate familial functions assumed by the Church: the Church gave spiritual birth (through baptism); assigned spiritual parents on whom major responsibilities were conferred and who were treated with regard to marital impediments as physical relatives; had a monopoly on education; sanctified marriage; administered the last rites. A confessor was father to his charge and had to give his consent for any major change in the person's life. A priest was "married" to his congregation; all believers were the children of the Church, ecclesiastics were married to Christ and the Church, and nuns were the brides of Christ.[17]

The codified justification of marriage took the form of a restatement of the Augustinian marital ethics with a special emphasis on the first of the three "goods" of marriage, namely, children. Ivo of Chartres, Peter Lombard, and Gratian effected the most influential compilations of the subject of marriage in the eleventh and twelfth centuries; this period also saw the rise of the controversy regarding the formation of marriage. The initial proponents in the controversy were the canonists of Bologna, supporting Gratian and the dialecticians of Paris, supporting Hugh of St. Victor and Peter Lombard. Gratian emphasized the importance of *commixtio corporum* as an essential component of a valid marriage while Hugh and Peter only considered it an accessory element—a change in the perspective that will have far-reaching ramifications, as we will see, in the thirteenth century rigorist position.

Courtly love

It is impossible to discuss medieval misogamy, and twelfth century misogamy in particular, without reference to that phenomenon which Gaston Paris termed *amour courtois,* and which Henry A. Kelly proposes to call a "code of courtly courtship."[18] Paris suggested in 1883 that courtly love made its first appearance in French literature in the *Lancelot* of Chretien as an illicit, furtive passion, characterized by the lover's constant fear of losing his lady or displeasing her, and C. S. Lewis' 1936 book, *The Allegory of Love,* accepts as given the concept of courtly love as a specialized upper-class code of behavior characterized by Humility, Courtesy, Adultery, and the Religion of Love.[19] Donnell von de Voort and D. W. Robertson Jr., on the other hand, offer an attack on the whole notion of courtly love, von de Voort proposing that, at least in English literature, "idealized immorality has no place in the prose and metrical romances"; and Robertson, reading Chretian's romances and Andreas Capellanus' *De arte honeste amandi* as ironic and humorous, broadsides against "idolatrous passion."[20]

While both camps of scholars promote too intransigent a theory, one thing is certain: in the late eleventh and twelfth centuries a type of literature appeared which, often in a stereotypic fashion, but sometimes in a personal mode, depicted the courtship or affair of a young man and a lady. In this body of literary texts, the beloved lady sometimes is shown as married and often is described in the feudal terminology of lordship. She is often older than the young man wooing her and of a higher social position, and his love for her usually has an ennobling effect on his character and frequently a negative effect on his purse. As Peter Dronke observes, this ennobling spiritualized love has a great deal in common with the peculiar tone of Christian mysticism,[21] but the type of love described also lends itself with great facility to ironic treatment.[22]

Clearly, this is not the place to ascertain whether Arabic influence, Cathar heresy, Mariology, Roman elegy, or "Ovid misunderstood" account for the occurrence of the courtly love code.[23] One thing, however, is clear: this code was substantially different from any of its supposed sources.[24]

In its most codified and intense form, courtly love was antigamous or at least not principally opposed to adultery. Georges Duby even suggests that courtly love was a "domestication" game directed, or at least tolerated, by the heads of houses as an "exaltation of gaiety, the game, and pleasure and as a summons to break the threefold injunction against abduction, adultery, and fornication, courtly love does assume the appearance of a threefold defiance of the power of those who arrange marriages.... But this defiance is only apparent."[25]

The misogamous attitude of courtly lovers is expressed by their assertion that love must be freely given and received and that the marriage bond is not conducive to this free exchange. A letter from Marie of Champagne dated May 1174, quoted by Andreas Cappelanus as expert testimony on the courtly code, reads:

> ... this is the doubt that has arisen between you: whether love can have any place between husband and wife. ... We declare and we hold as firmly established that love cannot exert its powers between two people who are married to each other. For lovers give each other everything freely, under no compulsion of necessity, but married people are in duty bound to give to each other's desires and deny themselves to each other in nothing.[26]

This is a very creative and highly paradoxical restatement of the Pauline statement concerning the purpose of marriage: marriage is a means of avoiding fornication with others; what takes place within marriage is different from fornication or, as Marie would have it, from love. Andreas even has one of his characters quote ecclesiastical authority to make an argument in favor of extramarital love. A would-be lover attempts to persuade his lady that she could not love her husband by saying: "For as the apostolic book teaches, a vehement lover of his own wife is judged an adulterer."

Capellanus' book, *De arte honeste amandi,* one of the best source books for several facets of the courtly love tradition, is a satiric, pragmatic, enigmatic Latin guidebook to the art of amatory persuasion. The tract was probably written for clerks but was definitely intended for an audience that had education, intelligence, and much free time (i.e., for the same audience as the works of philosophic misogamy). The book seems to exemplify the same literary purpose as Ovid's *Ars Amatoria*—after all, the twelfth century had been termed the *aetas Ovidiana*—namely, the writer's offer of instruction to those who wish to gain a mistress. Ovid emphasizes that he is not writing for those who are rich (they can easily acquire a mistress by lavish gifts) nor those who are lacking refinement (*cultus*) or are ridiculously boorish (*rusticitas*), but for polished young people with a facility for acquiring the *ars.* Like Ovid, Andreas has helpful hints both for the sophisticated young man and the sophisticated young lady of "good character"—only rich magnates, peasants, and boors are excluded from the profitable instructions of his pages. Peasants are excluded because, as Andreas says, "it rarely happens that we find farmers serving in love's court, but naturally, like a horse or a mule, they give themselves up to the work of Venus, as nature's urging teaches them to do." Furthermore, he adds, "it is inexpedient to teach them the art of love, because they may slack in their work and the farms . . . through lack of cultivation might prove useless to us" (Ch. 11).

Andreas outlines the valid reasons for acquiring love (beautiful figure, excellence of character, readiness of speech) and rejects those which he does not consider worthy of inspiring love (enormous wealth, readiness to grant what is sought). Wealth does not inspire love, Andreas says, because "real love comes only from the affection of the heart and is granted out of pure grace and genuine liberality . . . indeed the wantonness of such women [who love for money] is more polluted than the passion of harlots. . . . " Similarly, the easy attainment of one's goals is a sure sign, according to Andreas, that the woman "desires to sate her lust with anyone." He admonishes Walter, "It should be clear to you that where you find it easy to attain your desire you may be sure there is no love." Andreas then concludes that excellence (read, nobility) of character is the most valid reason for love but that articulateness is the best guarantee for inspiring love. He says:

> Character alone, then, is worthy of the crown of love. Many times fluency of speech will incline to love the hearts of those who do not love, for an elaborate line of thought on the part of the lover usually sets love's arrows aflying and creates a presumption in favor of the excellent character of the speaker. How this may be I shall try to show you as briefly as I can. To this end I shall first explain to you that one woman belongs to the middle class *(plebeia)*, and a second to the simple nobility *(nobilis)*, and a third to the higher nobility *(nobilior)*. ... So it is with men. ... In addition, among men we find one rank more than among women, since there is a man more noble than any of these, that is, the clerk *(clericus)*.

In Book I Chapter VII, Andreas specifically addresses himself to the "most noble" of men, the clerks:

> A clerk ought therefore because he derives his nobility from God to be a stranger to every act of love and to put aside all uncleanness of body, or he will deserve to be deprived of his special nobility granted him by God. But since hardly anyone ever lives without carnal sin, and since the life of the clergy is, because of the continual idleness and the great abundance of food, naturally more liable to temptations of the body than that of any other men, if any clerk should wish to enter into the lists of love let him speak and apply himself to Love's service in accordance with the rank or standing of his parents, as we have already fully explained in regard to the different ranks of men.

If we assume that the *De arte honeste amandi* was written for clerks and educated young men and ladies (i.e., for the schools and the court) as an entertaining, practical manual, then neither the linguistic medium (Latin) nor the final palinode, the *De reprobatione amoris,* are surprising.[27]

Andreas' book describes love as an illness, a suffering *(passio)* derived from the sight and meditation of the beloved. It is a state which, he says, can be recognized by pallor, lack of appetite, and a change in habit and mien. Moreover, love is a kind of voluntary servitude to which the lover subjects himself. The first two books of the *De arte,* provide model dialogues for men and women pursuing amatory persuasion, case studies, and judgments of courtly affairs, and urbane instructions. The last book of the work, however, is an unconditional indictment of women and love.

The third book is prefaced by an address to Walter: "now you [Walter] can lack nothing in the art of love, since in this little book we gave you the theory of the subject fully and completely, being willing to accede to your request because of the great love we have for you ... and ... for fear lest you might think us stupid." Walter is then encouraged to refrain from love because God abhors fornicators. Andreas proposes an ingenious explanation for the instituting of marriage to counteract lust. He says, "If God had wished the act of fornication to be without blame, He would have had no reason to order the solemnization of marriage, since God's people could multiply faster without it than by marrying." Heed my advice, Andreas concludes his catalogue of reasons against love, and embrace chastity! By love and the works of love men's bodies are weakened, Andreas says, and then presents Walter with an all inclusive, often contradictory, enraged attack on women. Women are greedy, grasping, avaricious, fickle, disobedient, proud, gluttonous, wanton, superstitious, and faithless. Greed takes the central place in Andreas' attack and recurs frequently in combination with the other vices.

In conclusion, by the twelfth century there were, in addition to the previously discussed ancient and patristic texts, several new misogamous currents readily available to writers of antimatrimonial treatises. The Cathars, Albigenses, and other eleventh and twelfth century Dualists deprecated marriage and the procreative ideal. At the same time and in the same location as the Cathars (Languedoc and Aquitaine), an ideology appeared, usually referred to as "courtly love," which celebrated love *outside* of marriage and rejected the generative purpose.

Just as the misogamy of the *amour courtois* is a product of polite society that favors refinement for its own sake, so philosophic misogamy is the product of a society or a segment of society which favors learning for its own sake—i.e., a society of professional intellectuals. It is the index of an age when scholarship as a professional activity is valued and pursued. As such, it is possible only in a period of relative order and civilization. It is essentially urban. Philosophic misogamy, unlike ascetic misogamy, is at home in the schools and at court rather than in monasteries. The other major requirements for the existence of philosophic misogamy are, of course, the same as for the other branches: a dim view of the intellectual, emotional, companionship value of marriage (as exemplified by Pauline and decretal traditions), a conviction of the biological, intellectual, and moral inferiority of the female sex (as evidenced by the exegetical tradition), a displeasure with a real or imagined improvement in the status of women (in this case, with the depiction of women in courtly literature) and, perhaps, with the reaction against the earlier economic clout of noblewomen as wives.

Philosophic misogamy attests to the upholding of the celibate ideal not for Everyman, but for a select elite of careermen, be it for religious, intellectual, or social reasons, and it emphasizes surrogate family ties in favor of physical marriage. The philosophic branch of misogamy advocates celibacy (not necessarily chastity) on the grounds that a wife and children are burdensome to the philosopher who should devote himself rather to his studies than to the everyday cares of family life. In its lack of interest in the chaste ideal, undiluted philosophic misogamy differs from ascetic misogamy that, as we have seen in the previous chapter, bases more emphasis on chastity than on celibacy, because chastity is the perfect, future-oriented, sinless state which enables Christians to devote all their energies to the contemplation and service of God.

Unlike general misogamy (which is addressed to Everyman), and ascetic misogamy (which in its medieval manifestations is addressed to priests and men and women in religion), philosophic misogamy is addressed to learned men. Consequently, the argument of tracts of philosophic misogamy usually runs as follows: learn by the example and wisdom of others, so that you may avoid the pitfalls of love, the greatest of which is matrimony, because it interferes with serious study and because it entails eternal servitude and ignominy; your bride should be Athena (or the Church), who elevates rather than degrades you.

Philosophic misogamy is the product of professional scholars and occurs as a corollary to the blossoming forth of medieval centers of learning: the urban cathedral schools and, later, the universities with their increased interest in the systematic and autonomous study of philosophy. It comes as no surprise, then, that one of the earliest medieval comprehensive texts of philosophic misogamy occurs in the writings of Peter Abelard, one of the first professional scholars of the Middle Ages, in the *Theologia Christiana* and in the *Historia Calamitatum* (c. 1132).

Secularism and satire in the works of Abelard, John of Salisbury, Walter Map, Hugh of Folietto, Peter of Blois, and Andreas Fieschi

Peter Abelard

In the *Theologia Christiana,* Abelard argues that pre-Christian thinkers had achieved salvation by their virtuous life and good intention. "Philosophers of 'old,'" he observes, "led a life of 'evangelical and apostolic perfection.'"[28] Their lives were characterized by temperance and charity, "everything being held in common." Furthermore, they showed continence and restraint: "inspired by such and similar reasons, the philosophers set themselves to a life of continence. They wished to have time for thought: they did not desire to reduce their forces by giving way before the distractions of women." Needless to say, the "such and similar" reasons are entirely honorable: to "avoid the snares of the world," "desire for divine contemplation," "acquisition of philosophy." Abelard combines the topos of misogamy with that of self-sufficiency by emphasizing that ancient philosophers" . . . had the perfection of anchorites in abstinence and manual work," for as Jerome says, "that philosopher is praised among the Greeks who can claim that everything which he uses, even to his cloak and ring, have been made by himself." Thus, Abelard emphasizes the importance of complete autonomy for the philosopher, the independence from material and marital ties.

The association of the two topoi had already been implied by Theophrastus whom, incidentally, Abelard quotes at length in support of his view of philosophy and marriage. Theophrastus, as we have seen, had suggested that taking a wife inevitably resulted in the need for acquiring material goods which would otherwise be unnecessary for the wise man. Abelard subsequently extols the total self-sufficiency of the philosophers. Abelard also suggests the essentially adulterous nature of marriage for a philosopher who is already betrothed to philosophy: "Socrates himself well knew this danger [marriage] and is an example of the importance to a philosopher of the blameless life, and of avoiding another union adulterously to that with philosophy herself." The Theophrastus fragment is followed up by several examples of pagan lay chastity drawn from Jerome's *Adversus Jovinianum*. Thus, the passage in the *Theologia* is fundamentally a learned florilegium on the subject of marriage in which the wisdom and virtue of pagan philosophers is favorably contrasted with the pitiful marital experiences of Adam, Samson, David, and Solomon. Abelard's purpose in this segment is to show that philosophy was always a matter both of knowledge and of morality, and that the moral fortitude of ancient philosophers is manifested in their celibate, communal, and self-sufficient way of life. In their total autonomy, pagan philosophers armed themselves against the vicissitudes of fate. The celibacy of ancient philosophers is an important piece in the mosaic prepared by Abelard, intended to show that a system of values has only limited usefulness unless it has been practiced, understood, and valued by rational mankind throughout the ages.

While the *Theologia Christiana* passage is fundamentally a theoretical statement on the inherent value and virtue of celibacy, primarily from a Christian but also from a rational, philosophic point of view, the treatment of the subject in the *Historia Calamitatum* is personal. Here not only the philosopher, but Abelard the philosopher is being dissuaded from marriage.[29]

The dispute concerning the authenticity of the correspondence between Abelard and Heloise is far from being settled. Etienne Gilson was able to show in 1938 that most of the arguments against the authenticity of the letters were unfounded, but the controversy was reopened in 1953 by the Basilian monk Joseph Muckle, the learned editor of the letters.[30] Scholars such as Benton who originally proposed a complex multiple-authorship theory, question the emotional probability of the letters. This is precisely the issue which Peter Dronke addresses.[31] He investigates Robertson's assessment that medieval readers saw Abelard's and Heloise's love as a "sordid affair," and that the collection was planned to show how Heloise grew "from a vain and amusingly unreasonable young girl into a mature and respected abbess." Regarding the first charge, Dronke is able to show that except for Fulco and Roscelin, whose reflections on the lovers do not contain moral condemnation, the mass of evidence is sympathetic, even "passionately compassionate" toward them.[32] Thus, Dronke concludes, "There is no a priori reason against taking the Abelard-Heloise letters at their face value. . . . We have no reason to doubt their authenticity on the ground that they express thoughts and emotions incompatible with what we know of twelfth century thought and emotions.[33] Dronke's case is further strengthened by E. Konsgen's publication of the MS Troyes B.M. 1452, a fragmentary collection of twelfth century love letters.[34] They are in tone, emotion, and attitude quite compatible with the emotional and intellectual atmosphere of the Abelard-Heloise correspondence. Consequently, there seems to be no inherent reason to question the authenticity of the correspondence on grounds of emotional improbability.

The part of the letters which concerns us here is Chapter 7 of the *Historia Calamitatum*, Abelard's first love letter. The *Historia* was written about 1132 when Abelard was abbot of St. Gildas in Brittany and Heloise abbess of the Paraclete in

Champaigne. The letter is an autobiography addressed not to Heloise but to a friend. It follows the classical genre of *consolatoria* (i.e., a statement that one's misfortunes, however great, have happened to greater men). Southern observes: "Abelard portrays himself throughout the affair with Heloise as half beast, half monk, sinking through sensuality into the filth of carnal sexuality, but rising through philosophy and bodily mutilation to the stature of a spiritual man."[35] While Southern's assessment of Abelard's self-portrayal is essentially correct, the characterization in the work is much less stereotypic than he suggests. The *Historia* is much more personal and mimetic than the classical *consolatoria* or contemporary hagiographic narratives and *exempla*. As Hanning points out, the *Historia* is a "profoundly innovative exercise in self-definition."[36]

Chapter 7 of the *Historia* presents the philosophic misogamic canon in an interesting setting. Abelard is recounting the standard authoritative arguments against marriage as he quotes Heloise, his mistress and, later, wife. Thus, the *dissuasio* is put in the mouth of a sympathetic, loving, educated, and intelligent woman whose persona provides a convenient and effective distancing device for the author. Even the shadow of doubt concerning the potentially selfish nature of the argumentation is thus removed and the irony of the situation heightened: the *dissuasio* is addressed not to a fictitious friend but to the author of the work, who, as we are reminded, refused to listen. Moreover, the validity of the arguments is confirmed because they are proposed by Abelard's mistress who, it is clear from the narrative context, has only Abelard's good in mind and assesses the situation not only with remarkable erudition and cognitive firmness but, as it turns out, with foresight. The masterful manipulation of the argumentation does not deny the authenticity and sincerity of the letter; rather, it shows Abelard as a perceptive and creative artist who reshaped his reality with keen literary and dramatic awareness as he wrote his recollection of Heloise's advice against marriage.

According to Abelard, Heloise disapproved of his marrying her for two reasons: the danger it entailed and the disgrace that was bound to result from it. Her uncle, she maintains, would

never be placated by the arrangements, and he would be lost to
both the Church and philosophy: "What curses, what loss to
the Church, what weeping of philosophers would ensue from
our marriage?" she asks. Then she begins her dissuasion. Like
Jerome who is the main source of her information, she commences with the Apostle's dictum: "Art thou freed from a
wife? Do not seek a wife. . . . I would have you free from care."
After this meager Scriptural exhortation, she immediately turns
to the testimony of philosophers: if Abelard will not listen to
the Apostle's and the Saint's advice, he "should at least listen to
the philosophers." On good patristic authority, Heloise cites
Theophrastus, Cicero, and Seneca and adds also *sua voce*, an
antithetical catalogue reminiscent of Jerome's *Adversus Helvidium* Letters 22 and 54 and of the Theophrastus fragment:

> To say no more of the hindrance of the study of philosophy . . .
> consider the status of the dignified life. What could there be in
> common between scholars and wet-nurses, writing desks and cra-
> dles, books, writing tablets and distaffs, stylus, pens and spindles?
> Or who is there who is bent on sacred or philosophic reflection
> who could bear the wailing of babies, the silly lullabies of nurses
> to quiet them, the noisy horde of servants, both male and female;
> who could endure the foul and incessant degrading defilement of
> infants?

She answers a possible objection that the rich could possibly
afford to put up with all these inconveniences in their spacious
houses, by saying that philosophers are different from rich men
who, "engrossed in riches and entangled in worldly cares, will
have no time for sacred and philosophical studies."

After quoting Seneca's advice to Lucilius that he devote
himself entirely to philosophy, Heloise comments on it: "What
those among us who truly bear the name monks endure for
love of God, that they, the esteemed philosophers among the
pagans, endured for the love of philosophy." Her subsequent
passage on the universality of the chaste ideal among Hebrews,
Gentiles, and Christians alike is a rephrasing of the corresponding passage of the *Theologia Christiana* and she adopts Augustine's description of what a philosopher is. She says: "It is

clearly shown that the wise men of the Gentiles, that is to say the philosophers, were so named rather in praise of their lives than of their learning."

Then Heloise prepares for a skirmish: Abelard should follow the good example of the pagans and avoid base pleasures as they did, ". . . lest such a Charybdis drag you down headlong and you shamelessly and irrevocably swamp yourself in such obscenities . . . if you do not regard the privilege of a cleric, at least uphold the dignity of a philosopher." Remember Socrates, she concludes, and quotes the familiar Jeromian account of Socrates' marital tribulation from the *Adversus Jovinianum*. Philippe Delhaye points out that Heloise is not particularly faithful to the spirit of the *Adversus Jovinianum* for, had she been in agreement with Jerome, she would have begged her lover to renounce their liaison.[37] But she fails to do so. Rather, she sets her *dissuasio* in a pagan philosophic rather than patristic framework and advocates freedom and dignity rather than asceticism. All in all, as L. Crane perceptively observes, the learned reasons against marriage put forth by Heloise are precisely those which compelled Abelard to keep the marriage secret.[38] More specifically, Abelard has Heloise recite the misogamous canon which focuses on the observation that marriage is an unsurmountable obstacle to the professional activities of a scholar, a destructive influence on his dignity, and an impediment of his freedom.

As a final attempt in her dissuasion, Heloise even tries to appeal to Abelard's sensuality: she would much prefer to be called his mistress, even his whore, than his wife, so that her charm and not marital chains would tie him to her. Delhaye singles out this statement of Heloise to document his assertion that the *dissuasio* was unlikely to have been delivered by Heloise. Yet her statement is in full agreement with every detail we know of Heloise's life and character.

To support her appeal, Heloise stresses the old adage, well known from the *Ars Amatoria* and repeatedly confirmed in the *De arte honeste amandi* that occasional separations would increase the pleasure they would have in each other's company.

Finally, she suggests that while their liaison is a betrayal of the philosophic ideal, it is not a complete destruction of it, as marriage would be.

In Heloise's last set of arguments no trace is found of a transcendental legitimization of sensuality (as would be evidenced in the proposal of pseudo-familial ties) nor of the didactic pragmatism of the misogamy of the preceding pages; her words are the unabashed, undisguised expression (as manifested in the enumeration of distractions marriage entails to the scholar) of eroticism. The Ovidian reminiscence in this, the *aetas Ovidiana,* is hardly surprising. That medieval readers were aware of Heloise's Ovidian arguments and her amatory talents is clear from the fact that a fifteenth century version of Capellanus' *De arte* was put in her mouth.[39]

As a text of philosophic misogamy, clearly indebted to the final chapters of Jerome's *Adversus Jovinianum* and to Theophrastus, Chapter VII is characterized by two major omissions: there is neither a catalogue of bad wives nor a set of *exempla in bono* of pagan virgins. The reasons, of course, lie both with the character of the persona and with the theme. Abelard was unlikely to put an invective of female misbehavior in the mouth of the wise and responsible Heloise. Regarding the theme, the whole point of the *dissuasio* is that not even the best of wives (i.e., Heloise) is compatible with the professional ideal of the philosopher. This is Abelard's very creative modification of the otherwise obligatory *rara avis* topos.

Regarding the omission of the *exempla in bono* for virginity, both the genre and the persona are responsible. Chapter VII is a tract of philosophic misogamy not so much interested in upholding the chaste ideal as it is in upholding the dignified celibate ideal for the philosopher. This omission is characteristic for most treatises of philosophic misogamy. Similarly, Heloise is not exhorting Abelard to chastity (in fact, she wishes to remain his mistress), but she is dissuading him from matrimony. Thus, the hierarchy of values established by Heloise places continence at the highest level but concubinage above marriage.

Delivering the dissuasive arguments against marriage via Heloise, Abelard is not only able to distance himself from the arguments, but he is thus able to present a masterful combination of *ratio* and *auctoritas;* personal judgment and authoritative precept. What Jerome, Theophrastus, Seneca, and others have said applies to the philosopher in general; what Heloise herself urges applies specifically to Abelard the philosopher.

The vocabulary concerning marriage and procreative intercourse in the *Historia Calamitatum* is Jeromian. Both Abelard and Heloise use the vocabulary of the gutter when they speak of marital relations, for example, talking of marriage as base voluptuousness (*turpes voluptates*), obscenity (*obscenitas*), indecency (*indecens*), and lamentability (*lamentabilis*), and of the marital life as characterized by childish squalling (*pueriles vagitus*), lullabies of the nurse (*nutricial nenias*), the constant filth of little ones (*parvi sordes assiduas*). The last part of the *dissuasio,* however, is pronouncedly Ovidian. In the passage concerning the enhanced joys of occasional meetings as opposed to the drudgery of everyday marital life, the language takes on an elegant Ovidian sensuality. Heloise argues that it would be sweeter for her to be called Abelard's mistress than to be known as his wife since then love alone would hold her, and if from time to time they would be separated the joy of their meetings would be all the sweeter because of its rarity. The dichotomy of the scatological (Jeromian) marital imagery and the sexual (Ovidian) imagery embody a perfect form-content bond. The word is what it denotes; the tradition upon which the thematology draws is also its linguistic medium.

John of Salisbury

Among Abelard's most distinguished students is the Englishman, John of Salisbury. Hans Liebeschutz describes him as "the most notable representative of that revival of learning which gave the title of medieval Renaissance to the twelfth century."[40] John of Salisbury studied with William of Conches and Gilbert de la Porrée, and heard Peter Abelard at Montagne Sainte Geneviève. He became subsequently secretary to Theobald, archbishop of Canterbury whose court was frequented by Peter of Blois. John's misogamous tract is contained in Book VIII of his *Policraticus, de nugis curialium et vestigiis philosophorum.*[41] The work, completed in 1159, deals with court and political affairs and is a book of moral principles illuminated by classical and Biblical examples and contrasted with the author's observation of contemporary courtly behavior. John criticizes courtiers for their love of hunting, magic, astrology, their interest in actors, their ambitious striving for social prestige, vainglory, and their addiction to voluptuousness in every form. The part criticizing voluptuousness is subdivided, according to the Jeromian model, into five vices, each dependent on one of the senses.

John's dissuasion from marriage is embedded in his list of capital vices. It comes under the heading of lust and immediately follows the attack on gluttony and is, in fact, treated as a twin vice: "As sobriety is necessary at banquets, so modesty must attend all things, since lust springs from satiety and manifold disasters from lust." These are the initial words of Chapter 2 of Book VIII of the *Policraticus* entitled "The Annoyance and Burdens of Wedlock according to Jerome and other Philosophers." As the title implies, the moral equivalence between philosophy, celibacy, and virtue has been affected. To John, as Delhaye observes, clerk and philosopher are identical terms.[42]

John commences his arguments against marriage and carnal pleasure by distinguishing between what Epicurus the philosopher actually taught and what his corrupt disciples and followers practice: "Whatever the meaning of the grunting of the drove of swine that followed him [i.e., those who advocate carnal pleasure], my opinion is that no philosopher approved such a filthy and dangerous view; much less Epicurus who was great enough to found a philosophical school of his own." The pleasure-principle is irreconcilable with the philosophic way of life, John believes—"it is the principle not of Epicurus but of Silenus."

The vice of lust is John's focus for the discussion of matrimony: "All lustful pleasure is therefore vile with the exception of that which is excused by the bond of matrimony. This, thanks to the license granted, covers any shame that may be inherent in it." And of shame, there is plenty, John continues with a restatement of the Pauline concession to marriage as a way to avoid fornication, for marriage is a veiling that hides "the shame of human frailty."

After stating the Pauline and patristic view, John continues with the misogamous arguments of the philosophic tradition: however honorable and useful marital union may be, it is more productive of worry than of joy. This precept is illustrated by an anecdote from Valerius Maximus reporting on Socrates' view of marriage. More clearly than his compatriot Hesiod, Socrates is reputed to have seen the disadvantages of both the marital and the celibate states. When asked by a young man whether he should marry, Socrates supposedly answered that either way the young man would regret it:

> On the one hand loneliness, childlessness, the dying out of your stock, and an outsider as your heir will be your destiny; on the other, eternal worry, one quarrel after another, her dower cast in your face, the haughty disdain of her family, the garrulous tongue of your mother-in-law, the lurking paramour, and worry as to how the children will turn out.

John, like the other Christian misogamous writers, emphasizes that those who are repelled by the "strict doctrine of Christian religion," may learn chastity and virtue from the pagans. John feels called upon to defend himself for his advocacy of celibacy and uses the obligatory distancing exclamation regarding the heretical condemnation of marriage: "Not that I would at all deprecate conjugal chastity but I am not at all inclined to think that the fruit of the 100th and 60th part should be united with the 30th." Thus, John repeats Jerome's number symbolism to establish a true hierarchy of values. He quotes the Theophrastus tract in full and concludes with an approving comment: "Such and similar are the remarks of Theophrastus. They in themselves are sufficient to explain the perplexities of the married state and the calamities that overtake its cherished joys." Some people, John is amazed to observe, are foolish enough to marry again: "Who could pity the man who once freed from the fetters fled back to chains?" Typically enough, John castigates not the sinfulness but the foolishness of second marriages. John is much milder in his condemnation of matrimony than his predecessors and contemporaries. He does not so much condemn the institution as he does its abuse, observes Delhaye, and he suggests that John systematically transfers the critique of the institution to a critique of abuse.[43] Yet John criticizes licentiousness in general and female corruption in particular. In fact, the *dissuasio* from marriage is only a convenient surrogate for an attack on lust.

Herodotus' observation that woman puts away her modesty when she takes off her clothes prompts John to relate a contemporary incident. With Juvenalian concreteness, he commences his indictment. A lawyer friend of his, he says, had a client in a divorce case. The lady in question very much disconcerted the lawyer by her audacity: she was alleging in the presence of friends and supporters that her husband was impotent (*frigidus*). When questioned by the lawyer about whether she was still a virgin, she answered in the affirmative. When asked whether her husband ever kissed and embraced her, she answered, "Yes." "How then do you know," asked the lawyer, "my chaste, wise and shy maiden, that he has not played the role of potent husband with you and performed the complete rites of matrimony?" The lady blushed, and John considers the self-indictment obvious. He comments on the incident with a curious aside: "But clerics are fortunate in that not one of them proves impotent or has in court been branded with infamy of this sort" ("Sed bene cum philosophantibus, id est cum clericis, agitur, quod nemo eorum frigidus est aut in iudicio perfusus huius modi macula"). In the context, John seems to suggest that philosophers (clerks) embracing a life of celibacy (not necessarily chastity) thereby avoid the possibility of public disgrace caused by an accusation of impotence in court by a wife who seeks divorce. At the same time, John's court *exemplum* may also contain a reference to the known licentiousness of clerks.

The presentation of the incident is very similar to Jerome's account of the virtuous Bibia in *Adversus Jovinianum* who, when asked why she never complained of her husband's bad breath, replied that she believed all men would smell that way. Thus, Jerome remarks, she proved her chastity beyond doubt, because obviously she could not have let any man come close enough to her to be able to smell his breath. John uses a similar argument for the opposite purpose, turning the *exemplum in bono* into an *exemplum in malo*, thereby introducing the type of embarrassing, emasculating wife into the misogamous canon by the *exemplum* of the wife who openly deprecates her husband's virility.

John's tract continues with the traditional Jeromian examples of Cicero, Philip, and Socrates' two wives. Then he comments on the frivolity of the female sex (*levitas*). To illustrate his point, he quotes the tale of the widow of Ephesus from Petronius' *Satyricon* almost verbatim and he prefaces it with a quote from Juvenal's Sixth Satire: "There are others who are most modest although the satirist calls the woman of perfect chastity a rare bird on earth, most like a coal black swan." John also quotes Eumolpus to the same effect, saying that " . . . there is no female so modest that she will not be stirred with passion at the advances of a stranger." But, John insists, Petronius is not the only one to ridicule the absurdities of women; Jerome attests to the fact that Euripides abused women in his plays and Epicurus advised the wise man against marriage. Like Jerome, John also has to affirm the divine origin, validity, and sacred nature of marriage, but that does not prevent him from condemning, all the more vehemently, sex. In view of the resurgence of dualistic heresies in the West in the twelfth century, it is not surprising that John feels compelled repeatedly to affirm the divine validity of marriage. Moreover, in view of the emergence of troubadour poetry and courtly love at the English court, patronized so lavishly by Queen Eleanor, the vehemence of John's castigation of lust and fornication is hardly surprising. As a serious churchman, an older man, and a man imbued with strong moral principles, he objected to Eleanor's newfangled ideas. He exclaims with Jeromian vigor and in Jeromian scatological vocabulary:

> If, therefore, the vexation of marriage, though the state is undoubtedly a good one as it was instituted by the Lord, is so great that the sage fears it, who except one bereft of sense would approve of sensual pleasure itself which is illicit, wallows in filthiness, is something men censure and that God without a doubt condemns?

The two forms of physical delight, namely gluttony and carnal love, "are characteristic of beasts; the one seems to possess the filth of swine and the other the stench of goats."

In agreement with Jerome, John asserts that modesty is the crowning virtue in women for when that is lost, all other virtues disappear. He quotes Jerome's eulogy of the chaste ideal from *Adversus Jovinianum* and then observes with regret that even though many writers repeatedly castigated female lust, they did not succeed in checking or blotting out this evil. What's more, to quote Juvenal (*Sat.* VI, 350–51), poor women are just as bad as the rich matrons. All in all, John concludes, those who cannot or do not wish to be continent deserve indulgence rather than glory, and if they do not practice moderation, then they deserve punishment, not indulgence.

John's tract, more than Abelard's and Jerome's, is a hybrid of divergent traditions. Like preachers of the ascetical tradition, John upholds the chaste ideal and considers marriage simply legalized fornication that is to be tolerated rather than glorified (thus restating the Jeromian hierarchy of values). These passages are scatological, referring to stench, filth, and excrement, or they use metaphors of bestiality. Like proponents of the philosophic tradition, John asserts that philosophy and marriage are mutually exclusive occupations because of the troublesome burdens of married life (thus emphasizing the philosophic-misogamous ideal of freedom from distractions). Finally, adumbrating the less-qualified return to classical models of general misogamy, John shows woman to be unworthy of her potential husband (thereby reiterating the general misogamous topos that no virtuous woman can be found). From Jerome's model, John adopts most of his *exempla in bono,* the authoritative tone, florilegian form, and scatological vocabulary. From the philosophical tradition, he takes the preceptual arguments; from the Juvenalian tradition, he takes the use of contemporary everyday documentation in his use of the example of wifely audacity (the *exempla in malo*) and the use of sexually ambiguous language. Even more than in Abelard's *dissuasio,* we find an equation of religion with human endeavor in John of Salisbury's tract. A philosopher, John argues, is a religious and, therefore, virtuous man whose aim in life is sacred study, hopefully unhindered by marital burdens. As Delhaye observes, there is no juxtaposition of pagan *philosophers* and *clerks*, because Salisbury uses the terms as synonymous. This equation offers a possible explanation for the well-balanced confluence of the different traditions in the work.

Walter Map

Much more influential and popular than either Abelard's dissuasion (1132) or John of Salisbury's *De molestis et oneribus coniugorum* (1159) is Walter Map's *Dissuasio Valerii Rufino ne ducat uxorem* (1180–90).[44] Map's letter, next to Theophrastus' tract, is the most widely quoted and used work of philosophic misogamy. The work had been attributed to Jerome (Migne prints it as *Epist*. 36 of Jerome in the *PL*), to Cyprian, and also to Valerius Maximus, but Thomas Wright more correctly prints it as part of Walter Map's *De Nugis Curialium* as do Map's later editors and translators.

The work's popularity is attested by the manuscript tradition. Pratt cites seven manuscripts surviving from the first century of the letter's existence (1180–1280) which contain *Valerius* and Theophrastus' *aureolus* and three manuscripts which hold Valerius, Theophrastus, and Jerome's *Adversus Jovinianum*.[45] Both John of Salisbury and Map included their *dissuasiones* in a work criticizing the court of King Henry II, and of the sixty Valerius manuscripts that Pratt examined, more than twenty contain commentaries on the letter.[46] The work is listed as an authoritative text on marriage, or rather on the trials and tribulations of marriage by such divergent sources as Chaucer's wife of Bath and Jean De Meung on the one hand, and the Dominican *Malleus Maleficarum* on the other.

Little is known of Map's life. Most of his biography is supplied by his friend Giraldus Cambrensis in his *Speculum Ecclesiae*, relevant portions of which are reproduced in Thomas Wright's edition of poems attributed to Map.[47] From there we learn that Map was a favorite of King Henry II who held him in high esteem for his learning, facility with words, and for his courtly manner (*facetia curialium*). He obtained several ecclesiastical benefices and was canon of the churches of Salisbury and Paul, preceptor of Lincoln and, finally, archdeacon of Oxford in 1197. Like John of Salisbury, as a young man he studied in Paris, and, like John, he returned to the English court. In 1179, he was sent by Henry II to the Third Lateran Council. Thomas Wright remarks: "All the information which can be gathered relating to him shows him to have been a wit and a man endowed with a marked taste for light, and elegant, literatures."[48] Or, as Pratt more recently observes about him, "Cosmopolitan and urbane, he was famous for his ready wit and entertaining anecdotes. He loved the classics but wore his learning lightly and used it with grace and ease."[49]

The *Valerius* had been circulated as a separate pamphlet before Map included it in his collection *De Nugis Curialium,* a title which either he or his editor borrowed from John of Salisbury's *Policraticus.* The tract is in the form of a letter, its proclaimed purpose to dissuade the writer's philosopher friend from marriage. The writer calls himself Valerius and his friend, who has red hair, Rufinus. As Delhaye observes, the letter consists of a series of paragraphs based on a fact or a *sententia* ending in a short apostrophe.[50]

The *Valerius* is probably the rhetorically most perfect *dissuasio* in the antigamous tradition and follows Quintilian's model closely.[51] Map sketches a pitiful picture of his friend, a man of "philosophic life," whom he observes to have undergone a marked change recently. "I observed him to be changed in habit, mien, and face, full of sighs, and pale, yet better dressed and speaking less and more thoughtfully, and proud of his unusual guise (or in unwonted aloofness): his old lightheartedness and accustomed pleasantry were gone. He said he was ill, and indeed, he was far from well." With this exposition Map achieves a triple purpose: first, he evokes the reader's sympathy for his sick friend; second, he projects a persona for himself of a concerned, altruistic, experienced friend; and third, he gives enough details to conjure up the prototype of the lovesick courtly gentleman of the romances. Several of the indicative attributes from Andreas Capellanus' guidebook are here: the pallor, the change, the dress, the love of solitude, the suffering, and the sickness.

Map's friend, however, is not wooing a cruel and distant lady, he is not burning in adulterous passion for his unattainable fair—no, Map is quick to disappoint our expectations: his poor friend is to be wived. His friend, Walter continues, is "the suitor, not the sage." As a devoted friend, Map is determined to leave no stone unturned in bringing him to his senses. With a masterful string of antitheses contrasting love and marriage as mutually exclusive states, Map assesses the situation: his friend is "on his way to be wived, not to be loved (*uxorari tendebat, non amari*); he would be, not Mars, but Mulciber." Or to put it differently, "he was on his way to death," and Map "was dying with him." This association of death and marriage, already familiar from Juvenal's Sixth Satire, caused some of the details of the Sixth Satire to be fathered on Valerius. Three of the manuscripts of the *Quinze Joies de Mariage* have a reference to "un docteur appelle Valere" for whom marriage was death and who is supposed to have said to his friend that it was far preferable to jump from a window than to marry.[52]

Valerius tried to persuade but was repelled . . . thus, he decided to "discharge every office of friendship" by writing a letter entitled *A Dissuasion of Valerius to Rufinus the Philosopher that He Should Not Take a Wife*. The text proper begins with a highly rhetorical justification for the virtuous purpose of the *dissuasio:* Valerius has nothing to gain by dissuading his friend; he has solely his friend's good in mind. He cannot keep silent, he claims to have a moral obligation to save his friend; he is the prophet of truth. He friend, Valerius is quick to point out, has many flatterers and mindless advocates of his pleasure but he and he alone will speak the truth. His friend is blind, he is on fire with passion, he does not see that what he is wooing is a chimera: "The three-formed monster is adorned with the face of a noble lion, polluted with the body of a stinking goat, armed with the tail of a rank viper." In other words, what appears to be noble and virtuous [lion] is actually sinful [polluted-goat] and dangerous [armed-viper].

The rest of the *dissuasio* musters carefully balanced and often ironic examples to demonstrate the undignified, sinful, and dangerous nature of women. The method of documentation is the favorite medieval device of *frequentatio,* a rhetoric figure meant to bring scattered references together to elaborate a principle. The *dissuasio* commences with two contrastive sets of dissuasive *exempla,* all meant to demonstrate the virtue and utility of celibacy by showing the disadvantage of its opposite. Three Old Testament *exempla in malo* (followed by the obligatory *rara avis* exception illustrated by three chaste and three unchaste women of antiquity) are set against three mythological *exempla in malo* (followed by the mythological *rara avis,* Pallas Athene). The Old Testament examples (Adam and Eve, David and Bathsheba, and Solomon) claim to exemplify female disobedience, bad influence and apostasy respectively. The mythological examples (Jupiter and Europa, Phoebus and Leucothea, Mars and Venus), show reduction to beastliness, loss of power, and ridicule as the effects of the love of women.

Ironically, after he had emphatically contrasted love and marriage as essentially different states (marriage being a much less desirable condition), Map's first six dissuasive *exempla in malo* contain only one instance (that of Adam) where a married couple is concerned. The choice of exempla has distinct iconographic implications. Jupiter, for example, is presented as a bull bellowing for Europa. The picture immediately conjures up the medieval notion that a man (or, in this case, even a god) who abandons reason and gives himself to vice ceases to be a man and becomes a beast. Thus, he forfeits his upright posture, a symbol of reason (Boethius), or he might even undergo an actual metamorphosis (Ovid). Especially ironic is the juxtaposition of the two iconographies: the courtly lover of the introduction is not exalted, as is expected, as a result of love but reduced to beastliness and ignominy. As a parallel to the Adam/Eve story (both tales initiating the respective demonstrative strings of Old Testament and pagan examples), the Jupiter/Europa story is intended to exemplify female seduction and the reduction of the male through female wiles to a pitiful state.[53]

The same ambiguity of theme and purpose holds true for the other four *exempla* as well. Intended to show the destruc-

tive and humiliating effect of marriage on men, these mythological *exempla* also illustrate male lasciviousness and cruelty
and, thus, qualify a sympathetic response to the supposed
victims.[54]

Another syntactical contradiction is raised by Valerius' contradictory use of preceptual setting and demonstrative mythological symbols. In the introduction, the reader's sympathies
are evoked for the writer's poor friend who was to be wedded
not loved, who was to be Mulciber not Mars. The parallelism is
clearly between Mars and love on one hand, and Mulciber and
marriage on the other. In fact, later in the tract, Mulciber the
married is shown to be excluded from the Olympian banquet
while Mars, the promiscuous, happily reclines there. In the initial set of dissuasive *exempla*, Mars is ironically called upon to
warn Rufinus against marriage; because of Venus, he found
himself in chains and became the laughingstock of the Olympians. The *exemplum* is clearly an illustration of the cuckolded
husband's revenge-motif, more appropriate to dissuade a young
lover from adultery than to show the detrimental consequences
of marriage. In fact, there is an ironic association of marital
chains and the chains of Vulcan that expose the adulterer Mars
to the rest of the Olympians, for Rufinus is admonished to
avoid the chains of Vulcan.

Valerius admonishes his friend to take his advice. The great
Julius Caesar, described in a pithy epithet borrowed from Juvenal, would have done better had he listened. The two illustra-
tions that follow are new to the misogamous canon and
contrast an unhappy married ruler and a happy unmarried Emperor. Then Valerius quotes Jerome's *Adversus Jovinianum:* Cicero said that "he could not spare time at once for a wife and
philosophy" and Valerius hopes that his friend will "copy the
prince of eloquence."

Valerius presents a heterodox but typical philosophic contrast of marriage and promiscuity by using, like Lucretius, a
medical metaphor. Promiscuous relationships are better than
permanent ties, he says, because "many fits of sickness with intervals of health are less injurious than a single ailment which
never ceases to vex with pain that cannot be cured." Map, however, modifies Lucretius' medical statement (*Luc. De rerum nat-*

ura 4, 1052–1120) that sexual desire is a sickness that cannot
be cured by intercourse. Again, the metaphor used for love is
the metaphor of *amour courtois;* sickness and suffering are the
standard courtly descriptions of love. This hierarchy of values
(continence best, promiscuous affairs next, and marriage last) is
identical with the one proposed by Abelard via Heloise and is
an essential argument of philosophic misogamy.

Drawing on Aulus Gellius, Valerius relates the story of
Pacuvius' tree (on which three of his wives hanged themselves)
of which a friend begged to have a cutting. "Friend," Valerius
says, "I too say to you, I fear you may be driven to beg cuttings
of that tree when they are no longer to be had." The Pacuvius
exemplum is an ironic inversion of the death-marriage equation
at the beginning of the *dissuasio,* because the thoughtful friend
of the addressee is regretting the loss of the wife-killing tree.
The testimonies of Sulpicius, Cato, and Metellus on the foolishness and inconvenience of marriage are called upon. Cato of
Utica probably best expressed the idea underlying the *dissuasio,*
namely, that if the world were without women, men's lives
would be almost divine. After cataloguing the wisdom of the
ancients, Valerius returns to the association of death and marriage echoing the initial equation of Rufinus' plans of marriage
with the road to death. Women murder their husbands both
out of too much love and out of too much hate: "Livia killed
her husband for hate, Lucilia killed hers for love.... Women
proceed by many diverse paths; but in whatever zigzags they
wander, in whatever blind ways they go astray, the issue is one
and the same, the goal of all their ways one—and that is mis-
chief." There is no hope. Woman harms you whether she actually wishes to or not: " ... woman dares all for what she loves
or hates, and is clever to do harm when she will—which is
always: and often when she wishes to help, hinders; whence it
happens that she does hurt even against her will." This precept
is illustrated by the tragic fate of the unfortunate Hercules who
died because of the poison of the unwitting Deianira. Again,
the story is derived from Ovid (*Met.* ix, 111).

Like John of Salisbury, Map has Valerius ask the rhetorical
question, "Did ever a woman sadden a constant and earnest

suitor by permanent denial? Did she consistently silence the supplicant's words?" Of course not, Valerius answers and proceeds to demonstrate the validity of his reply. Ironically, however, he does not use the likely illustration (as, for example, John of Salisbury, who followed up the statement by the example of the widow of Ephesus), but part of the canonic catalogue of virgin births (*exempla in bono*) to prove that neither age nor high walls can protect a maiden's virginity: "Gold made a breach in the defences of Acrisius' tower and undid the honor of Danae," and "a virgin verging on old age and eminent in repute for chastity, at last by a vision of Apollo conceived and bore Plato." The statement about Perictione is a verbatim quote from Jerome's *Adversus Jovinianum* where she is used as an *exemplum in bono* to exemplify the Christ-like virginal births of antiquity. Valerius, however, converts the incident into an *exemplum in malo* to show woman's lack of ability to resist a lover.

Valerius offers the by now traditional justification for using pagan examples: "Friend, are you more surprised or angry that . . . I intimate that heathen are to be imitated by you; idolaters by a Christian. . . . The unbelievers do much amiss, yet some things they do, which though in the doers they come to nought, might in us bear fruit abundantly." Valerius urges his friend to remain truthful to his first bride using the metaphor already familiar from Abelard, namely, that the marriage of a philosopher is adultery against the first bride, philosophy. He wants his friend to be the husband of Pallas, not of Venus. This dignified wedding, this hopeful and promising espousal is what prompted the letter. In effect, Valerius is proposing a pseudomarriage for a real wedding, spiritual marriage for physical nuptials. The substitution echoes the medieval Church's emphasis on surrogate parenthood—of spiritual rather than physical ties.

The conclusion of the letter reintroduces the medical metaphor: "Hard is the hand of the surgeon, but healing. Hard too is this discourse but wholesome, and I wish it may be as profitable to you as it is well-meant." If his friend needs more ancient testimony, Valerius concludes, then he can read

"Theophrastus' *Aureolus* and Jason's *Medea*," and he will find
that "there are hardly even a few things impossible to woman."
Finally, the letter ends with a prayer: "May God Almighty
grant you not to be deluded by the deceits of almighty woman,
and enlighten your heart that you go not with bedazzled eyes
whither I fear you may." The prayer concludes with a reference
to Juvenal I: "so that I may not be writing an Orestes, fare-
well!"

The structure of the *Valerius* is a carefully balanced string
of *exempla in malo*. Each paragraph ends in an apostrophe of
either admonition or indignation. Some of the apostrophes re-
cur verbatim at regular intervals. One of the most frequently
occurring apostrophes, "Loqui prohibeor et tacere non pos-
sum," became subsequently, as Lehmann points out, a standard
device of erotic parody.[55] Almost invariably the final apostrophe is an application of the moral of the paragraph to Rufinus
himself. Thus, the ancient illustrative example is turned into a
genuine medieval *exemplum*, complete with moral and application.

Map's treatise is a hybrid of the tradition of philosophic
and general misogamy. With Juvenal's satire, Map's letter shares
the use of ambiguity, contradiction, and irony. Like the Sixth
Satire, the *Valerius* is replete with *exempla in malo* that are often
ironic and that frequently backfire on the supposed victims of
the illustration. Unlike the Sixth Satire, however, the *Valerius*
has no contemporary everyday specificity; any topicality is the-
matic rather than detailed. Like Theophrastus' *Aureolus,* it is
highly preceptual; Map's language, like that of Theophrastus, is
sober and lacks the customary obscenities. The illustrative *exempla* or the dissuasive *praecepta* are, like Abelard's ancient with
very few Old Testament incidents. The Pauline epistles, the
surest indices of ascetic misogamy, are entirely missing. All
these observations suggest that the *Valerius* was written for the
school and the learned at court, rather than for the monastery.
For the budding young scholar, and the educated courtier, the
Valerius provides a wealth of classical and mythological allusions, a witty and clever turn of speech, a wealth of ironic and
enigmatic passages, and a fine rhetorical model.

The work must have been an immediate success. Map says that it was "greedily seized upon, eagerly copied, and read with vast amusement." Some people denied Map's authorship; "My only offense is," Map complains, "that I am alive." He then admits that he changed the names of the author and addresses of the letter for those of dead men, thereby giving the book an aura of antiquity. We have already noted the great popularity of Valerius Maximus in connection with John of Salisbury who uses the Roman writer as one of his chief sources of abundant quotations.

With Walter Map we have to ask the same question as with Jerome. Why did Map, writing a dissuasion against marriage, avoid using Juvenal's Sixth Satire directly? In the *Valerius* there are three borrowings from Juvenal: *Sat.* I, lines 60, 80; *Sat.* X, line 168, but none from the Sixth Satire. In the previous chapters, on the other hand, two quotations are cited from the Sixth Satire (lines 140 and 200). Consequently, lack of knowledge of the Sixth Satire cannot account for the hiatus. Rather, as in Jerome's case, it seems to be a conscious, planned omission. Again, while the methodology of the Sixth Satire was appropriate for the *Valerius,* its topography was not. Map's acclaimed purpose for the letter was the dissuasion from marriage of a philsopher not only because no worthy woman can be found to wed but also because marriage and the study of philosophy are incompatible occupations. To this end, Map presents the experience and wisdom of gods, heroes, and ancient philosophers, arguing that if better men than Rufinus succumbed to women, how much more careful should Rufinus be. The method of Map's argumentation is essentially the same as that of the contemporary popular fabliau, the *Lai d'Aristote,* in which Aristotle recaptures the moral of his humiliation by Philis by saying to his pupil:

> but now assuredly you see
> that I was right to fear for you;
> sheer youth might well consume you too,
> when fires of juvenescence rage,
> if I who am so full of age,
> cannot, by holding Love at bay,

> prevent his leading me astray
> so flagrantly as you've discerned;
> for all I've ever read and learned
> Love's cancelled in an hour here.[56]

Thus, the vivid examples of Roman matron's perverse and domineering behavior presents a different stratagem of dissuasion and would have lacked the intended universality of historical, mythological, and sententious arguments. This avoidance is a clear indication that medieval writers did recognize the different strands in the misogamous canon and utilized only those writers of the tradition whose misogamous purpose was similar to their own.

Walter Map's *Valerius* shows another important hiatus. There is no reference to 1 Cor. 7, or, for that matter, to any of the Pauline epistles, except maybe a vague allusion to 2 Cor. 12. Map is the first medieval misogamous writer not to expound on the Apostle's dictum (I Cor. 7:29), which had been quoted *ad nauseam* by other misogamous writers. Again, the reason is generic. Map is writing a witty tract of philosophic misogamy; he claims to be more concerned with his friend's intellectual, physical, and emotional welfare than he is with his salvation; he aims to delight, entertain, and impress rather than to exhort. The playful tone, the ambiguity of the *exempla,* the careful rhetorical structure are all clear indications of his purpose. Neither does Map quote the well-known Theophrastus fragment—he only refers to it as an authoritative text on marriage. Rather, he presents a whole set of new dissuasive *exempla,* most of which are inserted into the misogamous canon for the first time.

Essentially, Map is presenting a dim view of marriage and women while, at least in theory, he exalts love. Thus, his tract reads as a counter-gospel of courtly love. The ironic courtly love iconography of the setting of his poem would have raised expectations of a genuine romance in his audience, but Map presents the inversion of the eulogy of courtly ladies by cataloguing a remarkable multitude of wicked women. At the same time, he claims to be attacking marriage and not love, thereby providing a convenient camouflage for his attacks on women.

In Map's *dissuasio,* a confluence of a contemporary misogamic preoccupation (*amour courtois*) with an ancient theme (philosophic misogamy) and an eternal satiric topos (misogyny) occurs. As such, the work had great demonstrable and lasting appeal for a wide audience.

Both John of Salisbury and Map included their *dissuasiones* in works criticizing the court of Henry II. However, Map's work uses a misogynistic setting while John of Salisbury's is set in an attack against lust. Because both works were written for the same courtly audience (i.e., Henry II and Eleanor's court), the juxtaposition of their respective targets of attack is revealing. Henry's court was probably one of the first major "courtly" courts in Europe, and Eleanor's and her entourage's presence there assures us of the cultivation of troubadour poetry. John of Salisbury vehemently attacked the patronizing of "actors, jougleurs, etc.," and he expressed his indignation at the court where courtiers were busily employed in frolicking in one of the seven deadly sins. Thus, the setting for his misogamous chapters in the context of lust is hardly surprising. Lust to him is clearly one of the seven deadly sins in which courtiers find so much pleasure; and marriage, in its essence, is lust hidden by the "veil of matrimony." If lust must exist, John argues, it should at least be moderate and marital. The younger man Map, on the other hand, also criticizes the English court, but he finds different shortcomings: too much ambition and too little polish; even the Muses refuse to frequent so uninspired a court. His criticism, therefore, is less moral and more urbane than that of John of Salisbury. While both writers attempt to be teachers and entertainers, John is closer to the former (criticizing marriage in the context of lust) and Walter to the latter (reviling matrimony in the context of female atrocities). The alternative treatments might also, of course, reflect a change of situation at Henry II's court: in 1173, Eleanor supported the rebellion against her husband by their eldest son and was subsequently imprisoned in Winchester castle where she remained for the rest of Henry's reign. Consequently, the pronounced emphasis of Map's *dissuasio* on the wicked and potentially destructive effect of women (i.e., "woman harms even against her will") is hardly surprising in view of the fact that Map was one of King Henry's special favorites.

Hugh of Folietto

Hugh of Folietto's *De nuptiis libri duo* is also in the form of a letter.[57] Delhaye even suggests that Hugh knew and used Map's *Valerius* because he quotes some examples from Map and because he uses Map's technique of the paragraphal apostrophe.[58] Although Hugh's letter, addressed to a "very dear brother," is generally directed toward the monastic audience, the first part of the first book is an uncontaminated text of philosophical misogamy discouraging the addressee from carnal nuptials, and the writer utilizes all the traditional arguments and examples of the genre. Hugh was a canon regular of St. Augustine at the Foundation of St. Lawrence near Corbie. He was born ca. 1100, became prior of St. Lawrence, and died in 1174. Two works are generally attributed to him: the *De claustro animae* and the *De medicina animae,* which contains the *De nuptiis.*

De nuptiis begins with the favorite medieval misogynistic motif, "quid est mulier," a definition of what woman is. She is the abyss of death, her love burns all the more when she is married. Therefore, Hugh exclaims in the introduction, his friend ought to listen to the testimony of philsophers and saintly men who enumerate the burdens of wedlock. Hugh's first authority is, of course, Theophrastus whom he quotes at length. "Whom does Theophrastus not move to the quiet life of continence?" Hugh asks. Continence is the quiet life, he explains, because it is not disturbed by the suspicions of a wife, the expense of serving maids and the "perversity" of children. This life bears the "flower of cleanliness," the "fruit of purity," and gives the "fragrance of a good conscience." After this sketch of a garden of delights, Hugh exhorts his friend to listen to the experts because he does not know the inconveniences of wedlock from firsthand experience. The appropriate testimony of the married Cicero and Socrates (via Jerome) follow. Hugh then anticipates a possible objection. Someone might believe, he says, to have provided for concord by taking a poor wife.

Not so, Hugh argues, and cites the pitiful case of the famous Cato. Moreover Philip the king found the door of his wife's chamber locked, and Euripides' plays are full of bad women.

Hugh quotes the familiar Herodotus dictum that women put off their modesty when they put off their clothes, and he extrapolates on it:

> What a woman does without a witness, she forgets as if it never happened. If, however, there was a witness, she forces him to believe by her artful use of language (*artificio linguae*) that he had not seen what he actually saw. If she has not enough force to excuse herself with words, then she resorts to tears. She coaxes with her eyes, seduces with kisses, pursues with embraces ... and she wins.

Several new topoi are here added to the misogamous canon: the *lingua rhetorica* is joined to the cunning use of tears and the strategic utilization of the whole arsenal of female weaponry that lead to triumph over man. Furthermore, the eternal topos of female lust is linked with deception as it was in Juvenal's and Ovid's works and as it is in contemporary twelfth century oriental tales.[59]

Hugh's next topos is introduced by an already familiar precept, but he presents it with eloquent amplification: the love of beauty enervated the virile mind. Here Hugh combines the Platonic *amor formae* and the Jeromian *amor mulieris,* but retains the rest of the church father's dictum. His substitution is appropriate because the precept is illustrated by references to Plato, Lysias, Aristotle and Seneca. In a somewhat misleading sentence Hugh refers to these writers: "Aristotle and Seneca, I recall to have read, wrote books on marriage in which they both judge the love of beauty." The ambiguity of the statement is a clever appropriation of the proverbial peacock's feathers, in this case, from Jerome's *Adversus Jovinianum.* Hugh reports that Aristotle and Seneca said that love of beauty causes the oblivion of reason: the closest thing to a drug of insanity. It is not only horrible, but also least congenial to the minds of wise men since it disturbs good judgment, interrupts and debases one's thoughts.

Hugh quotes Seneca's example of an inordinately loving husband and comments upon it by quoting Jerome: "The origin of the love was honorable but not its magnitude, and Seneca said that he who loves his wife too ardently is an adulterer." The logical sequence of comments of the procreative ideal follow, and Hugh uses Stoic arguments to evaluate marital behavior. "Certainly those who say they marry for the sake of children ought to at least imitate the dumb beasts and after they had made their wives' bellies swell, not kill the children." Those, on the other hand, Hugh comments, who marry not to avoid fornication, but to fill their pockets, are even worse.

The first part of the letter concludes on an original note. Hugh introduces Xenophon and Columella into the misogamic canon. A marvelous book on domestic economy by Xenophon, Hugh says, treats of the division of labor in marriage. The husband ought to attend to civic duties (*cultus humanos*) and to work in the fields, while the wife ought to attend to the care of the home, the animals, and the fruit. Unfortunately, however, the work of women becomes boring and "those who were accustomed to work begin to turn dominating—for domination always follows idleness."

Hugh then presents similar testimony from Columella. Columella, when speaking of the extravagance (*luxus*) of women, says that it comes from idleness. Thus, he concludes, his friend has to decide which type of wife he wants: the idle, the domineering, or the one fatigued by labor. Idleness is followed by luxury, domineering by pride, fatigue from work by quarrels. Thus, Hugh concludes his syllogism, none of the alternatives is particularly desirable.

Part II of Book I musters Scriptural evidence against marriage. The catalogue is traditional, including generous portions from the Proverbs, Psalms, Ecclesiastes, and Genesis, interspersed with a few New Testament and patristic dicta and examples. While Part I is a dissuasion from marriage, Part II is a persuasion to take monastic vows. It starts, however, with a passage on repudiation: what to do if one already has a wife. Hugh gives a short history of the Church's position on permissible repudiation and quotes some cases to illustrate the law.

Hugh's treatise resembles Jerome's *Adversus Jovinianum* more than it does the other twelfth-century tracts. Like Jerome, he presents the greater part of his documentation from Scriptural sources, and like Jerome, he presents the pagan evidence as a separate (although ideologically identical) segment from the biblical and patristic testimony. Even the title and the separation into two books is reminiscent of Jerome, as is Hugh's intent to provide the *consensus omnium* of philosophers and saintly men on the subject of marriage. Clearly, Hugh of Folietto had a monastic rather than scholarly audience in mind for his tract. This is reflected in his clear separation of pagan and Christian evidence and his lack of total equation between philosophers and clerks. Furthermore, his major concern (i.e., the upholding of the virtue of continence) breaks through even in the philosophic part of his tract. Love of woman in any form is "lowly," filthy, and purely physical; continence, on the other hand, is exalted, clean, and tranquil. Thus, Hugh's asceticism contains dualistic ideas of body/soul, evil/good, filthy/clean controversies. Consequently, Hugh sketches a horrid picture of the abysmal filth of marital relations with the incarnation of corporeality, woman.[60]

Peter of Blois

Peter of Blois was a Frenchman by birth, educated in law in Bologna (1150) and theology in Paris (1155), but he spent most of his adult life in England, first in the service of the archdeacon of Salisbury, then of Archbishop Richard. In 1182, he was made archdeacon of Bath and never further promoted. Like John of Salisbury and Walter Map, Peter, too, was associated with the court of Henry II, and he, too, wrote a book criticizing the life and manners at the court. The book, the *Compendium in Job,* presented to Henry II in 1173, provides a contemporary adaptation of Job's sufferings to Henry's life. Peter of Blois' correspondence is among the few twelfth-century works that immediately became a success. Its long-lasting popularity is attested by the manuscript tradition: there are seven manuscripts from the twelfth century; forty-two from the thirteenth; thirty-nine from the fourteenth; and 112 copies from the fifteenth. Peter's letters were collected in 1184. To those who criticized him for publishing private letters, he replied that they were made available as models for beginners and contributions to the general welfare.

Peter's dissuasion, Letter 79 *Ad R. amicum suum,* like his other letters, is a clever scholarly and rhetorical exercise.[61] The title as well as many of the details are reminiscent of Map's *Valerius.* However, Peter is original both in his introduction and in his presentation of the evidence. A friend, he says, underwent a most pitiable conversion. He who used to detest the female sex from childhood on, and was the champion in maligning women, now fell into the pit which, until now, he was able to avoid. Out of his own free will he now bears conjugal chains. Thus, Peter comments, all women shall rejoice because they have triumphed over their persecutor: "The wolf is captured by the sheep and the astuteness of the fox is deceived by the simplicity of the hen." The setting clearly echoes the popular medieval paradoxical motif of the trickster tricked, or, in this case, the persecutor persecuted. Peter is appealing *de post facto* to his friend's sense of dignity, and he highlights the ignominy of the "fall" by pointing to the weakness of the victor and the strength of the victim. If his friend delights in his self-chosen servitude, then he deserves God's punishment. If not, then Peter pours forth his sympathy and bemoans his friend's fate. With exceeding fondness for *adnominatio,* Peter says: "Navigasti, uxorem duxisti, satius tibi fuerat in exilium duci, quam sic ducere." Great are the inconveniences of married life, Peter concludes; scarcely is there ever peace with a wife.

To illustrate his preceptual introduction, Peter turns to the testimony of philosophers. He quotes Valerius Maximus' account of Socrates' view of marriage (already familiar from John of Salisbury's *Policraticus*) and the parallel instance of King Phoroneus (first used by Map) who said that he would have lacked nothing, had he lacked a wife.

The inevitable Theophrastus fragment is then presented in a novel way. Peter glosses the *Aureolus* with a host of pagan *exempla* from the *Adversus Jovinianum* and with the new examples from Map's *Valerius.* He uses familiar *exempla in malo* to illustrate the Theophrastian *praecepta*. Thus, Peter's letter is the most intimate incorporation of the Theophrastus fragment into the misogamous canon.

The glossing of the *Aureolus* with pagan *exempla* is very effective. Theophrastus' dictum that it is difficult to support a poor wife and torment to put up with a rich one is illustrated with the example of Metellus, who said that he would rather belong to himself than to a wife. Theophrastus' statement regarding a happy family life (that it is impossible: if the husband is liberal the wife will be unchaste; if he is strict, he will be accused of suspiciousness) is explained by the Mapian instances of Livia and Lucilia, who killed their husbands out of an excess of hate and love respectively, and by Deianira, who killed hers unwittingly. Furthermore, he illustrates the ubiquitous notion that a woman takes off her modesty with her clothes by a reference to Juvenal's Sixth Satire. Peter suggests that had his friend read Juvenal's satire diligently, he would have been able to avoid such abject misery. Thus, Peter seems to consider the Sixth Satire not so much a tract against marriage as a textbook of female misbehavior and as an exemplary work on the plight of husbands.

The Juvenal reference is immediately followed by the example of Gannius from Map's *Valerius* without, however, Map's medical metaphor and comment attached to it which promote promiscuous attachments over marriage. Rather, Peter ends the quotation by reaffirming the validity and sacramentality of Christian marriage and contends that he is objecting only to his friend's nuptials. He is astonished at his friend's marriage because his friend used to be so eager in his studies and was so well-known as a philosopher. This interjection is followed by a well-chosen illustration of the sententia that philosophy and marriage do not mix. Cicero (via Jerome), Metodorus (via Salisbury), and Pacuvius (via Map), are called upon, and their testimony is concluded with an apostrophe concerning the necessity of Pacuvius' tree for the purposes of Peter's friend.

Peter's letter is unusual for several reasons. First, it is a *post facto dissuasio* because the addressee is already married. However, as a rhetorical exercise on the topos *an vir sapiens ducat uxorem,* the occasion was of less importance than the topos. Second, Peter is the first medieval misogamic writer to refer to Juvenal's Sixth Satire as a canonic text on the vices of women and wives. The inclusion might be a result of Peter's attempt at originality or his addressee's marital status. Another possible reason for the Juvenal reference could be the initial setting of the letter. Peter describes his friend's marriage as the triumph of women in the battle of the sexes: they succeeded in ensnaring him who was their most dangerous persecutor. Consequently, his friend's marriage was the result of malicious female plans and the *dissuasio* is directed to a victim of female wiles. Third, no Scriptural arguments are found in the letter. This omission corresponds to Peter's purpose; he says that he is disconcerted with his friend's marriage because he professed to be and was a great philosopher. Thus, the dissuasive arguments are directed toward a professional scholar and are entirely philosophic, historical, and rhetorical. Fourth, and most important, Peter is original in his incorporation of exemplary material into the Theophrastus fragment. This assimilation of materials from different sources into the organic whole evidences not only great stylistic awareness but also a facility with the works of misogamy and a recognition of them as essentially the same topographical expressions. As a work of philosophic misogamy, more dependent on Theophrastus than on Jerome, Peter's letter lacks even occasional use of scatology.

Andreas Fieschi

Andreas Fieschi's tract *De dissuasione uxorationis* belongs to the thirteenth century.[62] According to editor Pio Rajna, the writer was Andreas, nephew and chaplain of Pope Alexander IV.[63] The tract is a witty and elegant *dissuasio* in the philosophic misogamous tradition reminiscent of Map's *Valerius*. The setting is similar to Map's. An experienced man addresses a friend eager for marriage projecting an altruistic persona: "Expertus ad inexpertum loquor; in amicum amicus invehor"(1). Matrimony is lethal danger, the speaker exclaims, and his friend has neither Odysseus nor Perseus' mirror to protect him: "Nec ulixem portas in navibus, nec in cristallo Gorgones deridebis"

(2). Like the contemporary *De conjuge non ducenda* (to be discussed in the next chapter), Andreas' *dissuasio* is replete with nautical images: if his friend ties his anchor to woman, he will dash against hidden rocks; if he marries, he traverses over the monsters of the sea. He restates Jerome's warning that a woman's embrace enervates and weakens a man and observes, better men than his friend have succumbed to the wiles of women. The demonstrative *exempla* contingent on this assertion include the stories of Samson and Jupiter among gods and heroes and Holofernes among mortals. The persona emphasizes the advantage of the liberty of the celibate state. Happy is the life free from matrimonial chains, he says, and concludes with a rhetorical question: why would anyone desire to be a slave when he can be a free man? The bonds of matrimony are everlasting, the speaker observes, well aware of the insoluble nature of Christian marriage; only death will abolish them. Andreas interpolates the antithetical Theophrastian and Juvenalian catalogues of undesirable wives in an abbreviated and modified form:

> If she be chaste, she will be proud; if rich and noble, she will spurn the husband. A beautiful wife will be desired by many; an ugly one will be easy to conquer. Finally, if she be stupid, she will never put up with the scholar's reading and study.(7)

If marry you must, he says, marry Pallas Athene, then you shall never be alone: "nubat tibi Pallas, amice, scilicet virtus; quia numquam solus esse poteris, si solus cum virgine virginabis"(8). The substitutional marriage with Athene is advocated in an enthusiastic and eloquent panegyric on the beauty of pseudofamilial ties that bestow eternal joy and glory, the stellar glory of infinity upon the lucky man.

The *De dissuasione*, like Map's *Valerius* and Hugh's *De nuptiis*, is punctuated by apostrophes. Each segment begins with an invocation or direct address to the speaker's friend and concludes with an exhortation. The two chief dissuasive ideas, the beneficiality of liberty and the superiority of spiritual nuptials, place Andreas' tract fully within the philosophic misogamous tradition.

Conclusion

The contribution of the twelfth-century misogamous writers to the misogamous canon was an equation between philosophers and clerks as members of an intellectual and moral elite with clearly defined responsibilities for upholding the normative ideals of that elite.[64] Consequently, their *dissuasiones* are addressed to the professional scholars of the period, the clerks, whom they dissuade from matrimony on the grounds that marriage and philosophy are mutually exclusive occupations. All the *dissuasiones* are written by educated men, very much aware of their privileged state. Thus, the mode of expression usually adopted is one of indignation—standing on a lofty mountain top surrounded by the mist of literary and mythological allusions, surveying the vices and follies of mankind. All of the clerical writers under consideration present an idealized picture of themselves by projecting a *persona* clearly imbued with learning and superior to others. For these writers misogamy is to a large extent an exercise in self-definition; a clerk is superior to others not only because of his learning and vocation but because of his wisdom in avoiding, perceiving, and condemning the vices and follies of others. Among the follies of mankind, marriage, the concession to human frailty, ranks high.

This pronounced sensitivity of individual and professional worth raises yet another parallel with courtly literature. As Marc Bloch perceptively observes, the most profound effect of courtliness lay in the "spontaneous expression of class consciousness to which it gave rise." A similar exclusiveness is at work in the works of philosophic misogamy which, like courtly literature, depict an elitist cohesiveness for their audience.

The elitism of these twelfth-century misogamous texts is attested to by their almost exclusive appeal to an educated (i.e., Latin reading/speaking) audience. The texts were not translated into the vernacular but continued to be copied in Latin for the benefit, education, and entertainment of the same type of educated audience for which they were written. Furthermore, unlike most systems of values that are promoted by small interest groups yet claim universal applicability, works of philosophic misogamy refrain from preaching the general application of the ideals to all men. Philosophic misogamy perpetuates the idea that *one* wise man is worth a thousand foolish men. Thus, it rejects the criterion of quantity in favor of the criterion of excellence, which is achieved by study and leisurely reflection.

While the themes of the tracts are pagan, several contemporary echoes found their way into the works of philosophic misogamy of the twelfth century. Echoes of the *amour courtois* are the most pronounced, and they are invariably ironic. Except for Hugh and Abelard, all writers under consideration were associated with the court. John of Salisbury, Walter Map, and Peter of Blois were patronized by Henry II and their association with "the first major European court to encourage literature propagating the courtly ideal" was bound to result in a certain preoccupation with that ideal. The reactions of these three writers vary from the urbane irony of Walter Map who compensates for the relative mildness toward the ideal by an extensive catalogue of *exempla in malo* of female wickedness and worthlessness, to the indignant attack of Salisbury on general licentiousness, to the intellectual elitism of Peter of Blois. Most writers, but especially Walter Map, provide a wealth of scandalous details in the course of their *dissuasiones,* leaving the reader with the impression that entertainment at the expense of lofty courtly ladies was not the least of their literary purposes.

A predominant concern with all of these writers is the unnerving paradox of strong man brought low by weak woman. Thus, their *dissuasiones* are replete with animal metaphors, animal analogues (representing the inversion of "natural" order) and with the theme of servitude. For a physical marriage that inevitably causes the philosopher's descent to a lower level of living, the clerkly writers propose the surrogate marriage with Athene or Philosophy, which effects the opposite move; rather than being brought low (as they would be by a wife and family), philosopher bridegrooms are raised by their wife-substitutes to Olympic heights.

Another contemporary echo concerns the modified hierarchy of sexual values. Several of the writers under consideration in this chapter (Abelard, Map) maintain that occasional extra-marital affairs ("sudden fits of sickness") are preferable to marriage. While this point of view concurs with the opinion represented in some pagan writings, notably Lucretius' *De rerum natura*, it is in blatant contrast to the ascetic ideal as represented by Jerome. However, the modified hierarchy does represent eleventh- and twelfth-century theocratic policies; as Lea, Gilchrist, and others have shown, sacerdotal marriage was regarded by the Church a much more awful offense than the practice of concubinage and fornication.[65] As H. C. Lea perceptively argues,

> It was the married clergy who boldly proclaimed the correctness of their course, and defended themselves by arguments as well as by political intrigues and military operations. They thus became offenders of a far deeper dye, for the principles of the Church led irrevocably to the conclusion, paradoxical as it may seem, that he who was guilty of immorality, knowing it to be wrong, was far less criminal than he who married, believing it to be right.[66]

All of the writers in this chapter were men in high ecclesiastic positions. While they do not direct their *dissuasiones* exclusively to a priestly or monkish audience, their tracts nevertheless mirror the "official" policy of the Church. Thus, celibacy, singled out by the writers as the index of the philosophic ideal, is at the same time the pragmatic index of preferment and ambition. The substitute marriage with Athene proposed by these writers as the elevating counterpart to physical marriage is the metaphor for the organizational and promotional structure of their corporate employer: the Church.

❖ IV ❖

General Misogamy

Canon law, comedy, and clausura
in the late Middle Ages

Philosophic misogamy was clearly a mixed and, in some respects, a transitional form. In its more ascetic manifestations it still presented marriage as an obstacle to spiritual perfection: to grace and union with God. In those tracts that better reflect the ethos of the twelfth-century Renaissance—John of Salisbury's, for instance, which weighs equally prayer and study—marriage becomes a threat to man's earthly dignity and freedom. In particular, it is represented as a bar to his professional advancement in a context of intellectual careerism and increasing competition.[1]

By the mid-thirteenth century, with medieval Europe reaching its demographic peak, the cultural climate had altered even more dramatically in the direction of an urban market economy and a correlative secularism. Cathedrals replaced abbeys as the most magnificent churches, the workshop replaced the household as the center of economic production. The incorporated master as well as the courtier assumed prominence as the trend toward educational and political professionalism increased.

In such a world, the wit and humor of a Walter Map could more easily appear "unglossed" by the asceticism of Hugh of Folietto, and misogamous literature could be written without even a nod in the direction of otherworldly values. Works filled with humor, wit, and biting satire replace counsels to perfection. Gone, too, is any mention of the possibility for spiritual equality (achieved through sexual abstinence) of the sexes stressed under the ascetic dispensation of early Christianity.

As in the urbane Rome of Juvenal, several legal and philosophical trends herald the reemergence of works of general misogamy. In Juvenal's time, popular misogynistic and elitist (especially Stoic) celibate propaganda coexisted with the official, statutory advocacy of marriage by the state. In late medieval Europe, ecclesiastical endorsement of marriage for the multitude of Christians existed alongside elitist theological and canonical (clerical and celibate) distrust of sex, one of its major components. The threat of legally emancipated luxury-loving matrons loomed large in Imperial Rome and a storehouse of popular antiwomen literature was widely circulated and readily available to assuage if not to offset it. By the late thirteenth century, a misogynistic reaction to the relative gains in public power made by aristocratic women in the preceding centuries (see chapter 3) was in evidence.

Veneration of the ideal women, culminating in the cult of the Virgin, appears to have paralleled this general decline in women's public power.[2] The cult also seems to have fortified the belief in the moral and social dangers of women of flesh and blood.[3] One of the most striking iconographic examples of this latter trend is the figure of Frau Welt—an aristocratic lady if seen from the front; from behind, a cadaver eaten through by worms, frogs, and snakes. Frau Welt appears quite suddenly in the portal sculpture of numerous German churches in the thirteenth and fourteenth centuries, "just at the moment when the developing cult of the Virgin and the love ethic of the Goliards were supposed to have injected some positive notes into the medieval picture of the female sex."[4] Traditionally, the symbol of the pleasures of the world and the flesh had been the attractive *male* aristocrat, Mundus, Prince of the World—(Mundus, Prince of the World; John 12:32 and 14:30).

In sum, late medieval literature like that of Juvenal's Rome stressed the physicality of the female, her biological purpose, and essential instability. As in antiquity, the sequestering of women seemed to be the only relatively foolproof means of maintaining virtue. Even holy women were suspect; thirteenth and fourteenth century monastic "reform" for convents entailed provision for stricter supervision by male superiors and stern rules of enclosure.[5] Not surprisingly, it was classical authority, and especially the rediscovered theory of Aristotle, that provided new "scientific" justifications for the general inferiority, and necessary subordination, of the female.

Scientific misogyny

The credit for disseminating the Aristotelian view of woman as an imperfect male, and thus, by extension, a creature lacking in reason and morality, widely goes to Thomas Aquinas. It was Thomas who, by embracing in turn the androcentric Aristotelian biology, gave a "scientific basis" to earlier "patristic sexual pessimism." In Part I, Question 92 of his *Summa Theologica,* Thomas discusses the production of woman. In dealing with Aristotle's statement that woman is a misbegotten male, Thomas attempts to reconcile Aristotle's thesis and the account of Divine Creation:

> As regards the individual nature, woman is defective and misbegotten, for the active force in the male seed tends to the production of perfect likeness in the masculine sex; while the production of woman comes from defect in the active force or from some material disposition . . . as the Philosopher observes. On the other hand, as regards human nature in general, woman is not misbegotten but is included in nature's intention as directed to the work of generation.[6]

Thomas subsequently uses Genesis 2 to justify male supremacy: "Woman was made to be a help to man. But she was not fitted to help man except in generation, because another man would have proved a more effective help in anything else." Further, he speculates, "It would seem that husband and wife are not equal in the marriage act. For according to Augustine, the agent is more noble than the patient. Therefore, they are not equal in the act" (*ST* Pt. 3, Quest. 64, art. 5). Thomas emphasizes that woman is not different from man as to *res* (she, too, is a human being) but as to *signum* (what she represents). Thus, because priesthood is a sacrament both regarding *res* and *signum,* woman, in her state of subjection, cannot be ordained while men who are slaves can because their subjection is not by nature but by accident (*ST* pt. 3, Quest. 177, art. 2).

Biological antifeminism is, of course, not restricted to Thomas. Adelard of Bath reflects the consensus regarding the application of biological "science" to moral behavior. He suggests that the humidity in woman causes desire; the cold keeps blood from being digested so that blood must be purged through coitus because the seed is nothing but converted blood. His dictum is the "scientific" restatement of the familiar *ardens corpus* accusation levelled at women throughout the ages. This biological view of women permeated medieval physiologies, bestiaries, and works on gynecology as well. Trotula of Salerno's *Diseases of Women,* for example, asserts that women desire sex more than men because they produce seeds in their wombs that can be purged only through intercourse. Thus, because of the pressure in their wombs (caused by the overproduction of seeds), women are more desirous of coitus than men.

As a corollary to the attacks on lust, ancient (Aristotelian) and patristic (Jeromian) theories of the effects of sex were resurrected. As Herlihy observes, the view that frequent coitus shortens the male's lifespan originated with Aristotle.[7] Aristotle had already maintained that, among animals (i.e., sparrows), those males having frequent sexual intercourse age sooner, because they dry up more quickly, just as males that labor too much die more quickly.[8] Albertus Magnus in the thirteenth century restates the philosopher's dictum, applying it to humans. The Jeromian application of the topos to its intellectual consequences occurs in *Adversus Jovinianum* where the Church Father asserts that the love of a woman causes the effeminacy of a virile mind, and Pope Innocent III combines the biological and ascetic traditions:

> O extreme shame of lust, which not only makes the mind effeminate but weakens the body; not only stains the soul but fouls the person. . . . Always heat of desire and wantonness precede lust, stench and filth accompany it, sorrow and repentance follow.[9]

Canon Law—The rigorist position

The emphasis on Mary as virgin, an immaculate mother who had not only remained a virgin but who had herself been conceived without sin, had special significance for law and teaching on the state of matrimony. The height of Virgin worship not coincidentally corresponded to the renewed emphasis on clerical celibacy and the elaboration of a rigorist canonical position on marital relations (one that easily lent itself to parody) developed to suit both burgeoning cult and bureaucracy.

While the medieval misogamic texts are derivative of Jerome's works, in the formation of medieval marital ethics, as in the canon law, Augustine's moderate views rather than those of Jerome were embraced by Church authorities. Augustine maintains that physical sexuality is a gift of God and, as such, not entirely corrupt.[10] Marriage was not evil. Even marital intercourse, had it occurred in paradise (it had not according to Augustine), would have been accomplished without guilt or shame since in that uncorrupted state, coitus would have been passionless and controlled by reason. After the sin of our first parents, however, man was burdened with concupiscence as a result of that sin. Thus, he was no longer in total control of his passions and consequently no longer in full harmony with reason and nature. Concupiscence was most strikingly displayed in the sexual impulses. No sexual activity could take place without its corrupting effect, without passion and unruly desire which was both the consequence of, and the punishment for, original sin. The working of concupiscence or lust in the generative act transmitted original sin to offspring. Sin was thus conveyed by sexual activity in marriage and not via marriage itself—the evil of concupiscence did not take away the good of marriage. Sex in marriage, however, could only be fully blameless when concupiscence was mitigated by a marital good, that is, when desires were tempered by procreative intent or by the intention of "rendering the debt" exacted by one's spouse. Marital intercourse motivated by lust or to avoid fornication was a venial sin because "the intercourse that goes beyond this [procreative] necessity, no longer obeys reason, but passion."[11] Although intrinsically evil, conjugal sex to avoid the greater sin of fornication was a venial and not a mortal sin, because it was pardoned by the good of marriage.

Finally, Augustine accepted fully the Pauline injunction:

Therefore, married people owe each other not only the fidelity of sexual intercourse for the purpose of procreating children ... but also the mutual service in a certain measure, of sustaining each other's weakness, for the avoidance of illicit intercourse, so that even if perpetual continence is pleasing to one of them, he may not follow this urge except with the consent of the other.[12]

Augustine's interpretation of the Pauline dictum was to remain, with one exception, the norm for the greater portion of the Middle Ages. This exception is in the form of a slight, but important, modification introduced by Pope Gregory the Great.

A concise statement of his teaching is found in Gregory's letter to Augustine of Canterbury. It was in response to the latter's query concerning the propriety of entering a church directly after having had carnal relations with one's spouse:

Saying these things we do not assign fault to marriage. But because this lawful mingling of spouses cannot be done without pleasure of the flesh, one is to abstain [from entering the church at once]. This pleasure cannot be without fault. For not of adultery nor of fornication, but of lawful marriage was he born who said, "Behold I was conceived in sins, and in delights my mother bore me."(Ps. 50:7)[13]

For Gregory, the evil of marital coitus was not in the act itself, which may indeed be a "lawful mingling," nor in the concupiscence that impelled man to act irrationally. Instead, it was the sensual pleasure, even when only experienced incidentally, that tainted intercourse. Gregory's extreme distrust of pleasure is apparent. Taken literally, his theory would make every instance of marital intercourse, despite the motive, at least slightly sinful.

Gregory's rigorism was to lie dormant for many years, only to be revived by some like-minded canonists in the late twelfth and thirteenth centuries.[14] Canonical jurisprudence, which began to emerge as a discipline distinct from theology in the twelfth century, centered for years on the *Concordia discordantium canonum,* generally called the *Decretum.* Compiled around 1140 by the Bolognese monk Gratian, this law book was commented on and studied by most of the canonists of the later twelfth and early thirteenth centuries. In their formative elaborations of marriage law, Gratian and his early successors had accepted and developed Paul's concept of a conjugal debt and had consistently defended the right of spouses to exact their marital due. Emphasizing the continuing and obligatory nature of the conjugal duty, they demonstrated their commitment to the ideal of sexual reciprocity.[15]

Yet, by the later twelfth century, the Gregorian equation of marital pleasure with sin surfaced with renewed vigor. Huguccio (d. 1210), an important Bolognese canonist, was a representative and influential spokesman for the rigorist position. He expressed his distrusted of sensual pleasure in the most uncompromising manner. Huguccio maintained that carnal union could never take place without sin. He linked coitus to concupiscence, and concupiscence to pleasure: "Coitus is never without sin because it is always accompanied by a certain itch, and a certain pleasure."[16] Admitting that it was better to unite with one's spouse than to fornicate, he still refused to concede that sexual relations could ever be fully blameless. This restriction included intercourse motivated by such recognized purposes as procreation or rendering the debt—purposes which had not been considered culpable even by Huguccio's least indulgent predecessors. When defending his position against the charge of heresy levelled by some of his detractors, Huguccio claimed that his view was not at odds with orthodox tenets. Heretics, he countered, believed that all coitus was mortally sinful, while he regarded intercourse for "good ends" (payment of the debt or generation) as only venially sinful.[17] Huguccio succeeded in equating coitus with pleasure and venereal pleasure with sin. Given this nexus, the obvious question arose: could a spouse ever perform his marital duty (Huguccio had never denied that Paul's admonition still held) without sinning? Ingeniously, Huguccio answered in the affirmative:

> Returning the debt to one's wife is nothing more than making your body available to her. Hence, one often renders the debt to his wife in such a way that he does not satisfy his pleasure, and conversely. Therefore, in the aforesaid case, I can so render the debt to the wife and wait in such a way until she satisfies her

pleasure ... I can if I wish, withdraw, not satisfying my pleasure, free of all sin, and not emitting my seed of propagation.[18]

For Huguccio as for Gregory, the evil of intercourse was in the pleasure resulting from that act. If pleasure could be avoided, sin could be eliminated. Huguccio's particular solution, as later canonists would note, thwarted procreation because a husband need not emit his "seed of propagation." Because he considered sexual pleasure so grave a threat to morality, Huguccio was even willing to tolerate an obvious departure from orthodox teaching.

The rigorist stance had its appeal. It was reasserted by a number of other canonists, among them Pope Innocent III. Writing as a private theologian, Innocent declared: "Who does not know that conjugal intercourse is never committed without itching of the flesh, and heat and foul concupiscence, whence the conceived seeds are befouled and corrupted."[19]

The extreme rigorism of Huguccio threatened to undermine the orthodox tradition that upheld the essential goodness of marital sex, properly motivated. Such a position was bound to be challenged. By the early thirteenth century, Huguccio's reasoning was considered suspect in some circles. The ordinary gloss on the *Decretum*, first written between 1215 and 1217, evidenced this skepticism. The gloss frequently cited Huguccio's teaching as representative of opinions contrary to those found in the *Decretum*. When Joannes Teutonicus, author of the gloss, expressed his own views, he challenged those of Huguccio. In one instance, he launched a direct assault:

> Huguccio says that no coitus is possible without sin; hence, even he who renders the debt sins venially, because there is always pleasure in the emission of sperm. Huguccio holds others to sin because they are bound to render the debt ... following this reasoning, a man sins because of the need to follow a command.[20]

Needless to say, Joannes did not subscribe to this faulty reasoning. He asserted that rendering the debt was meritorious because it was the satisfaction of a just demand.[21] The *Glossa ordinaria* upheld the Augustinian notion that intercourse for procreation or for the return of the debt was lawful and blameless. Exacting the debt either through incontinence or lust might be a mortal sin, but it was punished as a venial one thanks to the mitigating effects of the good of marriage.[22]

The uncompromising rigorism of Huguccio and his followers seems to fall out of favor by the mid-thirteenth century. If it suffered a setback at this time, however, the doctrine certainly did not die completely. As late as the seventeenth century, a hard-line approach to sexuality that was in many ways similar to Huguccio's reappeared.[23] At that later date, as well as in the twelfth century, revived interest in the rigorist position was more than fortuitous. Why did the rigorist doctrine, in all its stark severity, emerge in the twelfth century? Why did it find adherents in an era far removed from the patristic age in which it was first enunciated?

The rigorist position took hold at a time when the whole complex body of marriage law was as yet in its formative stages. Most of Gratian's work would pass, with few changes, into the law of the Church. Gratian's teaching on marital formation and his embryonic doctrine of marital sacramentality, however, were to be considerably modified by his successors. The developed doctrine on both these vital areas tended to minimize the role of coitus, whether as the symbol of marital sacramentality, or as the element that ratified its formation. Development in these related areas of the marriage law signify and reinforce an inherent distrust of carnal relations. The conclusions at which the rigorists arrived could have appeared tenable in such an intellectual climate.

Gratian had confirmed a patristic and canonical tradition that gave consent the primary and initiating role in marital formation. According to the Roman law principle, "consensus facit matrimonium," consent exchanged between contracting parties, rather than sexual union, brought a marriage into existence.[24] The lawyers employed the Roman law theory of consent as a basis of canonical marriage law, in part, because it was consonant with Christian teaching.

Since the end of the patristic period, the perpetual virginity of Mary had been "something nearer a dogma than a pious opinion, and propriety had long represented her spouse as an aged man whose role was that of guardian rather than husband."[25] With the meteoric rise of the cult of Mary, the task was to uphold the true marital status of Christ's parents while denying the existence of sexual relations either at the time of Christ's birth or subsequent to it. The canonists could reckon this spiritual union a true marriage if they used the consensual theory, the basis of which was volition and not sex.[26]

In the final analysis, the canonists were not content with Gratian's teaching. Gratian had said that consent and not copulation initiated marriage but insisted that consummation perfected the union already established. Later writers, influenced by Peter Lombard and the Paris school, succeeded in establishing as doctrine the teaching that exchange of consent in the present tense alone made a perfected marriage. The primary role of carnal relations then was to initiate the duty of sexual reciprocity—the obligation to pay the marital debt. In terms of the essence of marriage, sexual relations were not essential. A mutual vow of continence, or an act of God that rendered one party incapable of paying the debt after consummation, could in no way impair the indissolubility of the union.[27]

The decretists managed to divorce the element of sex, an element they distrusted, from the essence of matrimony via the consensual theory. A similar line of development is evident in the lawyer's treatment of sacramentality. In this area as well, there was a departure from Gratian's stance—a departure that indicated a negative attitude toward sexual relations in marriage.

Unlike the doctrine of marital formation, the issue of sacramentality remained largely unresolved until the fifteenth century.[28] Without delving into the complexities of this theological problem, two notable canonical developments occurred in this period. According to Gratian, only the consummated marriage was sacramental.[29] Sexual union signified what Paul had referred to as the "magnum sacramentum" of the union of Christ and his Church. Paucapalea, Gratian's earliest commentator, reaffirmed this teaching when he commented on Pope Leo's statement that, without sexual union, a marriage did not have sacramental symbolism.[30] So, too, Pope Alexander III stressed the need for consummation: "only matrimony perfected by carnal union can be said to have the *sacramentum* of Christ and his Church."[31] Gradually, under the influence of theologians such as Hugh of St. Victor, the unconsummated union also gained a sacramental value, complete with its own novel signification. Rufinus, for instance, postulated a "two sacrament" theory of marriage, according to which the exchange of consent signified the union of the soul with God, while consummation represented the union of Christ and the Church.[32] By declaring that there were two sacraments in marriage, corresponding to consent and consummation respectively, Rufinus abandoned the position taken by Gratian. Consummation was no longer required for marriage to be a sacrament. As sacramental theology developed, the term *sacramentum* was reserved for those symbols that were effective causes of grace. In light of this development, Rufinus' double-sacrament notion could not remain acceptable. The theory of sacramental signification developed by Huguccio was more in accord with what would become the orthodox teaching on the matter. For Huguccio, there was only one sacrament, marriage, which contained two significations. Consent signified the union of the soul with God, consummation the union of Christ and the Church. In different terms, Huguccio still recognized the sacramentality of an unconsummated marriage.[33]

With minor revisions, and some differences of opinion concerning the exact number of significations in marriage, a theory that recognized the sacramentality of an unconsummated union was victorious. Gratian had reserved sacramental status only for unions that had been perfected by conjugal relations.

Although they could assign sacramental value to an unconsummated union, the canonists could not deny that consummation signified a sacred thing as well. Despite its symbolism, however, some prominent members of the Bologna school were not willing to admit the sacrament of matrimony to the ranks of the other six. They reasoned that marriage might indeed signify a sacred thing, but it did not necessarily produce grace as a consequence. Many of the canonists took this stand for two reasons. The first and most common was not a theological reason at all but rather a legal one. The canonists knew that money frequently changed hands during marriage negotiations whether in the form of a dowry or as a stipend for the nuptial benediction. If matrimony were to confer grace, the contracting parties would be guilty of simony. The *Glossia ordinaria* summarizes this argument:

> Note that matrimony does not belong to those sacraments that supply the consolation of heavenly grace, and for that reason money may change hands in regard to it ... the other sacraments are symbols of a spiritual thing and as such have in them its virtue. Matrimony is only a symbol.[34]

The second argument against the efficacy of the sacrament of matrimony cannot be dismissed as an attempt to wipe out a glaring ecclesiastical abuse. Instead, it once again has the tainted nature of the sexual act as its premise. Marriage, it was argued, could not produce grace due to the evil of concupiscence; it could only be a means of legitimizing what was innately sinful. This was the position Rufinus took. He submitted that the union of the sexes in marriage was only a symbol and that the "law of sin" that inhered in carnal relations prohibited the sacrament from being efficacious.[35] Even into the fourteenth century, noted canonists would still not reckon the marital sacrament a fully effective channel for grace. Joannes Andreae, for example, admitted that marriage enabled the recipients of its remedial grace to avoid sin and to live more easily as chaste spouses, but matrimony did not bestow a fresh influx of sanctifying grace as did other sacraments.[36]

Eventually, marriage was recognized as truly efficacious and as conveying a positive increase in grace. In the period when Gregorian rigorism flourished, this view was far from widespread. When both the developments regarding marital formation and those dealing with sacramentality are viewed together, one overriding theme emerges. Inheritors of jaundiced patristic notions about sex, the canonists were wary of allowing consummation to initiate or to symbolize marriage. Both the consensual theory and the doctrine of sacramental signification became law; both were departures from Gratian's more "natu-

ralistic" pronouncements. Obviously, to the extent that such canonical casuistry was known among the literate class, it was fair
ground for parody.

Popular Misogynistic Literature

As in Juvenal's *Sixth Satire*, the personae of late medieval satires subvert by ridicule the ideals of the two dominant classes
in their case, the aristocracy and the clergy. The ecclesiastical
model of marriage, dependent on the Augustinian ideal of
proles, fides, and *sacramentum,* is presented either as an antivalue
or its inversion is shown as common practice; so, too, canonical
rigorism is lampooned. In both cases, the ideal is presented as
an argument against marriage. Similarly, the aristocratic
courtly model provides the butt for many attacks, as the over-
populated literary gallery of cuckolded husbands, adulterous
wives, and lusty bachelors attests.

The storehouses of literary misogynistic sentiments in the
period were the sermons and other works of ecclesiastic writers, and the popular genres of the vernacular fabliaux and the
Latin *comedia elegiaca.* All of these genres contributed substantial materials for the topology of general misogamic satire
while works of philosophic misogamy from the previous century were utilized to a lesser degree.

Gerald Owst, in his pioneering research into the sermon
origins of medieval vernacular satire, maintains that wandering
preachers played an important role in disseminating pulpit satire and that their ideas fell on fertile ground.[37] Among the
preachers' favorite subjects of attack were, of course, women
and wives, and Owst lists the commonest epithets hurled from
the pulpit at women as "foolishness," "overmuch spekying,"
"instabilitas loci" (i.e., an attraction to the outside world),
"love of finery," disobedience, and a "certain unnatural condition of contrariety and wilfulness," in that order.[38] Emphasis
on the polluting effects of women does not lag far behind.
Bromyard in his chapter on *Matrimonium* restates the patristic
argument that while the Old Testament ideal was one of fecundity, the New Testament ideal is one of chastity. He exhorts his
audience: "So yf thou wolt be Cristes Clene childe, flee as

Cristes toward the companye of folyes women, ne be thou non to famylyer with non maner women." Similarly, the *Speculum Laicorum* repeats the familiar misogamous and misogynistic arguments the society of women ought to be avoided, "quia hominem illaqueat, . . . comaculat . . . et rebus et virtutibus spoliat" (because she traps man, stains man, and spoils him of his goods and powers).[39] One of the favorite topoi of homilistic misogamy which had passed into many branches of popular literature concerns the danger that woman represents.[40]

Not only sermons but other works by churchmen are replete with attacks on women. A large proportion of these antifeminist statements follow the form of the *Quid est mulier* guessing-game. Hildebert's definition is a case in point. He writes of woman as sordid and treacherous, of fickle and destructive disposition . . . venomous and deceitful to all[41] and even he is surpassed by Bernard of Cluny who describes women as "locusts of the soul . . . a guilty thing, or hopelessly fleshly thing . . . beautiful rottenness . . . a vessel of filth . . . a trench of lust, the arms of chaos, and tongue of vice."[42] Such and similar statements of Bernard led A. K. More to make the suggestion that in Bernard, the Church was sheltering a psychopath.[43] Hildebrant and Bernard are by no means the only churchmen thundering insults upon women—a glance at Wolff's and Moore's compilations will evidence dozens of similar indictments.[44]

Among the secular genres, both the fabliau and the *comedia elegiaca* specialized in tales of adultery. In fact, by the thirteenth century "fabliau" came to mean a story of cuckoldry. In the fabliaux women are sometimes treated as foolish, but almost always as lecherous. Noblemen and high prelates are treated with some deference while the parish priest, the friar, and the monk are the universal scapegoats of fabliaux. As Robert Harrison remarks about the village priest: "practically without exception he is depicted as a vain, covetous lecher, ready at the drop of a handkerchief to deflower a virgin, debauch a wife, or plunder a pyx or a poor box."[45] No wonder that in many works of general misogamy wives, monks, priests, and friars are often attacked together as a group. Similarly, the Latin elegiac comedy (we need only consider the *Lydia*) treats almost invariably of adultery; but, while the fabliau specializes in gross and drastic obscenities to raise a laugh, the Latin elegiac comedy is replete with puns, rhetorical subtleties, and suggestive innuendoes.

From a philological point of view, several traditions seem to be of importance for the occurrence of works of general misogamy: a misogynistic literary tradition upon which the writer can freely draw and which is recognized as such by his audience; an equally well-understood and recognized tradition of elitist misogamy; and the official upholding of the procreative marital ideal—in sum, a set of conflicting and contradictory intellectual, moral, and social signals. In Juvenal's Rome, popular misogynistic and elitist celibate propaganda coexisted with the official advocacy of marriage by the state. The same applies to works of medieval general misogamy.

Wykked Wyves: a tradition reasserted in *De conjuge non ducenda, Quinze joies de mariage,* and the Wife of Bath's "Prologue"

Because misogynistic works burgeoned in the thirteenth, fourteenth, and fifteenth centuries, and because most of these works also contain misogamous passages, our choice for representative examples is particularly difficult. Works that were particularly popular in the Middle Ages or later such as the *Roman de la Rose* (which includes passages of misogamy among a host of other concerns), the *Mirror of Marriage* (which, like the *Couplets sur le mariage,* is not a *dissuasio* in the strict sense, but an *altercatio* weighing arguments pro and contra marriage), the *Matheoli Lamentationes* (the enormous amplification of the *Chanson de mal mariage* taking its impetus from a problem of digamy and, by extension, attacking marriage), will be discussed but the focus will be on full-fledged *dissuasiones* of the general satiric tradition: the anonymous *De conjuge non ducenda,* with its vernacular adaptations, the *Quinze joies de mariage,* and finally, the most intricate and intriguing satire of them all, the Wife of Bath's "Prologue."

De conjuge non ducenda

The thirteenth century *De conjuge non ducenda* begins with what is usually the concluding benediction of scribes after having finished the copying of a manuscript: "Sit deo gloria, laus, benedictio."[46] As in the other famous occurrence of the same practice, Jerome's letter to Paulinus, the author or the scribe must have considered the copying work enjoyable and rewarding.

The thankful benediction of the first line is extended not only to God but also to his representatives, the angels Johannes, Petrus, and Laurentius. God in his great mercy sent his angels to save the narrator from the portals of hell, from miserable shipwreck, from eternal suffering, in one word, from marriage.

The poem's setting, a vision in the valley of Mambre, is replete with ironic implications. Mambre is known as the Old Testament *locus* where three angels appeared to Abraham prophesying his aged wife Sarah's impending parturition and the arrival of his longed-for son Isaac. Firm in his faith, Abraham believes the words of the angels even though they appear to be contrary to all probability. At the same time, the angels conversing with Abraham are on their way to test and destroy Sodom and Gomorrah—cities of vice, particularly of unnatural licentiousness. On Abraham's intercession, Lot and his family (the only virtuous people in the two cities), are to be saved from destruction by the angels. Thus, the topical implications raised by the Scriptural setting are twofold: a test of faith in the context of promised parenthood; and the salvation of the virtuous from destruction in the context of severe punishment for the sinful.

The angels' explicit purpose in the poem is to save the narrator from the "mouth of hell," i.e., from marriage, because marriage is servitude and because women are weak *(carnis fragilis)*, inconstant *(labilis)*, and proud *(numquam humilis)*.

The setting of the poem is also similar to Walter Map's *dissuasio*—in fact, the setting of the *De conjuge* is the actualization of the setting of the *Valerius*. Valerius claimed to be the prophet of truth who felt compelled to tell his friend of the dangers, burdens, and inconveniences of marriage because Rufinus' friends and flatterers failed to do so. In the *De conjuge,* not one but three voices of truth appear and, like Valerius, deliver the *dissuasio*. Golias, we are told, was encouraged in his plans for matrimony by false friends who, themselves miserable in their marital servitude, wanted a companion in misery. The setting of the poem concludes with a clever use of *traductio*, the repetition of the same word with different and, in this case, ironic implications. The angels are described as "quibus vox varia sed sensus unitas," which line is immediately followed by their accusation of women being "varia" (two-faced, inconsistent).

Whom the angels represent is still subject to debate. Wright identifies them as John Chrysostom (Johannes... *os habens aureum*), Peter of Corbeil (Petrus de Corbolio), and possibly Laurentius of Durham to whom, mistakenly, the *De conjuge* has been attributed by Fabricius.[47] However, Johannes is also referred to as "hic sicut aquila videt subtilia," the iconography of John the Evangelist. The two references are reconcilable, however, for the eagle iconography of John is derivative of his eloquence and the lofty style of his Apocalyptic Gospel. Moreover, it is possible that the author of the *De conjuge* wanted to project a composite figure rather than a specific person for his chief mouthpiece. We have already noted some of John Chrysostom's misogamous views in the second chapter. In the twelfth century several spurious antifeminist works were ascribed to him, not the least popular of which is a "quid est mulier" tract printed in Wright's *Reliquiae Antiquae*:

> What is woman? Hostile friendship; unavoidable pain; a necessary evil; natural temptation desirable calamity; domestic danger; delectable ruination... the gateway of evil; path of iniquity.[48]

John the Evangelist, on the other hand (as the author of the Apocalypse) is a most convenient symbol for the visionary setting and angelic delivery of the satire: especially so, as the twelfth and thirteenth centuries interpreted the Apocalypse in its eschatological meaning by means of popular vernacular and Latin commentaries of this Gospel. Here, too, doomsday is prophesied; doomsday which is equated with marital tribulation. Moreover, John the Evangelist is the misogamic messenger in at least one other medieval text of a later date. In one of the *Miracles de Notre Dame par Personnages,* a young canon vows to serve Mary. His uncle, however, chooses a bride of wealth and beauty for him whom the cleric agrees to marry. On his wedding night the Virgin summons John the Evangelist, and they descend to the young man's bedroom and reproach him for breaking his promise. The cleric repents and immediately leaves his bride to serve the Virgin.[49]

One other John (John the Apostle) might also figure in the echoes of the name of the chief misogamic angel. Starting with Bede, but especially well-spread in the thirteenth century (because of the incorporation of the belief into the *Legenda Aurea*) was the notion that the bridegroom at the wedding feast at Cana was actually John the Apostle who left his bride to follow the Lord.

The other two angels might have been chosen for several reasons. Peter of Corbeil (Petrus de Corbolio) was a Parisian teacher of Innocent III, the archdefender of the celibate and chaste ideal, and was Archbishop of Sens between 1199 and 1222. He was famous for his asceticism and his reform efforts. Laurentius, a third-century martyr, was the patron saint of couriers and might have been chosen for that reason.

At the same time, the choice of "Petrus" and "Laurentius" as the names for the lesser angels also provides a convenient opportunity for the author to play his favorite inversion game. Peter, for example, is described as deriving from the firmness of rock *(firmitas et petrae ratio),* and he is the one who condemns female *fragilitas* (weakness). Similarly, Laurentius, whose name is supposed to derive from the laurel which greens "in winter just as in spring" attacks female *labilitas* (inconstancy) and *stultitia* (stupidity). Both female vices are, of course, the direct inversions of the laurel's qualities: constancy and poetic or intellectual talent.

The topography of the poem

Petrus is the first angel to deliver his mock-sermon. He who marries, he begins, subjects himself to a great burden from which death alone can liberate him: the husband always serves; the wife always commands. Like an ass he has to work to feed his wife and children. Manifold and awful are the burdens of wedlock and, what is more, they completely wear out the poor husband. A wife always pretends to be unwell and sick, but he has to work continuously; as soon as he produces anything, it is immediately consumed. In a statement reminiscent of Theophrastus, Peter observes that many things are necessary for a married man, for him, his wife, the children. In order to fill their bellies, the husband is reduced to cheating and crime. Psychologically astute, the angel observes that the husband has to work so hard, that he even works in his dreams. By continuous work, as a direct result of marriage, the husband crucifies himself. The invocation of the crucifix iconography is a clever utilization of the theological/canonical analogy of marital relations and Christ. Paul and countless exegetes and preachers emphasized that "as Christ is the head of the Church, so man is the head of his wife." Consequently, the husband crucifies himself for the wife as Christ was crucified for mankind.

The chief idea of Peter's *dissuasio* is that a woman actually being or pretending to be weak is a constant drain on the poor husband: his energy, his goods, and his mental and physical well-being—and idea prevalent, as argued above, in thirteenth-century biological and ecclesiastical works.

Peter's speech is followed by Laurentius' *dissuasio* in which he castigates the stupidity, lasciviousness, inconstancy, and greed of women. If the husband does not provide for all her needs (and the nature of these "needs" is left ambiguous at first) then she turns to adultery (lines 87–88). Then Laurentius specifies her needs as being marital and sexual: a woman commits adultery to have clothes "ut vestes habeat" and to cool her burning entrails "ut refrigeret ardorem viscerum."[50] As soon as the husband's "substance" (again the word carries the double meaning) is used up, the wife turns to an adulterer. The

double entendre, as in Juvenal's work, is obscene; unlike those
in the Sixth Satire, it is metaphoric rather than mechanistic.
The sad result is, the angel observes, that because women are
adulteresses and their guilt can be easily hidden, the poor
deceived husband has to support a prostitute and bastards
(lines 102–12). The maritime imagery of the introduction
(marriage is shipwreck) recurs in the context of adultery: just
as a ship leaves no trace after crossing the sea, so the adulterous wife cannot be found out after the event has taken place.
Consequently, Laurentius takes Petrus' suggestions a step further. Not only does a wife drain her husband's energy, goods,
and vitality, she also deceives him and makes his paternity
doubtful.

Johannes is the last to speak. He commences his *dissuasio* by
defining marriage as double servitude of body and spirit. The
husband is a "bos venditus," a sold ox subjugated by perpetual
labor. He is also likened to an ass bearing all the burdens that
are caused by a deceitful, envious, proud wife. In this context
of servitude, Johannes mentions (in what sounds like an echo
of Thomas's *Summa Theologica*) the purposeful creation of
woman as a helpmate (*in adjutorio*) for the propagation of the
race (*ut salvet generis humani semina*); but in everything else,
the angel concludes, she is a burden to man. In spite of her
obvious inferiority, woman is still domineering; what is more,
she wishes to usurp the male's right to rule (*semper domini vult
esse domina*). Johannes continues his speech by demonstrating
how woman perverts her God-given purpose. In a passage as
savage, as categorical, and as obscene as the corresponding passages in Juvenal's Sixth Satire (but clearly referring to sex *se-
cundum naturam* only), the angel delivers his indictment of
insatiable female lust, insisting that woman is never satisfied by
one man (lines 149–57)—she is capable of exhausting a na-
tion. Having to pay the marital debt too frequently kills the
husband. Thus, it is not expedient for anyone to marry. After
the indictment of the adulterous, lascivious wife, Johannes echoes the Salomonic misogamous catalogue. Women fight with
their *lingua gladius*, they, like smoke and rain, expel the husband from his own home, they are quarrelsome and are more

difficult to live with than a fierce lion. This last observation occurs also in the *Disciplina Clericalis* under the attributes of the "mala femina."[51]

Johannes' third and last argument is the already familiar equation of death, marriage, and suffering. He who takes a wife accepts death—woman is more bitter than death and while death comes in a short hour, the anguish of marital troubles lasts for a long time. "How shall I define marriage," the angel asks, "but as Tartarus." Neither condition has any hope of remedy, and they both consist of suffering, pain, and punishment. Therefore, he concludes with an apostrophe, "avoid marriage."

The accusations are all-inclusive; all nubile women are under attack as is the institution of marriage. As a text of general misogamy, the *De conjuge* is in full methodological, ideological, and topographical agreement with the prototype of this branch of misogamy, Juvenal's Sixth Satire. As in the Roman satire, so in the *De conjuge,* the *dissuasio* is delivered by friendly, sympathetic, altruistic personae to a supposedly less experienced young man contemplating marriage. As in the Sixth Satire, the idea underlying the dissuasive arguments is that no worthy woman can be found to wed, and that marriage entails the servitude and ultimate destruction of the husband. As in the Sixth Satire, so here, the two chief dissuasive ideas are "mundus inversus" (i.e., domineering wives), and insatiable female lust (with all its familiar repercussions of adultery, illegitimacy of heirs, and constant deception). Even the method of inversion and repetition are present in the *De conjuge*. The author not only inverts such standard values as divinely ordained female fecundity but, by providing the ironic Old Testament setting in Mambre, he creates a constant undercurrent of irony. At the same time, the poem shows the inversion of the procreative ideal with all its ramifications: children, the major *bonum* of marriage, are burdensome; they wear out the husband and lead him to resort to crime in order to feed them; they are frequently bastards without the knowledge of the poor husband who is made a fool in his paternal affections for someone else's child.

The narrator of the poem is not likely to be a nobleman, a cleric nor a man of means. Rather, he seems to be a man living slightly above the subsistence level because God's messengers repeatedly suggest that a wife and children would necessitate not only his continuous hard labor but also the possibility that he may have to resort to cheating, crime, and dishonesty to fill his family's bellies. The implication appears to be that the addressee is an artisan of some trade, or, possibly, a peasant. Thus, the poem appeals not only to an educated audience who would appreciate and enjoy the text's ironic subtleties and complex Scriptural echoes, but also to a bourgeois audience who would enjoy the poem's topography and its coarse obscenities—in one word, to Everyman. This hypothesis is supported by its great popularity and translation of the poem into at least two vernaculars (English fourteenth century, French late thirteenth century), a fate which did not befall the erudite texts of philosophic misogamy that were clearly written for an educated readership.

Similarly, the poem lacks any direct mythological, literary or Scriptural allusions. What literary and Biblical echoes there are, are paraphrased but not identified. Thus, the poem is fully intelligible without any understanding of the subtleties and ironies of the setting and the presentation. All of these observations suggest that the author was consciously trying to project a persona less educated and of a lower social class than himself.

The title and the name of the addressee vary in the different manuscripts of *Golias* is the most common (*Gilbetus, Galuius, Gauterus* are the others). Who this Golias was is open to conjecture, but it is quite likely that the author of the poem (himself perhaps a travelling scholar or its scribe) chose the name in full awareness of its connotations, for by the thirteenth century Golias was a generic name for the *Vagantes*.[52]

In the *De conjuge*, Golias, the addressee of the three *dissuasiones*, does not reveal himself as addicted to either one of the vices associated with his name. What he does share with his apocryphal namesake is his abhorrence of material needs and matrimonial troubles to which abhorrence the three angels eloquently appeal. Significantly, no castigation of promiscuous relationships is found in any of the speeches and, in fact, the lover whom the adulterous wife takes and supports is described in rather enviable terms. He has all the joys but none of the encumbrances of wedlock. The implied comparison of the enviable lover with the miserable husband is subtly but perceptibly stated.

A minor, but nevertheless revealing, omission might argue for clerical authorship of the *De conjuge*. As in Andreas' *De arte honeste amandi*, so in the *De Conjuge*, accounts of female wiles and cunning are missing. This omission is particularly surprising in view of the great popularity of the topos toward the end of the twelfth and in the thirteenth centuries in the fabliau, homiletic, and exemplary literatures of the period and in the oriental compilations of the age. Could it be that the author considered himself or his estate immune to female cunning? Clerks, particularly clerk scholars who had to live by their wits, were famous for their cunning and wiles. In the popular contemporary fabliau, for instance, the scholar clerk (as opposed to the lecherous secular priest or the greedy and lustful monk) almost invariably succeeds in his stratagem against jealous husbands and in his quest for women who take his fancy. Thus, it is possible that the omission of this very popular accusation might reflect both the literary tradition and a confidence of a clever secular cleric. In any case, the author is a fine stylist, a man with pronounced rhetorical polish and a fondness for wordplay, who shows particular preference for *adnominatio*. The rhymed quatrains with strong central caesurae are ornamented by alliteration and the occasional use of simple and compound hyperbaton. Like Map's and Peter of Blois' *dissuasiones*, the speeches of the *De conjuge* all end in an apostrophe exhorting Golias not to marry.

A full-fledged satire in the general Juvenalian misogamic tradition, *De conjuge* ridicules both celibate and marital propaganda while catering to contemporary prejudices. As such, it is an ironic and—to some—entertaining catalogue of *exempla in malo* of the trials and tribulations of wedlock caused, naturally, by wicked wives. Like Juvenal's persona, *De conjuge*'s three angels dissuade a young man from matrimony *not* because of an ascetic or philosophic ideal in mind, but because no woman is worth marrying and because, in one word, marriage is hell. Therefore, the satire had wide appeal. To an educated, Latin literate audience, the poem appealed by its rhetorical polish, well-sustained irony, and wealth of allusions, as well as by its topography.[53] To both an uneducated audience and to a secular-courtly bourgeois audience (for whose benefit the translations were made), the poem appealed by reiterating popular details of female vice and misbehavior and highlighting female lust and insubordination which are, incidentally, the two most popular motifs of the fabliau (cuckolded husband; *mundus inversus*).

Roman de la Rose

The *Roman de la Rose* is probably the most important (in the sense of its popularity and influence) vernacular poem of the Middle Ages and Jean de Meung's reputation as a savage misogynist was almost instantaneous and long lasting.[54] Geoffrey Chaucer, for example, was reproached by the God of Love in the Prologue to the "Legend of Good Women": "Thou hast translated the Romance of the Rose, / That is an heresye ayeins my lawe."[55] The *Roman* even occasioned the first sustained literary discussion on women, the *Querelle du Roman de la Rose* (initiated by Christine de Pisan), at the turn of the fourteenth and fifteenth centuries.[56]

All of the misogynistic and misogamous statements of the *Roman* are put in the mouths of unsympathetic characters. What is more, these unsympathetic characters are stock-figures of medieval comedy delivering stock-tirades. In the Jaloux's speech, even more than in the *De conjuge*, the double-edged sword of irony is prevalent; wicked wives as well as celibacy promoters who created them as literary types are satirized. The Jaloux, for example, uses such standard authorities as Juvenal, Valerius, Theophrastus, and Ovid. As Lionel Friedman points out, the Jaloux's antifeminism is neither "realistic" nor "bourgeois" but conventional and learned: "Just as he is clerical in his sources, our Jaloux is clerical in his expression.... In all respects, he shows a far greater reflection of the medieval schools than of an observation of contemporary life."[57] Yet, while the Jaloux recites the canon of philosophic misogamous arguments as part of his *dissuasio* from marriage, he offers no surrogate relationships in favor of physical ones—his *dissuasio* lacks one of the very essential elements of philosophic misogamy, namely, substitutionalism. The Jaloux is also a notorious wife-beater and a man who reveals himself as more addicted to physical needs, desires, and comforts than to learning. Thus, the satire on women and marriage is only one aspect of the Jaloux's speech—another is the satire on him and what he himself represents.

The jealous husband's *dissuasio* is delivered in chapters 41 through 44 of the *Roman* in the context of the contrast of love and seignory. Amis introduces the Jaloux's speech by observing that true love cannot endure as long as men treat their wives like property: "True love cannot for long endure when such / Reciprocal annoyances exist / And men treat their own wives like property... " / (8463–66). After complaining of his sad fate, the Jaloux delivers a *dissuasio* in the philosophic misogamous tradition. He assumes the tone of spontaneous indignation—which would suggest that he is speaking the simple truth. However, he so frequently and prominently displays irony, learning, and rhetoric that his "simple honesty" is not credible. Many of the canonic authorities and arguments are present. Theophrastus, who, according to the jealous husband, thinks a man a fool who takes a wife and whose *Aureole* should be studied in schools, is quoted at length and with amplification. The fragment is followed by the obligatory *rara avis* exclamation and the observation that no Lucretias and Penelopes are left today. Particularly interesting is the Jaloux's amplification of the Theophrastian "cat in a sack" motif:

> Most inconsistent is the wont of men
> When they would marry; often I'm amazed
> That such a risky custom they should use.
> Whence comes their foolishness I do not know,
> Unless from madness or insanity.
> I never see a man who buys a mare
> Act so unwisely as to close the deal

> Without observing her unblanketed.
> If she is covered, he will strip her bare
> That he may see her parts and try her out.
> But one will take a wife without such test,
> All unaware of solace or regret,
> For better or for worse, without a chance
> Of finding faults in her, provided that
> She no displeasure give before they're wed.
> But when the knot is tied, her spite appears;
> Then first does she reveal the vice she has;
> Then first the fool perceives her evil tricks
> When late repentance will avail him not.
>   (8661–77)[58]

Men who wish to marry, he continues, are insane because, according to Valerius: "He who weds / Afflicts himself with many a hard mischance / And fear and care"(8637–39). Valerius wrote to dissuade his friend from matrimony praying that God may protect Rufinus from being caught in the net:

> Valerius is not ashamed to ask
> To what end thinks the fool that he will come
> Who either in this land or overseas
> Makes love to evil women, who abound
> Thicker than flies, or bees about a hive.
> Who trust in such frail twigs lose body and soul.
> Valerius, who grieved when he perceived
> That Rufinus, his friend, would take a wife,
> Spoke these hard words: "May God omnipotent
> Forbid that e'er you're caught within the net
> Of woman, who is powerful to crush
> All things by her destructive artifice!"
>   (8731–34)

Juvenal also wrote a poem to dissuade his friend Postumus from marriage. The Jaloux quotes the example of King Phoroneus (via Map) and uses the testimony of the Abelard-Heloise correspondence as a misogamic argument. The Jaloux praises Heloise highly as a wise, loving, and well-educated woman. His respect for her, we are soon to discover, is based on her *dissuasio* from marriage, and he quotes at length her reasons for wishing to be Abelard's mistress rather than his wife. He comments on her speech with obvious envy:

> In turn confesses Peter Abélard,
> Who loved the abbess of the Paraclete,
> That Héloïse wished never to agree
> That he should take her for his wedded wife.
> She was a wise, well-educated maid,
> Well loved and loving, yet with arguments
> She taught her lover wedlock to avoid.
> Her letters pointed out how hard are found
> The circumstances of a wedded life,
> No matter how discreet the wife may be.
> Not only had she read and studied books
> But learned of woman's nature in herself.
> That he should love her she made her demand
> But also that he'd claim no other right
> Than what was granted freely, of good grace,
> Without supremacy or mastership;
> That he might study freely, without tie
> Though hers, while she, in science not unversed,
> Pursued her studies, too. She said at least
> Their joys would be more pleasing when they met,
> Their solace would by absence be increased.
>
> (8825–30)

He concludes by saying that Abelard should have listened to her (just as the Jaloux himself should have listened to Theophrastus) and that marriage is an evil bond, "Mariages est maus liens" (9125–30).

After exhausting the philosophic misogamous canon, the Jaloux turns to the topography of general misogamy and delivers a personal lamentation on the vices of wives, particularly his own. Wives are coquettes, luxurious; they reject the husbands' amorous advances; they love finery. Beauty and chastity are always at war, and chastity almost always loses. In chapter 44, the Jaloux gives a catalogue of *exempla in malo* demonstrating how women have always deceived men. Introducing it by his own sad tale of frustration and cuckoldry—his wife is only cold when he seeks her solaces; for her lovers she burns in lechery. The Jaloux quotes Juvenal and concludes:

> Cold comfort gives us Juvenal, who says
> Fornication is the least of women's sins,
> Whose nature urges them to greater crimes.
> We read how mothers-in-law cooked poison broth
> For daughters' husbands, and with spells and charms
> Worked many other might deviltries
> Unthinkable, which I cannot rehearse.
>
> (9143–47)

The examples of Hercules and Samson are called upon to show how strong men are brought low by women. The Jaloux then concludes his learned *dissuasio* with an anticlimactic threat to break his wife's ribs and to sell all her finery. Amis then relates how the jealous husband beats and abuses his wife, stopping only when he is out of breath. The friend very wisely concludes that seignory of this sort is in no way conducive to love: "Love dies when seignory exalts its head." Amis seems to be suggesting that as long as husbands mistreat their wives and misuse so totally their seignory, wives will continue to rebel and to react to such tyranny. Henry A. Kelly very appropriately observes that:

> If Amis has a favorable view of marriage in theory, in practice he is pessimistic: Lovers who marry may find that in spite of themselves their love is no longer able to endure; for the man beforehand acted as servant and she was mistress, but now he acts as lord and master over his onetime lady.[59]

If the Jaloux represents *auctoritas*, La Vieille (the Duenna) exemplifies personal experience. She advocates living according to Nature (a Nature which she defines as antithetical to law and monogamy) and proposes several animal analogies. Young men, constrained by religious or marital ties, are birds in a cage and fish in a net. To live according to nature, so she argues, men should behave in the same way as animals do (i.e., mate indiscriminately). Her argument is a clever inversion of a favorite attack of churchmen on the licentious behavior of men who "behave like neighing horses and braying asses rather than men."[60] At the same time, La Vieille's argument is also an ironic *sophisma;* her statements are true literally but not figuratively. Of course, man should live according to Nature (in the

Stoic sense), but we have already seen how naturalness in La Vieille's sense (i.e., bestial lechery) was regarded by the penitential writers and the decretists—it was said to be the worst and most severely penalized sin throughout the Middle Ages.

La Vieille's speech is set in the mythological framework of the *Tale of Mars and Venus,* a dissuasive misogamous *exemplum,* well known from Map's *Valerius.* After telling of Vulcan's deed, which she describes as foul and foolish, La Vieille remarks:

> Women are freeborn; they've restricted been
> By law, that takes away the liberty
> That Nature gave them. Nature's not so fond,
> As we should see if her intent we scanned,
> That Margot she would bring into the world
> Solely for Robichon, nor Robichon
> Solely for Agnes, Margot, or Perette.
> Rather, fair son, we're made, beyond a doubt,
> All women for all men, and all the men
> For all the women, interchangeably. . . .
>
> (13875–86)

Her reference to woman as "freeborn" (*franches*) is enigmatic, implying as did thousands of pagan and Christian antifeminist currents that women, unlike men, are born without a sense of conventional morality. She continues her speech by pointing out that the very nature of indissoluble marital bonds (i.e., the net) is such that it encourages adultery, because women seek to be free as they were born. She proposes to live according to Nature and explains her meaning by the image of a bird in a cage pining away in desire for its freedom. The same, she says, is true of monks whose cage is the cloister. She then introduces the image of a net that catches many a foolish fish and compares it to the captivity of monks. Each creature behaves according to nature: a cat need not be taught how to catch mice, a stallion need not be instructed how to find a mare. . . .

> The bird that's captured in the forest green,
> Shut in a cage and nourished carefully,
> And fed delicious food, may seem to sing
> With happy heart, in your opinion;
> And yet it longs to be among the boughs

Out in the woods, which naturally it loves,
And howsoever well it may be fed
Would much prefer to flit among the trees.
Ever it pines and struggles to get free. With all
    the ardor which fulfills its heart
It treads its food beneath its feet, and seeks
Throughout its cage, in greatest agony,
To find some door or other opening
Through which it may escape into the woods.
Know well that every damosel or dame,
Whatever her environment may be,
Has the inclination naturally
To long and search for roadways and for paths
By which to come into that liberty
Which all of them forever wish to have.
    I tell you it is so with everyone
Who in a cloister takes his place, for he
Will afterward to such repentance come
That scarce he fails to hang himself for grief.
He's inwardly tormented; he complains;
He lamentation makes.

                                    (14077–96)

Again, the preoccupation with lifelong matrimony is pronounced. Lifelong ties are unnatural, she observes, because men are fundamentally like beasts:

And what I say of horses—gray or brown—
And mares, of bull and cow, or ram and ewe
Is that (doubt not, fair son) each one desires
To seek a mate; and every female longs
For every male, and each gives free consent.
The natural appetite is just the same,
Upon my soul, in every maid and man,
Though law impose some moderate restraint.

                                    (14102–03)

After her discourse on the unnaturalness of both enforced celibacy and the marital state, La Vieille returns to her mythological framework and observes that Venus deserves but little blame for loving Mars. Actually, she points out, it was Vulcan who suffered from the affair; the lovers, perceiving that their liaison was common knowledge, made no more pretense about it and acted openly and without shame.

While the Jaloux mustered *auctoritas* to deliver his learned *dissuasio* in the framework of a personal jealous outrage, the Duenna provides personal experience and observation to comment on a mythological tale of ridiculous jealousy. Thus, the tract of philosophic misogamy is balanced by a *dissuasio* of general misogamy both of which are replete with irony and both of which constantly backfire on their unsympathetic narrators. The Jaloux describes the stock wicked wife of the misogamous tradition as his own, and La Vieille ridicules and labels the celibate clerical ideal and the secular monogamous ideal as "unnatural." Thus, the views propounded are not only anticlerical, but also antifeudal.

Both the Jaloux and La Vieille are comic stock characters exposing their shortcomings in their tirades that are intended to vindicate and support their points of view: the Jaloux reveals himself as the cuckolded wife-beater and La Vieille as the lecherous and venal duenna.

Matheoli Lamentationes

The *Roman de la Rose* was not the only medieval work maligning women that Christine de Pisan castigates. Her book *Le Livre de la cite des dames* (1404–05) was occasioned, she tells us, by her reading Matheolus' *Liber de infortuniis suis,* better known as the *Matheoli Lamentationes.*[61] Why are women depicted as so clearly inferior to men, so vicious and so foolish, she ponders, if not out of malice?

The work she refers to is a thirteenth-century, enormously long Latin work by a clerk named Matheolus who was unfrocked for bigamy (i.e., for marrying a widow), and laments his misfortunes in four books containing 10,508 half-lines of alternately rhymed verses. As the title implies, the speaker assumes the role of an indignant, victimized man who is impelled by righteous wrath to air his complaints. His woe, so eloquently and copiously stated, springs from having committed bigamy and from having a shrewish wife. The first and greater woe reduced him from a prestigious and respected social position to social insignificance—not even a cobbler wants to be his friend (16–19). His second woe, he tells us, results from the vile disposition of his wife, Petra. Petra's greatest fault is not the customary unfaithfulness but a proclivity for tormenting her husband with requests, complaints, and willful contrariety. Of her faults, Matheolus presents an amplified catalogue interspersed with exclamations of woe and regret. Women are unstable, contrary, always ready to go on pilgrimage just to get out of the house (the familiar *instabilitas loci* topos); they are shrewish, annoying, quarrelsome, vain, gluttonous, cruel, stupid, prone to lying and domineering. Petra's contrary behavior, as representative of all wives, is amply illustrated by interpolated dialogues, descriptions, and reflections. A wife, the reader is warned by the familiar topos, destroys her husband. Matheolus states with his customary thoroughness the inversion of woman's role as a helpmate to her husband: combining scattered biological, religious, and philosophical views of the destructiveness of intercourse which the speaker systematically transfers unto women. "Woman destroys, annihilates, kills, takes away, strips away, embitters the body, one's strength, soul, force, sight, and voice"(1780–81).

Matheolus proposes an amplified (500 lines) rejection of the diverse and generally upheld reasons for marriage by presenting them either as antivalues or as illusionary values. People marry, he says, to perpetuate themselves and to continue the family name (a rather vainglorious ambition, the writer comments). But marriage is no guarantee for having offspring (1786–89). Even if marriage is concluded for the right (i.e., ecclesiastically approved) reasons, the author is eager to point out, children often hope for the death of the parent so that they may receive their patrimony sooner. They might well be bastards and their rearing entails many a burden (1811–18). Others marry for company so that they may avoid solitude. But what kind of companionship marriage provides, Matheolus knows too well: marriage is a heavier burden than the torments of hell: "onus lacrimosum connubiale . . . gravius quam tormentum stigiale." Moreover, those who marry because of the beauty of the wife are foolish because beauty fades but the mat-

rimonial bond lasts forever. Those who marry for money become servants to their wives. Like Juvenal, so Matheolus
exclaims that it is just as bad to take a rich wife as it is a poor
one (1993–2008). It is most lamentable when a young man
marries an old woman. He makes a fool of himself and is rid-
iculed by all. When an old man marries a young girl, she will
wear him out demanding the marital debt. This particular evil
Matheolus knows too well; if he does not pay his conjugal debt
to his energetically demanding wife because he no longer has
his old vigor, then she pulls out his hair. It is equally unfortunate for a young man to marry a young wife. He probably will
not be able to provide for her sufficiently, and she will take a
lover. Finally, when an old man marries an old woman, they
act contrary to custom and decorum, because Venus and old
age do not mix and because they cannot hope for children
which, supposedly, is the only reason for marriage. Moreover,
if the husband wants children, but the wife does not, there are
many ways by which she can thwart his desires. In sum, there is
no valid reason for marriage.

The method of Matheolus' *dissuasio* from marriage is the
same as that of Juvenal's Sixth Satire; it is the categorical inversion of commonly accepted values by either presenting them as
antivalues or demonstrating their illusionary quality. Here
again, the medicine of *contraria contrariis* is applied to cure the
madness of marital aspirations. The categorical rejection of all
ecclesiastically sanctioned and generally approved reasons for
marriage requires, as in Juvenal's Sixth Satire, an antithetical
string of paradoxical syllogisms: wives either bear children that
are burdensome, or they prevent the desired fatherhood of husbands; they are either poor or rich, either young or old, but in
all cases, they are the wrong choice for the bridegroom. None
of the proposed reasons for matrimony are valid or particularly
desirable, thus young men should forego marriage.

Book III of the *Lamentationes* is the most original and the
most interesting part of the work. Matheolus, in his projected
persona of a modern Job, accuses God of incompetence and
malice for instituting matrimony; he even raises the question of
Divine cowardice—had Christ dared to take a wife, she might

have expelled him from Paradise. Day and night, he says, he is tormented and crucified. Therefore, he is compelled to speak: Alas, he says God made a mistake; had he taken a wife, though, himself, the state of affairs would look quite different indeed. "You did not dare to take a wife, Christ," he exclaims, "for had you done so, she would have expelled you from Paradise. (2395–97) This blasphemous reckoning with God for his blunder in matrimonial matters is original with Matheolus. Not only does he accuse God of a mistake and Christ of cowardice, but he proposes a solution: because God had hopelessly messed things up by instituting matrimony, let him (Matheolus) at least try out a wife for six months, and then let him be permitted to take her or leave her. The argument for open-eyed, experimental marital selection is not new to the misogamous tradition; Theophrastus' *Aureolus* and its literary progeny listed its opposite as a dissuasive reason against marriage.

While the direct address to God accusing him of incompetence in matrimonial matters is original with Matheolus, both the comparison to Job and the idea of the unnaturalness of marriage were popular in twelfth and thirteenth century literature. Peter of Blois wrote *Compendium in Job,* comparing the trials and tribulations of Henry II to Job, and the unnaturalness of marriage was amply propounded by La Vieille in the *Roman de la Rose.*

The *Matheoli Lamentationes* is one of the most bitter and certainly the longest tirade against women and marriage. It is a pronouncedly eclectic and learned work, utilizing the whole topography of the misogamous canon, yet claiming to rely on personal experience rather than authority. All three branches of misogamous literature are present in the work. The misogamous topoi are amplified and repeatedly supported by specific examples of wifely misbehavior that are presented as Matheolus' personal experiences. The work became popularized through Jean Le Fevre's 1371–72 translation into French.

Quinze joies de mariage

One of the last genuine works of medieval general misogamy, the *Quinze joies de mariage,* is an anonymous satire from the turn of the fourteenth century which occurs, at least in one manuscript, together with the Matheolus.[62] The date of its composition lies between 1372 and 1461. The *cent Nouvelles Nouvelles* (1461) includes the *Quinze joies* together with Juvenal and Matheolus among the "histoires anciennes" concerned with the wiles of women and the burdens of marriage, but Le Fevre's French translation of the Matheolus was known to the author of the *Quinze joies,* thus providing the *terminus a quo.*[63] A strong consensus of critical opinion places the work at the end of the fourteenth century; however, no consensus exists regarding the authorship of the *Quinze joies.*[64] Antoine de la Sale, Lemonde, Samer, Bellemere, Lerse, and Clermont had been put forward as possible candidates for authorship, but all of these theories have been subsequently discredited.[65]

The framework of the satire is the prayer to the Virgin Mary enumerating her fifteen joys. This particular prayer, as Joan Crow observes, gained popularity in France in the fourteenth and fifteenth centuries while shorter prayers (enumerating five or seven of the joys) were of older origin and in Latin.[66] The vernacular longer poems were frequently included in the *Books of Hours* destined for meditation, and one of the most famous versions of the Prayer is Christine de Pisan's "Les XV Joyes de Notre Dame."[67]

The fifteen joys of Mary are used as a prayer and a meditation—a *persuasio* to moral improvement by reflection and imitation. Conversely, the *Quinze joies de mariage* is a *dissuasio* from marriage by means of meditation and contemplation of the miseries of married life.

The fifteen joys of Mary are all androcentric or, more precisely, *Christocentric* (the center and example of her joys in Christ). The *Quinze joies de mariage,* on the other hand, is gynocentric (the center and cause of the marital sufferings is the wife). Similarly, the joys of Mary are frequently combined with physical suffering and pain (childbirth, crucifixion), and they are "joys" in a somewhat hidden, mysterious way. The "joys" of the satire are perceived as actual joys by the poor deluded husbands; only to the detached "objective" observer do they reveal themselves as pain and suffering.

The syntactic parallels between the meditations on the joys of Mary and the *Quinze joies de mariage* include the formulaic beginnings and conclusions of the respective "joys" and the exhortations for personal application of the meditative material. As for the possible sources of the *Quinze joies*, Jean Rychner lists the *Aureolus,* the *Valerius,* the *Roman de la Rose, Matheoli Lamentationes,* and the *Miroir de Mariage* and the plots of many a fabliau. Unlike its specific predecessors, *Quinze joies* contains many learned florilegian catalogues. Similar plots in the fabliau are resolved differently. For example, in the fabliau the situation of the husband catching his wife *in flagrante delicto* is usually resolved by the turning of the tables on the wretched cuckold. This is achieved, usually in an instant, by some mechanical device employed to deceive or terrorize the husband. In the *Quinze joies,* however, the guilty parties extricate themselves by gradually brainwashing the husband into believing that what happened did not actually happen (i.e., by repeated applications of the same medicine). In the course of this complex and intricate plan of deception, the culprits and their helpers expose themselves in their selfish, corrupt, and pitiless venality.[68]

The *Quinze joies* begins with a prologue introducing the ubiquitous image of the trap:

> Many have toiled and strained, invoking both logic and authorities to show that a man can find greater earthly happiness by living untrammelled and free than by enslaving himself of his own will. They agree that only a doltish man living joyously and sensually in the freedom of youth would, of his own volition and initiative, and quite unnecessarily, seek out the entrance of a confining, sorrowful, and tearful prison, and force his way inside; for once he's there, the prison's iron doors are slammed shut behind him and secured with heavy crossbars, and he's so closely kept that by no means, whether by bribes or prayers, can he escape. Now this fellow seems all the more dim-witted to have imprisoned himself since he'd beforehand, from within the jailhouse walls, the crying and moaning of its inmates. (Prologue)

Marriage is a trap, he continues; it is like a net in which fish are caught by bait.

The prologue is followed by fifteen domestic episodes, each depicting one of the "joys" of the wedded state, and each is punctuated with the phase "et finera miserablement ses jours." The episodes are further held together by the ubiquitous presence of the trap image and by the stock figure of the poor, innocent, deceived husband whose character and personality we find little changed from "joy" to "joy." He is almost invariably referred to as "bon homme" and "jeune homme"; he is persistently victimized, outwitted, taken advantage of, and cuckolded, and the few times that he gets angry enough to take revenge, he can only resort to blind violence and beat up his wife, "which does not solve anything and leaves him to be the loser again." Throughout the episodes, the author suggests that men age faster and wear out more quickly than women because of the hardships they have to endure—an Aristotelian view, popularized, by Albertus Magnus:

> Then, too, it often happens that the young man, who's lusty and full of sap, marries a good and honorable young woman, and that they guzzle as much as they can of love's pleasures for one, two, three years or more, till at last their youthful ardor cools. Yet the wife's appetites don't wane as soon as her mate's, whatever his station in life, for she doesn't have all his troubles, toil, and tribulation; why, even if he did nothing but play and romp, he'd still run down sooner than his wife. Now it's quite true that a women is sorely beset for so long as she's pregnant or bearing children, and that during childbirth she suffers untold grief and pain. But all this is nothing compared to the travail a reasonable man must endure when pondering any of his important undertakings. And as for the discomfort of pregnancy or childbirth, it impresses me not a bit more than that of a hen or goose laying an egg as big as my fist, and this through a hole too small for my pinkie just a moment before. One process is just as great as the other in Nature's scheme. Thus you'll see the hen remain plumper than the cock, despite the fact that she lays daily; for the rooster is so stupid, he spends the whole day scratching for food to bill-feed his mate, while her sole concerns are eating, gabbling, and resting easy. And the same holds true for good, respectable husbands, I say it to their credit. (57, 58)

We may not be able to ascertain the name of our author, but at least his gender seems to be clear beyond reasonable doubt.

The passage reflects the major preoccupation of the writer; it is the same concern that we have already noted in Semonidas' satire, and more recently, in the *De conjuge:* marriage is a drain on the husband's goods, his financial, physical, and emotional well-being.

The organization of the book resembles Juvenal's Sixth Satire in its repetitious and at times protean structure. The first joy depicts a young man, cheerful and innocent, who enters the trap (i.e., marriage). His wife presses him for a gown and, using all the tricks she can muster, she finally gets it. The husband buys on credit and is soon ruined. He is excommunicated and languishes in discomfort until the end of his miserable days. The motif known, among others, from the first argument of the *De conjuge,* is amplified, particularly concerning the wife's bedtime strategies to obtain a gown.

The second joy combines the motif of the cuckolded husband with the familiar sermon-topos of *instabilitas loci.* The wife, ever eager to get out of the house and go to feasts and on pilgrimages, uses these opportunities to entertain her lover. The trusting husband is cuckolded and when he finally finds out and beats her, things only get worse, and he suffers until he dies. The third joy depicts the wife's pregnancy, her unreasonable cravings for delicacies and attention. She and the voracious hunger and thirst of her gossips are an enormous drain on the husband's finances. Material desolation is the subject matter of the fourth joy as well; the poor husband, used up and weary, has to provide for his marriageable daughters, and has no comfort from his scolding wife. The fifth joy presents the sorry situation of a good man who married above his estate and is humiliated, cuckolded, and despised by his wife. She loves finery, and when she cannot secure it from her husband, she obtains if from a lover. Joy six describes the annoyances caused by a wife who is a bad hostess and who openly scorns her husband's friends in a much amplified vein but similar to Juvenal's Sixth Satire. The seventh joy offers some authorial comment on the adulterous nature of wives in a passage strongly reminiscent of La Vieille's sermon on living according to nature: In marriage, every wife believes "In the privy matter ye wot of, her husband is the sorriest and feeblest man in this world." He further comments on what we have seen to be the "scientific" biological view of female lasciviousness, i.e., that no one man suffices for a wife.... "I deem that if one man sufficed not one woman, God and Holy Church would have ordered that each woman had two men or as many as would suffice her." Women are always dissatisfied with their husbands and hold them the sorriest of all men. Men are different, our author observes; they always deem their wives to be the very best. In an age when men were to take proprietary pride in their wives and wives were to fear and obey they husbands, the author's observation is psychologically astute.

Joy eight repeats the *instabilitas loci* topos: the wife has wanderlust and wants to go on pilgrimages; and joy nine depicts a shrewish wife, a favorite character of many fabliaux, who immediately takes over mastery when the husband falls sick. The tenth joy presents the situation of a star-crossed couple; the wife by some witchcraft or charm cannot love her husband and when they are separated and cannot remarry, she turns wanton much to her husband's dishonor and sorrow.

The eleventh joy concerns an unsuspecting young man who is cunningly baited to marry a pregnant girl (skillfully pretending to be a virgin), and the twelfth joy burlesques a henpecked husband. Both topoi are well known from the fabliaux but they are amplified with a host of domestic details intended to caricature as much the sheepish husband as the shrewish and domineering wife.

The thirteenth joy concerns a happy couple. The husband, however, has to go to fight and is taken captive overseas. The wife remarries and when the first husband finally returns their lives end in misery. In the fourteenth joy the husband is a young widower who marries an older widow. She is greedy and jealous, shrewish and experienced. Thus, she makes life unbearable for him. The final joy, which the author considers the greatest and "most extreme dolor," is the popular fabliau topos of a husband finding his wife *in flagrante delicto*. With the help of her mother and her gossips, a plan is hatched to brainwash the poor husband. Needless to say, the plan succeeds.

The conclusion to the fifteen joys is short and concise. It is a satiric palinode boasting of the writer's ability to write a convincing tract from the opposite point of view and maintaining that, in fact, his book does honor to women.

> After all, anyone who truly understands what I've written here will see that the husband doesn't always get the short end, and that's a credit to the ladies.
>
> Now I've written this at the request of certain ladies; if they're unsatisfied and want me to apply myself to write in their behalf, in their favor, to the detriment of men, and from a feminine point of view, then I'm their man! Indeed, I'd have a lot better stuff than this considering the great wrongs, woes, and injustices that men heap on women everywhere and in general, both groundlessly and by superior force—after all, women are naturally weak and defenseless, inclining always to serve and obey. If this weren't so, men wouldn't know how to live, nor could they even survive. (115, 116)

One expects a final "cuius contrarium verum est" after the line of the palinode, but the suspense is left unresolved. The palinode is a masterpiece of satiric *sophisma,* a technique so well employed by Jean de Meung's La Vieille. What the author says is literally true but metaphorically wrong. His book, he says, is in fact a praise of women, because men always have the worst part. Literally, this statement summarizes the plots of the fifteen joys, in every one of which the husband is victimized. But, because it is the husband who supposedly deserves the narrator's sympathy, the moral of the episodes gives the wifely villains the "worse part." Similarly, it is true that in several of the tales men do resort to physical force to chastise their wives, but those beatings are the acts of frustrated outrage and avail nothing. The concluding catalogue of qualities of the "weaker sex" are the hilarious inversions of precisely those qualities which are satirized in the book as the endemic characteristics of wives. In the fifteen joys, women are depicted as domineering and invariably victorious over their husbands; they neither obey nor serve them but tyrannize them as long as they live.

The *Quinze joies de mariage* is not an ostensibly learned work. The customary catalogues of mythological, historical, and biblical *exempla* are missing. There are no *auctoritates* invoked or consulted, and no florilegia of misogynistic or mis-ogamous sententiae are included. Rather, the author, like Juvenal's persona, presents a vivid contemporary setting for his catalogue of exaggerated wifely misbehavior. His easy, conver-sational style, ornamented with extensive use of dialogue, be-comes the vehicle for well-known and popular satiric topoi. He makes fun of the misfortunes of husbands who are too easily deceived and too conveniently tamed, and he caricatures wives as comprised of nothing but perfidy, greed, cunning, lechery, ambition, and vanity. The techniques of dissuasion by inversion is explicit in the work. Throughout the fifteen joys, wives are depicted as exactly antithetical to what the palinode describes them as being and as they are exhorted to be. Moreover, the marital models are shown to be antivalues. To use Franc Vou-loir's false friends' convenient enumeration of the joys of the feudal and ecclesiastical models of marriage, it is advisable to marry because rich men should have heirs; because it is better to marry than to burn; and because marriage keeps a man from temptation.[69] In the *Quinze joies,* heirs are shown to be a con-stant drain on the poor husband's goods and energy; wives care so well for their old or sickly husbands that they isolate them completely from running their houses and meeting their friends; finally, the poor husband still "burns" in matrimony because wives are convinced that their own husbands are the worst possible lovers.

Miroir de Mariage

More than any of the other vernacular works of general misog-amy, Eustache Deschamps' *Miroir de Mariage* draws on the philosophic and ascetic traditions of misogamy.[70] In fact, Franc Vouloir, the addressee of both the marital *dissuasio* and *persuasio* of the work, decides to listen to Repertoire de Science and em-brace "spiritual nuptials" rather than earthly marriage. As such, the *Miroir* belongs to the elitist group of misogamous writings according to its topography but to the later *altercatio* according to its form. However, the *Miroir* is an interesting transforma-tion of the genre, and thus deserves a short discussion.

The *Miroir* is a *debate* weighing the advantages and disadvantages of the married state. The advantages are put forth by Franc Vouloir's (personification of Free Will) false friends, Desir, Folie, Servitude, Faintise, restating the standard lay and ecclesiastic reasons for marriage. The setting, thus, is reminiscent of Map's *Valerius* and the *De conjuge* and foreshadows the tale of January and May in the *Canterbury Tales*. Franc Vouloir, like the addressee of the *De conjuge*, considers that husbands, jealous of his freedom, try to persuade him to matrimony. Furthermore, the setting provides the model, as J. L. Lowes argues, for Chaucer's "Merchant's Tale."[71] Repertoire de Science, the addressee's true friend, however, dissuades him from earthly marriage by a long letter composed for Franc Vouloir's edification and his salvation. Again, both the epistolary form and the altruistic, didactic purpose are reminiscent of Map's *Valerius*. The letter's structure, however, echoes Hugh of Folieto's *De nuptiis libri duo:* first, Repertoire de Science condemns matrimony because no woman can be found worth marrying (i.e., the misogynistic general dissuasive argument); second, he urges Franc Vouloir to embrace a spiritual marriage because spiritual unions are by far superior to physical ones (i.e., the substitutional philosophic and ascetic dissuasive argument). Correspondingly, while the letter abounds in *exempla in malo* of wifely misbehavior, it is, however, clerical in its emphasis on the superiority of spiritual marriage. The monastery is safe, a sure means of attaining salvation. This consideration prompts Franc Vouloir to decide in favor of celibacy. As John C. McGalliard remarks,

> In the end Franc Vouloir rejects marriage as an integral part of worldliness, which he decides to renounce. He recalls that it was as easy for a camel to go through the eye of a needle as for a "riche mondain" to enter "en paradis." In serving the world and the flesh one may lose paradise.[72]

Very appropriately, Repertoire de Science draws heavily on Theophrastus' *Aureolus* and Jerome's *Adversus Jovinianum,* but unlike his predecessors, he is allegorical—like the rest of the *dramatis personae,* he is a moral abstraction. As such, Deschamps' work is a transformation of the dispute *an vir ducat* uxorem into a psychomachia of reason and appetites, with reason attaining the palm of victory.

Deschamps' catalogue of wicked wives is extensive, and it is strongly reminiscent of the *Roman de la Rose*. Women are lascivious, Repertoire says; as soon as the husband dies, they are on the lookout for a replacement (ch. 51); mothers-in-law act as bawds for their daughters and teach them all the tricks of the trade (ch. 37, 51); maids play into the hands of their mistress and deceive the poor husband (ch. 51). Wives are talented in extricating themselves from deserved accusations—when guilty, they reproach their innocent husbands for their own sins (ch. 51). Wives, because of their love of finery, demand costly garments, and when they dress up to be seen, they endanger their chastity. At home, Repertoire observes, they also have their demands, which exhaust the body and which, if unmet, brand the husband a defrauder!

In his 7,000-line letter, Repertoire de Science considers marriage inadvisable for scholars and knights (i.e., the *miles scientiae* and the *miles armati*) just as marriage is not permissible for the clerical class (the *miles christiani*). For others, marriage is advisable and necessary to sustain the race. Thus, Repertoire's *dissuasio* is clearly elitist even though his documentation is augmented with *exempla* of general misogamy. Because of its *debat* form, however, the *Miroir* has more in common with its fifteenth- and sixteenth-century works than it does with the earlier *dissuasiones* which were only concerned with one side of the issue.

The Wife of Bath's "Prologue"

We have defined the methodology of general misogamic satire as a dissuasion by inversion employing everyday specificity, exemplary documentation, and current misogynous topoi rendered by an experienced persona who is ironically unreliable and whose attacks on women and wives frequently backfire on him. All of these observations hold true for the Wife of Bath's "Prologue" in Chaucer's *Canterbury Tales*.[73] In addition to her full utilization of the general misogamic canon, Dame Alice also manages to incorporate into her speech the standard arguments of the philosophic and ascetical branches of misogamy in a masterfully ironic way which not only incriminates her but ridicules the arguments of the misogamous canon.

The Wife of Bath's "Prologue" is usually recognized as the exposition commencing the marriage debate in the *Canterbury Tales*. Kittredge, more than seventy years ago, called attention to the "marriage group" as a dramatically integrated unit within the *Canterbury Tales*.[74] He argued that the discussion begins with the Wife of Bath's Prologue and Tale, and is resumed by the Clerk's Tale of patient Griselda, the Merchant's cynical Tale of May and January, and is concluded by the Franklin's proposal for a compromise. Others since Kittredge (Hinckley, Neville, Lawrence), while endorsing Kittredge's view on the existence of the *débat*, have suggested the inclusion of the Nun's Priest's Tale, the Squire's Tale, and Melibeus in the marriage group.[75] Lawrence even suggests that the Wife of Bath is not initiating the controversy but is defending herself against an attack by the host which was levelled at her in the context of the tale of Melibeus.[76]

Some modern scholars question the very existence of a marriage debate in the *Canterbury Tales*.[77] Yet the four tales (of the Wife, the Clerk, the Merchant, and the Franklin), seen in their literary and historical context, provide a traditionally developed *altercatio* on the subject of marriage, complete with *exempla in bono* (Clerk), *exempla in malo* (Merchant), and resolution (Franklin). The focus of the discussion is *maistrie*, the fight for the breeches, which is initiated by the Wife in advocacy and demonstration of female dominance *(mundus inversus)*, by the Clerk's demonstration of female submission *(ordo naturalis)*, by the Merchant's demonstration of female perfidious supremacy and is resolved by the Franklin's advocacy and demonstration of marital equality.

Scholars emphasize the Wife's advocacy of marriage. Dame Alice's prologue, however, is a *dissuasio* disguised as a *persuasio*. The tone of her speech is sustained irony, and her method of argumentation is the systematic inversion of the aristocratic and ecclesiastic models of marriage augmented by three sets of well-known misogamous arguments: the ascetic, the philosophic, and the general *corpora*. In diametrical opposition to the ecclesiastical model, the Wife of Bath advocates (and practices) multiple marriage (inversion of *sacramentum*); ostensibly ignores the procreative precept *(proles);* she has a very selfish conception of the marital debt *(fides)*. Regarding the aristocratic model, Alice usurps the rights of the feudal *pater familias* by consolidating all economic power in her hands; she is neither "courtly" nor demure.

That at least one of the pilgrims recognized the "De conjuge non ducenda" nature of Alice's prologue is clear from the Pardoner's interruption of her speech. He says: "Now dame,' quod he, 'by God, and Seint John! / Ye been a noble prechour in this cas. / I was aboute to wedde a wyf, allas! / What sholde I lye it on my flessh so deere? / Yet hadde I levere wedde no wyf to-yeere!"(163–68). The Pardoner's perception of the *dissuasio* nature of the Wife's speech comes as no surprise: he is the likeliest character among the pilgrims to have recognized the misogamous florilegium and to have tried to look for the *integumentum* in her speech. The Pardoner is the most cunning, most corrupt, and most professionally deceitful of the pilgrims; he prides himself on his ability to outwit and deceive others by his sophistry, and, finally, aside from the Wife and the Parson, he is the only exegete among the pilgrims. He is a bachelor who has travelled, presumably through university towns, where *disputationes* on the subject *an vir ducat uxorem* were eagerly practiced. He also pretends to be learned, but his erudition consists of stock phrases of sententious Latin commonplaces that he acquired not by genuine learning but by incidental accretion. No wonder, then, that the Pardoner immediately recognizes the topography of the Wife's prologue as belonging to the *dissuasio* tradition, for she uses standard commonplaces of the misogamous tradition.

The Wife of Bath commences her prologue by asserting that experience, not authority, taught her the woe that is in marriage: "Experience, though noon auctoritee / Were in this world, is right ynogh for me / To speke of wo that is in mariage"(1–3). Of marital experience she has had a great deal, for like the Samaritan woman, the Wife has had five husbands.

Robertson observes that Alice's marital condition may be icon-ographically based on the story of the Samaritan; the Samari-tan listens to Christ but the Wife is deaf. Augustine's glosses on the passage explain that Christ came to save the Samaritan in the sixth hour (sixth age) but the Wife's response and echo of the passage is ironic: When she says "Welcome the sixth" she does not mean the sixth (perfect) age, but her sixth husband.[78] She was told that Christ teaches monogamy (i.e., only one marriage in a lifetime), but she rejects that ideal in favor of the Old Testament teaching to increase and multiply. Thus, she glosses the New Testament with the Old Testament and inverts the ascetic misogamous ideal by superimposing the Genesis passage over Christ's teaching. (Her practice is the exact inver-sion of the patristic evolutionary theory of the supremacy of the chaste ideal that glosses the Old Testament with the New Testament).

Dame Alice's reasons for marriage, however, have little to do with the procreative ideal: it is the remedial rather than the procreative purpose that she is interested in. As Robertson points out, she is ludicrous in her reference to Genesis 1:28; she is not interested in generating children but in multiplying her pleasure.[79] In promoting her marital ideal, the Wife inverts the methodology of ascetical misogamy when she presents a catalogue of Old Testament and New Testament *exempla in bono* for the wedded state. She applied the Scriptural lesson to her own marital history. "Yblessed be God that I have wedded fyve, / Welcome the sixte when that evere he shal. / For sothe, I wol nat kepe me chaast in al"(44–46). Alice's examples for the married ideal are familiar ones: they were used by Jovinian and violently rejected by Jerome in his *Adversus Jovinianum,* which is the Wife's major source of information for the first part of her speech. This first part (lines 1–130) is the direct inversion of the ascetical misogamous canon as far as the doc-umentation is concerned. The delivery of the arguments and the Wife's authorial intrusions, however, project a persona which is the stock female character of the ascetic misogamous canon: Dame Alice is the personification of the *ardens corpus* accusation hurled at wives by preachers of asceticism. Like most competent misogamous writers, the Wife takes quotes out of context, and she disregards parts of quotes that do not suit her immediate purpose. Like most misogamous writers, for example, she cites only the first part of Paul's logion concerning the marital debt: "The husband's body is not his but his wife's." Doing this, she reveals herself to be just what the misogamous and misogynistic traditions accused women on being: the personification of carnality.

Alice uses Jerome's analogy of wheaten and barley bread (wheaten bread, chastity; barley bread, marriage) and with a skill as sophisticated as St. Jerome's she turns the negative imagery into positive for her own purpose: "Lat hem be breed of pured whete-seed / And lat us wyves hoten barly-breed / And yet with barly-breed, Mark telle kan / Oure Lord Yhesu refresshed many a man"(143–46). Not only does Alice suggest a parallel between her five marriages and Christ's multiplying of five loaves of bread for the hungry, but she uses a sexual metaphor for the comparison. Then the Wife summarizes what she considers to be the essence of marriage:

> In wyfhod I wol use myn intrument
> As frely as my Makere hath it sent.
> If I be daungerous, God yeve me sorwe!
> Myn housbonde shal it have bothe eve and morwe.
> Whan that hym list come forth and paye his dette.
> An housbonde I wol have, I wol nat letter,
> Which shal be bothe my dettour and my thral,
> And have his tribulacion withal
> Upon his flessh whil that I am his wyf.
> I have the power during al my lyf
> Upon his propre body, and nought he.
> Right thus the Apostle tolde it unto me,
> And bad oure housbondes for to love us weel.
> Al this sentence me liketh everydeel.
>
> (149–62)

In this speech, the Wife uses the ironic inversions of arguments of ascetic misogamy, while she at the same time personifies the canon's topography. At the end of her speech the Pardoner interrupts her. He calls her a good "preachour" (i.e., a likely person to deliver a sermon of ascetic misogamy) and says that he is dissuaded from marriage by her speech. Part II of Alice's *dissuasio* (188–28) is a satiric tract of general misogamy. She tells of the "tribulacion that is in mariage" (of which she claims to be an expert) and admonishes the Pardoner to refrain from making up his mind on marriage until he has heard her whole speech. The context of her *dissuasio* is the story of her five husbands: three good and two bad. The "good" husbands were rich, old, and very much "bound unto" her (197–200).

Alice sets forth in detail her strategy for taming her old husbands and receiving all their property and wealth, and she apostrophizes on the general application of her policies: "A wys womman wol bisye hire evere in oon / To gete hire love, ye, ther as she hath noon. / But sith I that they hadde yiven me al hir land, / What sholde I taken keep hem for to plese. / But it were for my profit and myn ese?"(209–14). Her report utilizes many of the standard dissuasive reasons against marriage: wifely jealousy, *instabilitas loci*, sexual mercenariness, scolding, shrewishness, lasciviousness, vanity, adultery, greed, and lust for dominance. She proudly lists her achievements that gained her total mastery over her husbands: she chided them so frequently that they were "ful glad" when she spoke fairly to them. Like Juvenal's matrons, the Wife, too, gives curtain lectures accusing her old husbands of fictitious crimes of lechery. Some misogamous topoi she presents in a double quotation. The Wife quotes herself quoting her husbands:

> Thou sayst som folk desiren us for richese,
> Som for oure shap, and som for oure fairnesse,
> And som for she can outher synge or daunce,
> And some for gentilesse and daliaunce,
> Som for hir handes and hir armes smale.
> Thus gooth al to the devel by thy tale!
> Thou sayst men may nat keepe a castel wal,
> It may so longe assailed been overal.
> And if that she be foul, thou saist that she
> Coveiteth every man that she may see;
> For as a spaynal she wol on hym lepe,

Til that she fynde som man hire to chepe.
Ne noon se grey goos gooth ther in the lake.
(257–63)

The argument, developed in animal analogies, is familiar from La Vieille's speech and is presented by the Wife not as a path to follow (as the topos was put forth by the Duenna) but as a fictitious accusation levelled at wives quoted by Alice.

Most of the double-quoted arguments are derivative from Theophrastus' *Aureolus,* probably, via Eustache Deschamps' *Miroir de Mariage* and Jean de Meung's *Roman de la Rose.*[80] They include the envy of the neighbor's wife's clothes, the blind selection of a partner in marriage, a wife's insistence on praise for her beauty, the troublesomeness of her in-laws, the accusations of false suspicions by the wife, and finally, a direct use of a Theophrastian dissuasive topos by the Wife. Theophrastus said that a wife will insist upon taking over the mastery in marriage and if she is not given complete dominance she will accuse the husband of mistrust. If he gives over all power, however, he will be treated as a servant in his own house. The Wife's autobiography exemplifies precisely this. After having delivered the first part of her double-quotations of misogamous commonplaces, she concludes addressing her old husband: But tel me this: why hydestow, with sorwe / The keys of thy cheste away fro me? / What helpith thee of me to enquere or spyen? / I trowe thou wouldest loke me in thy chiste" (308–17), again typifying the Theophrastus topos.

The second part of her double-quoted arguments uses the *Communis ager* of misogyny, accusing wives of adultery, vanity, *instabilitas loci, ardens corpus,* and likening women's love to hell, fire, and a worm in a tree. All of her chiding gradually bore fruit, and Alice became master of her three old husbands, reminding them to bear their woes patiently:

> Ye sholde been al pacient and meke,
> An han a sweete, spyced conscience,
> Sith ye so preche of Jobes pacience
> Suffreth alwey, syn ye so well con preche ...
> Oon of us two moste bowen, doutelees,

> And sith a man is more resonable
> Then womman is, ye moste been suffrable.
>
> (434–37; 440–42)

Unlike La Vieille's speech and the *Quinze joies,* the Wife's *dissuasio* is replete with learned allusions and with arguments of ascetic, philosophic, and general misogamy. While the Wife presents these arguments as absurd and ridiculous, she exposes herself as personifying the larger portion of her presented arguments.

As a *dissuasio* in the general satiric tradition, the second part of the Wife of Bath's prologue resembles La Vieille's speech (with which it shares a modified [marital] version of the advocacy of multiple relationships) and the *Quinze joies* (with which it shares the theme of wifely supremacy over good-willed and sheepish husbands). Because the *Quinze joies* could have been written as early as 1372, the possibility of direct influence cannot be ruled out. Like the husband *(bon homme)* of the fifteen joys, so the composite character of the Wife's "good" husbands is tamed and subjugated by Alice's shrewish, nagging, and sexual mercenariness. Like the husbands of the fifteen joys, so Alice's husbands submit more or less happily to their subservient fate; as Alice suggests, they might have even considered their tribulations joys.

The discussion of Alice's fifth husband, the clerk Jankin, provides the Wife with the very appropriate setting for her *dissuasio* of philosophic misogamy. Jankin had a favorite book of "wykked wyves," a book the prototype for which apparently did exist in Oxford and other medieval universities. The compilation of Jankin's book included such standard works of philosophic misogamy as Theophrastus' *Aureolus, Valerius,* Heloise's *dissuasio,* and also the *Adversus Jovinianum,* Ovid, the parables of Solomon and countless *exempla in malo* of wives. The catalogue is reminiscent of the Jaloux's lament, particularly regarding the inclusion of Heloise's *dissuasio* among the philosophic misogamous canon. As the Jaloux's catalogue, so the Wife's is a learned clerical catalogue ironically presented by a persona having neither education nor aspiration for learning and philosophy. In fact, the conclusion of the Wife's account of

Jankin's book parallels Amis' account of the Jaloux's speech. Alice, upset at Jankin for so obviously enjoying the book, tears it
apart, thus provoking Jankin to physical violence. Jankin, like
the Jaloux, beats her, but unlike the Jaloux's wife, Alice fights
back, and the fight results in Jankin's signing over all power to
Alice. What Amis theorized about marital relationships (i.e.,
that as long as husbands treat their wives badly and like property, they will resort to vicious behavior) is actualized and enacted by the Wife. As soon as Jankin relinquished his power
and seignory, however, Alice became "meek as a lamb," and
they very appropriately burned the book, as one ought a heretical tract.

Ritamary Bradley observes that the "Prologue" is an ironic
mirror of marriage: the Wife's ironic testimony is built on the
contrast between exemplary or mirror values and realistic
detail.[81] In addition, the iconography of the mirror holds true
for Alice's character: she has more in common with the clerkly
examples of wicked wives than she apparently realizes—like a
mirror she reflects popular prejudices. But the Wife of Bath is
not only a "funny parody of a woman invented by woman-
haters," but also a woman of great and fascinating individuality
whose competent struggle for dominance is a struggle against
millennia of contempt and scorn. The fictitious Alice is a contemporary of Christine de Pisan, and she too initiates her own
Querelle: the *Querelle de mariage.* Alice's *Querelle* is directed not
only against the *Roman* and *Matheolus* but against the entire
literary and social tradition of misogamy.

Thus, the Wife of Bath's "Prologue" provides a worthy
conclusion to our survey. The "Prologue" comes at the end of a
long tradition, and it already heralds a new one; it combines
masterfully a satire on and a topology of the three distinct
strains of misogamy. More than the other contemporary eclectic *débat,* the *Mirroir de Mariage,* the Wife's "Prologue" clearly
follows the methodologies of the different branches of misogamy: Alice relies equally on pagan and medieval *auctoritates,* ex-
egesis, and experience. She is also a living example of the stock
domineering wife, the perennial winner in the fight for the
breeches. Yet Dame Alice is not an entirely unsympathetic

character. Admittedly, her struggle for "maistrie" is the target for scorn, but her frank exposure of her licentiousness and venality makes not only her, but those "learned clerks" whose figment of imagination she is, the butt of the satire.

In justifying her worldly ideas and ways, the Wife of Bath constantly implicates herself, but she is no hypocrite. The confluence of the three misogamous traditions and their ironic treatment in the Wife of Bath's prologue attests to a change to a more secular and various society. All three misogamic traditions are equally satirized, as is Alice, the lustful domineering wife. The Wife of Bath, for all her shortcomings, is probably no more malicious than the learned men who wrote about her for centuries.

Conclusion

We have seen some incorporation of general (i.e., Juvenalian) satire into the misogamous works of the twelfth century, but it is with the rise of cities and the bourgeois culture in the thirteenth century and later that we encounter full-fledged satiric works of general misogamy. Indeed, the clearest textual indication of the secularism and urbanity of later medieval misogamy is the rediscovery and use of Juvenal's Sixth Satire both as a source of exempla and as an overall literary model.

The parallels between late medieval misogamic literature (genesis, purpose, and ideological setting) and Juvenal's Sixth Satire is striking. Both settings are essentially urbane; both are essentially antiauthoritarian; both are essentially antiestablishment. As in Juvenal's Sixth Satire, the sexual antagonism of medieval works of general misogamy is framed by antagonism toward the propertied classes. The butts of the Sixth Satire's attacks are rich matrons—the embodiment of the propertied class—and liberated women; medieval works of general misogamy exhibit an antagonism towards the aristocracy, aggressive, independent women, and the Church's hierarchy via the ideals represented or promoted by these dominant groups. Similarly, the technique of dissuasion by inversion also occurs in the thirteenth- and fourteenth-century *dissuasiones*.

Like Juvenal's Sixth Satire, medieval general misogamous works attack marriage not as an institution incompatible with any professional or religious ideal, but simply and directly as incompatible with a man's physical, economic and emotional welfare. Thus, marriage is presented not as a fall from a dignified ideal (philosophic misogamy) or as a fall from perfection (ascetical misogamy), but as a continuous state of pain, suffering, and misery that is to be avoided by any sane person. Moreover, while works of philosophic and ascetical misogamy rely heavily on *auctoritas* (be it pagan or Biblical), tracts of general misogamy, like satire in general, have an aura of realism and rely on experience and the use of current topoi. Consequently, works of general misogamy are usually delivered by indignant personae who do little more than catalogue the misdoings of wicked wives.

Works of ascetic and philosophic misogamy are elitist and substitutional—works of general misogamy are not. The elitist misogamous works uphold the ideals of their respective hierarchies and offer spiritual nuptials and surrogate family ties in place of physical matrimony.

General misogamy upholds wifelessness, per se, as a *desideratum*. It pokes fun at celibate propaganda as eagerly as it ridicules the woes of marriage. While the texts maintain that marital tribulations result from that perennial pest, the wife, the husbands in these misogamous satires do not entirely escape the satiric barbs. Furthermore, the implications of general misogamous satire are that all pretensions to and regulations of marital affairs, all selective codes of behavior, are ludicrous because, as the Wife of Bath suggests, they come from precisely those people who know least about them.

CONCLUSION

In *Women, Production and Patriarchy in Late Medieval Cities*, Martha Howell concludes her discussion of the general decline in women's economic status in the late Middle Ages by surveying some of the contemporary literature. In the comedies and satires of the period, she finds ridicule and scorn and charges of sexual aggressiveness levelled against women who challenged the masculine preserve of the market place or who trespassed the all-male realm of higher education. These literary "entertainments" suggest an unusual hostility toward aggressive women that in some measure attaches to their positions in market production. The literature seems to validate the shifts being made at the time, shifts from an atmosphere in which women were increasingly being shut out of the market economy. "But," Howell cautions, "are we justified in seeing these implications? Are examples such as these representative of late medieval and early modern urban society or do they simply repeat literary conventions held over from other cultures?"(183)

If the conventions germane to medieval misogamy are any indication, links between life and literature are clearly justified. As we have seen, misogamous literature ran the gamut from pornographic excess to homiletic sincerity and the motifs that surfaced in a specific era did so neither randomly nor as artistic flourishes divorced from authorial experience.

Ascetic antimarriage tracts reflected the thoroughgoing dualism and revolutionary spirit intrinsic to the early Christian experience. They were inimical to Juvenalian rhetorical flourishes. Instead of bawdy, premised on the special provocative appeal of women, Jerome used scatological imagery that suggested a much broader distrust—all the appetites, not just sex; all flesh, not just woman's.

Philosophic antigamy, by comparison, was written in a social context that was increasingly secular and, with increased population pressures, competitive. As the chief corporate employer, the Church encouraged the substitution of loyalties based on shared work and goals for those derived from blood ties and kin networks. Antimarriage literature became a potent propaganda tool in the hands of Gregorian reformers devoted to clerical celibacy as a means of "husbanding" finite resources of landed wealth and public influence. The revival of classical literary and legal models that advocated pseudo familial ties (marriage to Pallas Athena) for the philosopher were appropriate storehouses for the writers of philosophic misogamy.

Finally, conditions in the late Middle Ages engendered a very real responsiveness to the letter as well as the spirit of Juvenalian satire. Impersonal government administration and the pull of a market economy began to alter the character of the family and to diminish the sphere of public influence and power for women. Once again, classical sources could validate contemporary trends. The urbane wits who penned the general misogamous tracts of the thirteenth and fourteenth centuries once again took up the poetic devices and stock themes that had endeared Juvenal to the threatened patriarchy in imperial Rome. Filled with attacks on lustful and aggressive wives, general misogamy was also a highly sophisticated and ironic look at the venality and cowardice of husbands. Capitalizing on the urbane, if jaded, sensibilities and the classical erudition of their educated readers, the authors of general misogamy wrote "entertainment" based on human foibles. Nevertheless, they courted danger if their work became popular (and it did).

For later readers who lacked a nuanced and allusive frame of reference, the virulent antifeminism of so many misogamous tracts became the single attraction. It is the misogynistic legacy which Christine de Pisan so pointedly and, as it happened, presciently, described in her debate on the *Romance of the Rose*:

Moreover, the poet speaks so unnecessarily and in such an ugly way of married women who deceive their husbands, a matter of which he can scarcely know from experience and of which he speaks very categorically. Of what use is this, what good can come of it? I think it is only a hindrance to peace and well-being by making husbands who listen to such nonsense, if they pay attention to it, suspicious and mistrustful of their wives. Heavens, what an exhortation, and to what purpose?[1]

ABBREVIATIONS
OF FREQUENTLY CITED WORKS

Sources often cited in the body of this work are listed below. Unless otherwise noted, in-text translations are by the authors.

Adv. Jov.: St. Jerome, *Adversus Jovinianum,* in *PL* 23

Au. Gellius: Aulus Gellius, *The Attic Nights,* 3 vols., trans. John C. Rolfe (Cambridge, MA: Harvard University Press, and London: William Heinemann Ltd., Loeb Classics, 1927)

Aug. De bono: St. Augustine, *De bono coniugali,* Latin text from *CSEL* 41; English translation, *The Fathers of the Church,* Vol. 27, ed. R. J. Deferrari, trans. C. T. Wilcox (Washington: Catholic University Press, 1955)

Cat. Con.: Sallust, *The Conspiracy of Catiline,* trans. S. A. Handford (Baltimore: Penguin Classics, 1970)

CCL: Corpus Christianorum, series Latina (Turnhout, Belgium: Brépols, publication on-going 1953–pres.)

CSEL: Corpus scriptorum ecclesiasticorum Latinorum (Vienna: publication on-going F. Tempsky, 1866–pres.)

Seneca, *De beneficiis* (Leipzig: B. G. Teubner, 1900–05), 4 vols., *L. Annaei Senecae opera quae supersunt,* ed. Carl Hosius et al. [Leipzig: B. G. Teubner, 1898–1907]

Decretum: Gratian, *Decretum,* in *Corpus iuris canonici,* 2 vols., ed. Emil Freidberg (Leipzig: B. Tauchnitz, 1879; rpt. Graz: Akademische Druck- u. Verlagsanstalt, 1959)

Dig.: Digestum seu Pandekta, in *Corpus iuris civilis,* 3 vols., ed. Krueger, Mommsen, Schoell, and Kroll (Berlin: Weidmann, 1872–95)

Diog. Lives: Diogenes Laertius, *Lives, Opinions and Remarkable Sayings of the Most Famous Ancient Phlosophers,* trans. by several hands (London: R. Bentley, 1696)

Enn.: Plotinus, *The Enneads,* ed. and trans. Stephen MacKenna, revised by B. S. Page (London: Faber and Faber, 1956)

Gaius: Gaius, "Institutes of Gaius," trans., Samuel Parsons Scott, *The Civil Law* (Central Trust Co., Cincinnati: 1932)

Inst.: Quintilian, *Institutes of Oratory,* trans. J. S. Watson (London: H. G. Bohn, 1856)

Liv.: Livy, *The History of Rome,* ed. C. Weissenborn and M. Muller (Leipzig: B. G. Teubner, 1901)

Luc. De rerum: Lucretius, *De rerum natura,* ed. W. E. Leonard and S. B. Smith (Madison: University of Wisconsin Press, 1961)

Meditations: Marcus Aurelius, *Meditations,* (Chicago: Henry Regnery, 1970)

Met.: Ovid, *Metamorphoses,* trans. Mary M. Innes, (Baltimore: Penguin Classics, 1955)

PG: Patrologiae cursus completus . . . series Graeca, 167 vols., ed. J. P. Migne (Paris: J. P. Migne, 1857–76)

PL: Patrologiae cursus completus . . . series Latina, 221 vols., ed. J. P. Migne (Paris: J. P. Migne, 1844–64)

Sat.: Saturae D. Junii Juvenalis, ed. Ulrich Knoche (Munich: M. Hueber, 1950); English translation, *The Sixteen Satires,* trans. Peter Green (Baltimore: Penguin Classics, 1967)

ST: Thomas Acquinas, *Summa Theologica: The Basic Writings,* ed. A. C. Pegis (New York: Random House, 1945)

Suet.: Suetonius, *The Twelve Caesars,* trans. Robert Graves (Baltimore: Penguin Classics, 1957)

Tac. Ann.: Tacitus, *The Annales of Imperial Rome,* trans. Michael Grant (Baltimore: Penguin Classics, 1956)

Val. Max.: Valerius Maximus, *Factorum et dictorum memorabilium libri novem,* ed. Karl Kempf (Leipzig: B. G. Teubner, 1888)

NOTES

Introduction

1. The term *celibacy* is used throughout to denote the unmarried state with no reference to regulated sexual morality. One need only look at the numerous eighteenth- and nineteenth-century diatribes against licentious celibate men to recognize just how recently the connotation of sexual abstinence became associated with the word.

2. Much of the newest research focuses on the special importance of that choice for women. Current studies of single women span the centuries and include Martha Vicinus, *Independent Women: Work and Community for Single Women 1850–1920* (Chicago: University of Chicago Press, 1985); Janice Raymond, *A Passion for Friends* (Boston: Beacon Press, 1986); Jo Ann McNamara, *A New Song: Celibate Women in the First Three Christian Centuries* (New York: Haworth Press, 1983). For the Middle Ages classics such as Lina Eckenstein, *Women Under Monasticism* (New York: Cambridge University Press, 1896, rpt. 1963) are now joined by a growing list of regional studies and monographs; see for example the works of Suzanne Fonay Wemple and Caroline Walker Bynum.

3. Ernst Bickel, *Diatribe in Senecae philosophi fragmenta,* Vol. 1, *Fragmenta de Matrimonio* (Leipzig: B. G. Teubner, 1915); Philippe Delhaye, "Le Dossier Anti-Matrimonial de l'*Adversus Jovinianum* et son Influence sur Quelques Ecrits Latins du XIIᵉ Siècle," *Mediaeval Studies,* 13 (1951), pp. 65–86; Henry C. Lea, *History of Sacerdotal Celibacy in the Christian Church,* 4th ed. (New York: University Books, 1966); August Wulff, *Die Frauenfeindlichen Dichtungen in den Romanischen Literaturen des Mittelalters bis zum Ende des XIII, Jahrhunderts* (Halle a. S.: Druck von E. Karras, 1914); Francis L. Utley, *The Crooked Rib an Analytical Index to the Argument About Women in English and Scots Literature to the End of the Year 1568* (Columbus: Ohio State University Press, 1944); Theodore Lee Neff, *La Satire des*

Femmes dans la Poésie Lyrique Française du Moyen Âge (Paris: V. Giard et E. Briere, 1900); Arthur Moore, *Studies in a Medieval Prejudice: Anti-feminism* (Diss., Vanderbilt University, 1943); Katharine M. Rogers, *The Troublesome Helpmate, a History of Misogyny in Literature* (Seattle: University of Washington Press, 1966); Angela Lucas, *Women in the Middle Ages* (New York: St. Martin's, 1983), p. 117. Diane Bornstein, in the *Dictionary of the Middle Ages* (ed. Joseph R. Strayer) entry *Anti-feminism*, notes the genre distinction in passing (New York: Scribner, 1982).

4. Among the Cathars, for example, women were allowed to preach and teach and attain the *consolamentum* (i.e., be counted among the "perfect"). See, for example, Steven Runciman, *The Medieval Manichee* (Cambridge, England: Cambridge University Press, 1955); Gottfried Koch, *Frauenfrage und Ketzertum im Mittelalter: die Frauenbewegungen im Rahmen des Katharismus und des Waldensertums und ihre sozialen Wurzeln* (Berlin: Akademie-Verlag, 1962); and Walter Wakefield, *Heresy, Crusade and Inquisition in Southern France* (London: Allen & Unwin, 1974).

5. See Edvard A. Westermack, *A Short History of Marriage* (New York: MacMillan, 1926); John T. T. Noonan, *Contraception* (Cambridge, MA: Belknap Press of Harvard University, 1966); David Herlihy, *Medieval Households* (Cambridge, MA: Harvard University Press, 1985), especially pp. 116–17.

6. St. Methodius, *The Symposium*, trans. and ann. by Herbert Musurillo, Ancient Christian Writers, No. 27 (Westminster, MD: Newman Press, 1958).

7. Peter Abelard, *Historia Calamitatum*, ed. J. Monfrin, 2nd ed. (Paris: Libraire Philosophique J. Vrin, 1962).

8. *Theophrasti aureolus liber de nuptiis*, in St. Jerome, *Adversus Jovinianum PL* 23, 313–15; *Joannis Sarisberensis Episcopi Carnotensis Policratici sive de nugis curialium et vestigiis philosophorum libri VIII*, ed. C. Webb (Oxford: Clarendon Press, 1909) Libri VIII, p. 9; Peter of Blois, *Epist.* LXXIX, *PL*, 207, pp. 243–46.

9. For example, St. Jerome, *Adversus Jovinianum*, PL 23, (J. P. Ming, series editor), *Epist.* 22, *CSEL* 54; Tertullian, *De monogamia, De continentia; CCL* 1–2; St. Augustine, *De bono conjugali*, *CSEL* 41.

10. *Saturae D. Junii Juvenalis*, ed. Ulrich Knoche (Munich: Hueber, 1950).

11. Quintilian says (*Inst.* III 5, para. 5–8):

Item convenit quaestiones esse aut *infinitas* aut *finitas*. Infinitae sunt quae remotis personis et locis ceterisque similibus in utramque partem tractantur, quod Graeci thesin dicunt, Cicero propositum . . . finitae autem sunt ex complexu rerum, personarum, temporum ceterorumque; hae hypotheseis Graecis dicuntur, causae a nostris . . . amplior est semper infinita, inde enim finita descendit, quod ut exemplo pateat, infinita est "an uxor ducenda," finita "an Catoni ducenda" ideoque esse suasoria potest.

12. Ernst Curtius, *Europäische Literatur und Lateinisches Mittelalter*, 5th ed. (Bern u. Munchen: Francke, 1965), p. 164.

13. On this subject see, for example, Ray Petry, *Christian Eschatology and Social Thought* (New York: Abingdon, 1956); J. N. Sevenster, *Paul and Seneca* (Leiden: E. J. Brill, 1961); Otto Pfleiderer, *Primitive Christianity* (Clifton, NJ: Reference Book Publishers, 1965); and Frederick Wilhelmsen, *Christianity and Political Philosophy* (Athens, GA: University of Georgia Press, 1978).

14. See Walter Ullmann, *Law and Politics in the Middle Ages* (Ithaca, NY: Cornell University Press, 1975); and Henry C. Lea, *Sacerdotal Celibacy.*

15. Jerome, *Adversus Jovinianum* is the text most frequently used and quoted by writers of misogamy. Passages from it occur in Héloise's *dissuasio* from marriage (Peter Abélard, *Historia Calamitatum*, 2nd ed. [Paris: J. Monfrin, 1962]); *Joannis Sarisberensis Episcopi Carnotensis Policratici sive de nugis curalium et vestigiis philosophorum libri VII*, ed. C. C. Webb (Oxford: Clarendon Press, 1909); and in Hugh of Folietto's *De nuptiis libri duo*, *PL* 176.

16. This highly influential branch of misogamous literature, with its select audience, is outside the purview of this study. Monastic anti-marriage literature contains numerous tracts written by men but addressed to religious women, such as the thirteenth century *Hali Meidenhad* and the *Ancrene Riwle*. See John Bugge, *Virginitas* (The Hague: Martinus Nijhoff, 1975); Angela Lucas, *Women in the Middle Ages* (New York: St. Martin's Press, 1983).

17. On similar arguments in favor of a celibate clergy, see Henry C. Lea, *Sacerdotal Celibacy*, and J. Gilchrist, *The Church and Economic Activity in the Middle Ages* (New York: St. Martin's Press, 1967).

18. Cf. Walter Map's "Valerius," *The Latin Poems Commonly Attributed to Walter Map*, ed. Thomas Wright (Hildesheim, 1968);

and Peter of Blois, *Epist.* LXXIX ad R. Amicum suum, *PL* 207, 243–46.

19. *Walter Map De Nugis Curialium Courtiers' Trifles,* trans. and ed. M. R. James (Oxford: Clarendon Press, 1983), p. 309.

> This bride you once betrothed with the flower of your springtime [i.e., Philosophy, Athena]; now, in your summer, she looks that you should bring forth grapes: do not in her despite marry another, lest the time of vintage you bring forth wild grapes. I would not have you be the husband of Venus, but of Pallas. She will deck you with precious necklaces, will clothe you in a wedding garment. Those espousals will be brilliant with Apollo for groomsman.

20. Cf. Juvenal's Sixth Satire, where Postumus, "moechorum notissimus olim" (42) is encouraged to remain in his present (unmarried and adulterous) state.

21. *Les Quinze Joyes de Mariage,* ed. Joan Crow (Oxford: Blackwell, 1969); Eustache Deschamps, *Le Miroir de mariage, Oeuvres Complètes,* ed. Gaston Rynaud (Paris: Firmin Didot, 1894), Vol. IX. When the composition is in Latin as, for instance, the *De conjuge non ducenda,* it becomes popularized in vernacular translations (*The Latin Poems Commonly Attributed to Walter Map,* ed. Thomas Wright, Hildesheim, 1968; Wright prints several English and French translations also). See F. Utley, *Crooked Rib.*

22. Anderson's observation about Juvenal's Sixth Satire, "Anger in Juvenal and Seneca," *University of California Publications in Classical Philology,* 19, no. 3 (1967), p. 136, i. e. that he uses *omnis* and *nullus* with suspicious ease, applies equally well to medieval works of general misogamy. Similarly, most works of general misogamy capitalize on the persona of the unreliable narrator, the persona of the ridiculously indignant man.

23. In his reply to Domnio concerning his critics (*Nicene and Post-Nicene Fathers of the Christian Church,* ed. P. Schaff trans. W. H. Freemantle, Grand Rapids, MI: Wm. Eerdmans, 1892, pp. 74 and 75), St. Jerome exclaims in a masterfully satiric passage:

> But he [his critic] refuses to write, and fancies that abuse is as effective as criticism, then . . . he must hear at least the echo of my cry, "I do not condemn marriage, I do not condemn wedlock." Indeed—and this I say to make my meaning quite clear to him—I should like every one to take a wife who, because they get frightened in the night, cannot manage to sleep alone.

24. Peter of Blois, *Epist.* LXXIX, *PL* 207, 244.

25. Compare, for example, St. Jerome's reference to fornication as the "eating of cow-dung" (*Adv. Jov,* I 48) with Juvenal's reference to sex with inferiors as the loosening of an actor's fibula (*Sat.,* VI, l. 73).

Chapter 1

1. On the history of Roman marriage, see, for example, Charles Seltman, *Women in Antiquity* (New York: H. Martin Press, 1957); J. P. V. D. Balsdon, *Life and Leisure in Ancient Rome* (New York: McGraw-Hill, 1969) and *Roman Women: Their History and Habits* (London: Bodley Head, 1962); Jerome Carcopino, *Daily Life in Ancient Rome* (New Haven: Yale University Press, 1940); Sarah B. Pomeroy, *Goddesses, Whores, Wives, and Slaves: Women in Classical Antiquity* (New York: Schocken Books, 1975); Henry C. Boren, *Roman Society* (Lexington, MA: Heath & Co., 1977); Otto Kiefer, *Sexual Life in Ancient Rome* (New York: Dutton & Company, 1935); Alan Watson, *The Law of the Ancient Romans* (Dallas: Southern Methodist University Press, 1970).

2. Pomeroy, *Goddesses,* p. 157.

3. Pierre Grimal, *Love in Ancient Rome,* trans. Arthur Train, Jr. (New York: Crown Publishers, 1967).

4. Ibid., p. 81.

5. Cassius Dio, *Dio's Roman History* bk 54, cap. 16, trans. E. Cary (New York: Loeb Classical Library, 1924).

6. Pomeroy, *Goddesses,* p. 164.

7. Cited by Reay Tannahill, *Sex in History* (New York: Stein and Day, 1980), p. 125.

8. Ibid., p. 169.

9. L. P. Wilkinson, "Classical Approach to Population and Family Planning," *Population and Development Review,* 4 (1978), p. 443.

10. On the mystery cults see, for example, J. Carcopino, *Daily Life;* A. G. Mackinnon, *The Rome of St. Paul* (London: The Religious Tract Society, 1930).

11. J. Carcopino, *Daily Life*, p. 121.

12. Verena Zinserling, *Women in Greece and Rome* (New York: A. Schram, 1972), p. 8.

13. Otto Kiefer, *Sexual Life in Ancient Rome*, p. 46.

14. The marital legislation of Augustus reflects the growing concern with the decrease of the indigenous upper class populations. His legislation, known as the *Juliae rogationes*, included the *lex sumptuaria*, the *lex de maritandis ordinibus*, and the *lex Papia Poppaea* (18 B.C. to A.D. 9), all aimed at increasing the number of suitable marriages between men and women of the senatorial families, at encouraging the rearing of children, and at regulating divorce. Augustus' law imposed property and civic disqualifications for celibacy on men between twenty and fifty, for childlessness on men older than age twenty-five and on women older than age twenty. He ruled that widows must remarry within two years and divorcees within eighteen months. Unmarried men were not allowed legacies and childless couples only one-half of what was bequeathed to them. Adultery became the matter of public courts, no longer that of the family. The legislation was the first Roman statutory assertion of civic and legal control over marital affairs: it regulated divorce and emphasized the importance of suitable marriages for the upper classes. To this end, Augustus also created the *jus trium liberorum*, which gave parents of three or more children a privileged status regarding taxes and political opportunities. The same law exempted women with three children from the need for a legal guardian.

That this ideal held up by state and moral authorities was not widely practiced is clear from the demographic data and from literary and historical sources, and from the fact that marital legislation and laws against adultery and sodomy continued to be enacted. According to Tacitus (*Ann.*, 3, 25), Augustus' law failed to increase the number of marriages and the rearing of children, and, more specifically, Pliny the Younger implies in a letter that the honorific and financial benefits that a childless person might expect from those who wish to be his heirs far outweigh the light penalties imposed by Augustus' legislation (*Epist.* 4, 15). Moreover, Suetonius writes that the knights protested against Augustus' marital legislation. Suetonius, "Augusus," 34 in *The Twelve Caesars*, trans. Robert Graves (Baltimore: Penguin Classics, 1957).

15. On the Stoic distinction, so important to later marriage law development, see James A. Brundage, "'Allas! That Evere Love Was Synne': Sex and Medieval Canon Law," in *The Catholic Historical Review*, 72, no. 1 (January 1986), pp. 1–13.

16. Aside from the slaves attending to his garments, jewelry, and entertainment, the rich Roman usually had several slaves competing over his toilet and his table: the bathers *(balneateres)*, masseurs *(aliptae)*, the hairdressers *(ornatores)*, and the barbers *(tonsores)*; his cooks *(coci)*, bakers *(pistores)*, pastry cooks *(libarii)*, dining room attendants *(tricliniares)*, and others.

17. See, for example, J. Carcopino, *Daily Life*, p. 70ff.

18. These statements have been so often reiterated that they have become axiomatic. See, especially, Gilbert Highet, *Juvenal the Satirist* (Oxford: Clarendon Press, 1954), p. 91.

19. W. Anderson, *The Rhetoric of Juvenal*, Diss., Yale University, (rpt. 1966, p. 256), describes the prologue:

> The thematic importance of this prologue sets the tone for the next 265 lines; the most important word is *Pudicitia*. Juvenal has personified the quality into a goddess. The personification and the general tone of epic formality gives the prologue a solemnity unusual in Juvenal's first book. Note that all line references can also be found in Juvenal, *The Sixteen Satires*, trans. Peter Green (Baltimore: Penguin Classics, 1967).

20. See, for example, Sallust *(Cat. Con.*, 2.5), Seneca *(Epist.* 90.8).

21. The association of woman's full occupation with virtue is traditional. See, for example, Hesiod, *Works and Days*.

22. Anderson, *The Rhetoric of Juvenal*, p. 258:

> As the prologue ends, the satirist has occasioned uncertainties. Part of the uncertainty is concerned with the ambiguous juxtaposition of the vignettes drawn from elegy and those from the world of the past. Part of the uncertainty is also directly related to the idealization of the past. The past is not automatically superior to the present.

23. Ibid., p. 258.

24. Suetonius says Domitian divorced Domitia because of her love for the actor Paris but that he could not bear the separation and

soon took her back, alleging that the people demanded it. Juvenal has several other scornful references to people surrounding Domitian, notably Tuscus (*Sat.* IV. l. 99), Catullus Messalinus (*Sat.* IV. ll. 113–15).

25. William S. Anderson, "Anger in Juvenal and Seneca," *University of California Publications in Classical Philology,* 19, no. 3, (1964): p. 137.

26. Ibid., p. 145.

27. See, for example, K. Schneider, *Juvenal and Seneca* (Würzburg: 1930). Clarence Mendell, *Latin Poetry and the Age of Rhetoric and Satire* (Hamden, CT: Archon Books, 1967), p. 154, on the other hand, proposes that actually Juvenal is neither:

> To Juvenal, satire is the scourge of vice. He has none of Horace's genial view of the world around him nor any of Persius' moral earnestness in propagating the Stoic faith. Such philosophy as he expresses is certainly Stoic but he resembles far more the Cynic teacher of hell fire on the street corner than the arm chair philosopher. He is really neither. He is the angry victim of a society which to him appears almost wholly vile, but his protest seems often to be not so much against the moral implications of vice as against the discomfort and degradation which it inflicts on men like himself. Like Lucan with his personal political fanaticism, Juvenal with his personal hatred of a degenerate society brings to the aid of his denunciation all the weapons of rhetoric wielded with the skill of a sincere and infuriated expert.

28. See again Brundage, "Allas! That Evere Love Was Synne': Sex and Medieval Canon Law," in *The Catholic Historical Review,* 72, no. 1 (January 1986) pp. 1–13, and *Essential Works of Stoicism,* ed. Moses Hadas (New York: Bantam Books, 1961), p. 26. Subsequent references to the latter are by page in the text.

29. The Stoics taught that man must not live for himself alone, but for society. The consciousness of the connection between all rational beings finds eloquent expression in the writings of Marcus Aurelius, the last of the great Stoic philosophers. The possession of reason for him was at once love of society (*Meditations* vi, 14, x, 2); he says that rational beings can only feel happy when working for the community (*Meditations* viii, 7); and that all rational beings form one social unit, one body of which individuals are organic members. Hence, he concludes that the social instinct is a primary instinct in man (*Meditations* vii, 55) and advocates that the good man must pro-

mote good and repress evil by partaking in political life. The Stoic emphasis on man as the organic part of the body politic with clearly defined duties and responsibilities, both civic and moral, has its direct reflection in the Stoic view of marriage: marriage and the procreation of children are natural and, moreover, both are the civic and moral duty of the Roman citizen.

30. See, for example, Tertullian, *De cultu feminarum*, 1 in *CCL* l. The fact that the Roman spectacula occasioned more than female lasciviousness is clear from the fact that, as Julius Rosenbaum, *Geschichte der Lustseuche im Alterthume*, 6th ed. (Halle a. S.: H. W. Schmidt, 1893), pp. 11 passim, remarks, several prostitutes were lodged near the Circus Maximus "... with the purpose of soliciting the men whom the sadistic pleasures of the games had raised to a high pitch of sexual excitement."

31. Theodor Hopfner, *Das Sexualleben der Griechen und Römer* (Prag: Universitätsbuchhandlung, 1938), p. 370.

32. Balsdon, *Roman Women,* p. 207.

33. The comparison with Ovid may not be so farfetched. Gilbert Highet, "Juvenal's Bookshelf," *American Journal of Philology* 72 (1951), pp. 369–94, argues very persuasively that Virgil, Martial, and Ovid were the writers who influenced Juvenal most.

34. Juvenal's use of exempla in the Sixth Satire as proof for his *loci communes* is extensive. As Fritz Gauger, *Zeitschilderung und Topik bei Juvenal* (Diss., Greifenwald, 1929), argues, Juvenal's extensive use of demonstrative exempla clearly responds to his rhetorical purpose, for the audience demanded exempla from the rhetor. Gauger also points out that most of Juvenal's exempla are contained in Valerius Maximus, with the exception of the exempla of *impudicitia* which are found in Seneca.

Chapter 2

1. Superstition and religious excess were high on Juvenal's list of wifely vices. Next to *impudicitia*, the Sixth Satire devotes the greatest number of dissuasive arguments to the misdirected religiosity of Roman matrons. As we have seen, Juvenal's emphasis clearly reflects the fact that there were hundreds of Oriental mystery cults in Rome popular with imperial women because they undercut the worship of

the more male-oriented indigenous religions. Christianity was one of these cults, but given the prominent leadership roles offered to women by its competitors, not to mention its persecuted status, it would seem to have been a very unlikely choice for any Roman woman. In fact, however, Christianity became *the* religion for women, for slaves, and for others among the socially disenfranchised. See Jo Ann McNamara, *A New Song: Celibate Women in the First Three Christian Centuries* (New York: Haworth Press, 1983).

2. Norman Cohen, *The Pursuit of the Millennium* (New York: Oxford, 1972), p. 23; on Christian eschatology see also Ray Petry, *Christian Eschatology and Social Thought* (New York: Oxford University Press, 1972).

3. In fact, at least one study, J. N. Sevenster, *Paul and Seneca* (Leiden: E. J. Brill, 1961) sees Christian eschatology as the crucial differentiator between the theology of the early Church and Senecan Stoicism.

4. Clement, however, interpreted the eunuch saying as referring to remarriage; Justin understood it as prohibiting second marriages.

5. George H. Tavard, *Women in the Christian Tradition* (Notre Dame, IN: University of Notre Dame Press, 1973), p. 40.

6. *Alexandrian Christianity*, ed. J. E. L. Oulton and H. Chadwick, Library of Christian Classics, vol. 3 (Philadelphia: Westminster Press, 1954).

7. For possible correspondences, see H. G. Highet, *Juvenal the Satirist* (Oxford: Clarendon Press, 1954), p. 183.

8. Cohen, *Pursuit*, p. 26.

9. For further information on early heresies see, for example, John Gunther, *St. Paul's Opponents and Their Background* (Leiden: E. J. Brill, 1973).

10. Quoted by John T. Noonan, *Contraception* (Cambridge, MA: Harvard University Press, 1966), p. 113.

11. Clement of Alexandria, for instance, attacks Gnostic heresies because they set a too ascetic tone and insist on continence on the grounds of hatred of what God has created. See James A. Brundage, *Law, Sex and Christian Society in Medieval Europe* (Chicago: University of Chicago Press, 1987) p. 66. Thus, while upholding the celibate

ideal when practiced for the right reason (i.e., glorification of God), Clement disapproves of it when practiced for the wrong reasons (i.e., the dualistic condemnation of the physical reality).

12. Joseph E. Kerns, *The Theology of Marriage* (New York: Sheed and Ward, 1964), p. 15, lists some of the decisions of the Council of Gangra: (1) If anyone disparages marriage, shuns a faithful, God-fearing wife who sleeps with her husband and speaks as though she cannot enter the Kingdom of God, let him be anathema...; (9) If anyone is a virgin or celibate but is avoiding marriage because he regards it as moral disorder... let him be anathema; (10) If any one of those who are celibate for the Lord's sake casts aspersions on those who take wives, let him be anathema.

13. David S. Wiesen, *St. Jerome as a Satirist* (Ithaca, NY: Cornell University Press, 1964), p. 2; E. K. Rand, *Founders of the Middle Ages* (New York: Dover Publications, 1957), p. 112, also sees Jerome as a "satiricus scriptor in prosa." Even E. K. Rand, whose chapter "St. Jerome the Humanist" is a eulogy of Jerome, has little to say about the *Adversus Jovinianum*. Rand observes: "Many even in Jerome's day thought that his reply [to Jovinian] had gone too far; but then as now, his sarcasm must have been read with relish. They contain, I am sorry to say, a smart excoriation of poor woman and I shall pay no attention to them whatsoever"(p. 126).

14. Wiesen, *St. Jerome*, p. 122.

15. Ibid., pp. 113, 151.

16. Ernst Bickel, *Diatribe in Seneca philosophi fragmenta,* Vol. I, Fragmenta de Matrimonia (Leipzig: B. G. Teubner, 1915).

17. Harold Hagendahl, *Latin Fathers and the Classics: a Study on the Apologists*, Acta Universitatis Gothoburgensis Goteborgs Universitets Arsskrift, vol. 64 (Goteborg: Elanders Boktryckeri Aktiebolag, 1958), p. 156.

18. Highet, *Juvenal the Satarist*, p. 183.

19. Hagendahl, *Latin Fathers and the Classics*, p. 184.

20. Ibid., p. 144.

21. English text from *Nicene and Post-Nicene Fathers of the Christian Church*, Vol. 6, ed. P. Schaff, trans. W. H. Freemantle (Grand

Rapids, MI: Wm. Eerdmans, 1892); Latin references are to the *PL* 23 or the *CSEL* 54.

22. Ilona Opelt, *Hieronimus' Streitschriften* (Heidelberg: Carl Winter Universitätsverlag, 1973), p. 47.

23. Hagendahl, *Latin Fathers and the Classics*, p. 150.

24. Bickel includes a critical edition of *Adversus Jovinianum* with spaced out letters indicating St. Jerome's sources; Porphyry and Seneca lead the list.

25. Hagendahl, *Latin Fathers and the Classics*, p. 153.

26. As Winfried Trillitzch, "Hieronymus und Seneca," *Mittellateinisches Jahrbuch*, 2 (1965), p. 44, observes: "Um etwaige Gedanken zugunsten der Ehe nicht aufkommen zu lassen, fügt Hieronymus Excerpte aus Theophrastus' goldenem Ehebüchlein an," thereby suggesting that the fragment is included as a balance to the preceding examples of female marital fidelity.

27. Robert A. Pratt, "Jankyn's Book of Wicked Wives," *Annuale Medievale*, 3 (1962), pp. 5–27.

28. Richard Heinze, *Virgil's Epische Technik* (Stuttgart: B. G. Teubner, 1965), p. 126, attributes this equation to specifically Roman thought: "Das ist spezifisch römische Denkweise: der *virtus* des Mannes entspricht als sittliches Ideal die *pudicitia* der Frau."

29. Bickel suggests that the Theophrastus fragment and most of the information on Aristotle are taken from a now lost work by Porphyry and that the rest of the exempla and loci communes are excerpts from Seneca's lost tract *de matrimonio*. Most scholars agree that chapters 41 through 49 of the first part of the *Adversus Jovinianum* contain, as Hagendahl observes, "mere extracts from antique learning; in no other work of Jerome's are pagan topics massed together to such an extent" (Hagendahl, p. 147). The reason for this high concentration of pagan matter lies with the subject matter. After exhausting the Pauline corpus for misogamic statements and ransacking the Bible for examples of the chaste ideal, only three bodies of misogamic literature were left: the ascetical tradition, the pagan (predominantly philosophic) works, and the contemporary dualistic heresies. Jerome does refer to and draw upon ascetical works, such as Tertullian's writings, and he quotes copiously from ancient misogamic works. Certainly, for Jerome, with his reputation as a man of learning, it was

both safer and more appropriate to turn to ancient authority than to express *sua voce* the same misogamic views which were even at this time considered heretical. This is why almost all of Jerome's arguments are put in the mouth of someone else: Juvenal has his persona do the dirty work for him; Jerome has his authorities.

30. Henry C. Lea, *Sacerdotal Celibacy in the Christian Church* (Philadelphia: J. B. Lippincott, 1967), p. 47.

Chapter 3

1. Rosemary Ruether, ed. "Virginal Feminism in the Fathers of the Church," in *Religion and Sexism: Images of Woman in the Jewish and Christian Tradition* (New York: Simon and Schuster, 1974) p. 169; James A. Brundage, *Law, Sex, and Christian Society in Medieval Europe* (Chicago: University of Chicago Press, 1987) pp. 80–81. For Augustine, see St. Augustine, *De bono coniugali, CCSL* 41 (Turnhout, Belgium: Brépols, 1953-pres.); English text in *Nicene and Post-Nicene Fathers of the Christian Church,* Vol. 6, ed. P. Schaff, trans. W. H. Freemantle (Grand Rapids, MI: Wm. Eerdmans, 1892).

2. Dom Jean Leclerq, *The Love of Learning and the Desire for God* (New York: Fordham University Press, 1982), p. 106ff.

As a spiritual New Jerusalem replaced an imminent earthly second coming in early medieval dogma, the new monasticism contained the potentially implosive asceticism of the Fathers. The passion for self-transcendence rooted in a distrust of the flesh could still be fully satisfied, but via hermetic withdrawal or conventual religious life. It is, as Leclerq observes, this continuity with patristic culture, this "prolongation of patristic culture in another age and in another civilization," that gives medieval monastic culture its specific character.

3. Francis and Joseph Gies, *Women in the Middle Ages* (New York: Crowell, 1978), p. 17. The Germanic codes of law, such as for example, the *Leges Alamannorum* and the *Lex Ripuaria,* treat rape, adultery, and wife-stealing as serious offenses infringing on property rights. The *Leges Alamannorum,* for instance, provides for a penalty of twelve solidi for a man who stripped a woman, and forty solidi if he raped her. The *Lex Ripuaria* proscribes the penalty of 200 solidi for the murder of a young girl but 600 solidi for the death of a woman in her childbearing years.

4. References to the early and twelfth-century penitentials are to the following editions: *Scriptores Latini Hiberniae*, ed. Ludwig Bieler (Dublin: Dublin Institute for Advanced Studies, rpt. 1963); *Medieval Handbooks of Penance*, ed. and trans. by John T. McNeill and Helene Gamer (New York: Octagon Books, 1965); Alanus de Insulis, *Liber Poenitentialis* (Louvain, Belgium: Editions Nauwelaerts, 1956); *Bartholomew of Exeter's Penitential* (edition of the Cotton MS), ed. A. Morey (Cambridge: Cambridge University Press, 1937).

5. The misuse of the *dos* is also punishable offense in the penitentials. The *Penitential* of Theodore of Canterbury, for example, severely condemns the practice of fathers who sold their beautiful daughters several times and refused to repay the money when they failed to deliver the bride.

6. The *Penitentialis Vinniani* (*PV*), for example, prescribes seven years' penitence for those who repeatedly fornicate either *in terga* or *suis labiis;* those clerics, on the other hand, who seduce and impregnate a girl and then kill the offspring are punished by three years' of penitence only. Similarly, for those who help or cause their mistress to abort (and the practice is almost invariably referred to as *maleficia*), the penitence is only one-half year on bread and water and two years without meat and wine (*PV*, 20). The penitential of Saint Columban proscribes ten years penitence for sodomitic practice (*PV*, 3) but only one year for abortion for clerks (one-half year for laymen, two for deacons, three for priests) (*PV*, 6). If the child is born, however, the punishment is a much more substantial seven years (*PV*, 2). Those who are *moechantes labiis* are ascribed penitence for four years if they sinned once, seven years if more frequently. Sodomites have to do penitence for seven years, but the proposed penitence is less for abortion or even for homicide.

7. David Herlihy, *Medieval Households*, (Cambridge, MA: Harvard University Press, 1985), p. 56.

8. For the classic overview of the era, see, Charles Homer Haskins, *The Renaissance of the Twelfth Century* (Cambridge, MA: Harvard University Press, 1927). See also *Renaissance and Renewal in the Twelfth Century*, ed. Robert L. Benson and Giles Constable, (Cambridge, MA: Harvard University Press, 1982). More on population, manufacture, and trade surfaces in studies such as J. Gilchrist, *The Church and Economic Activity in the Middle Ages* (New York: Macmillan, 1967).

The demographic factors of increasing population, increasing commerce, and a substantial surplus of nubile women is well-documented for the twelfth and thirteenth centuries and may have contributed to the decline of the lady's status. Countless sources substantiate this general decline in women's political and social power in the late medieval period: Eileen Power, "The Position of Women," *The Legacy of the Middle Ages*, ed. G. C. Crumb and E. F. Jacobs (Oxford: Clarendon Press, 1926), pp. 401–34; Jo Ann McNamara and Suzanne Wemple, "The Power of Women Through the Family in Medieval Europe, 500–1100," *Feminist Studies*, 1 (1973), pp. 126–41; and idem, "Sanctity and Power: The Dual Pursuit of Medieval Women," *Becoming Visible: Women in European History*, ed. R. Bridenthal and C. Koonz (Boston: Houghton Mifflin, 1977), pp. 90–118; Suzanne Wemple, *Women in Frankish Society* (Philadelphia: University of Pennsylvania Press, 1981); David Herlihy, *Medieval Households*.

9. Herlihy, *Medieval Households*, p. 98.

10. McNamara and Wemple, *The Power of Women Through the Family in Medieval Europe, 500–1000*, p. 96.

11. Georges Duby, *Medieval Marriage, Two Models From Twelfth Century France*, trans. Elborg Forster (Baltimore: Johns Hopkins University Press, 1978), pp. 12–17. For some cautions about this model theory see Herlihy, *Medieval Households*, p. 86.

12. Steven Runciman, *The Medieval Manichee* (Cambridge, MA: Harvard University Press, 1960), p. 116.

13. John T. Noonan, *Contraception* (Cambridge, MA: Harvard University Press, 1966), p. 180.

14. Ibid., pp. 181 ff.; see also Runciman, *Medieval Manichee*, pp. 117 ff.

15. Gilchrist, *The Church*, p. 99; Henry C. Lea similarly maintains (p. 149) that the advocacy of celibacy was a result of centralization. He says,

> Yet a motive of even greater importance than this rendered matrimony more objectionable than concubinage licentiousness. By the overruling tendency of the age, all possessions previously held by laymen on precarious tenure were rapidly becoming hereditary.... Had marriage been openly permitted to ecclesiastics, their functions and benefices would

undoubtedly have followed the example. An hereditary caste would have been established, who would have held their churches and lands of right; independent of the central authority, all unity would have been destroyed, and the collective power of the Church would have disappeared.

16. Quoted by Georges Duby, *Medieval Marriage,* p. 13.

17. Brocke, *Marriage,* pp. 22, 23; and *Penitentialis,* as we have seen, justify their very severe penitential prescriptions for the rape of a nun by emphasizing that she is the bride of Christ.

18. Henry A. Kelly, *Love and Marriage in the Age of Chaucer* (Ithaca, NY: Cornell University Press, 1975), pp. 40ff.

19. C. S. Lewis, *The Allegory of Love: A Study in Medieval Tradition* (London: Oxford University Press, 1936).

20. Donnell van de Voort, *Love and Marriage in the English Medieval Romance* (Nashville, private edition, 1938); D. W. Robertson, *Abelard and Heloise* (New York: Dial Press, 1972) and *A Preface to Chaucer, Studies in Medieval Perspectives* (Princeton, NJ: Princeton University Press, 1962).

21. Peter Dronke, *Medieval Latin and the Rise of European Love Lyric* (Oxford: Clarendon Press, 1965).

22. Courtly love as both a mode of expression and a code of behavior was much less spiritualized than some scholars would have us believe. Clearly, when Jakes d'Amiens in his courtly book on love counsels rape when suasion fails (many women actually prefer violence, he says, because it relieves them of responsibility) he is referring to *amor* as carnal love and *passio* as physical desire. Furthermore, when Andreas Capellanus insists that only those who are "able to perform the works of Venus" are fit to become lovers, he has physical rather than spiritual love in mind.

23. See the eclectic introduction to *The Expansion and Transformation of Courtly Literature,* ed. N. Smith and J. Snow (Athens, GA: University of Georgia Press, 1980).

24. In fact, Alfred Jeanroy's creative hypothesis about the origin of "courtly love" is very appealing (*La poésie lyrique des troubadours,* I, pp. 61–100). He supposes that one day in the eleventh century a hungry minstrel arrived at a castle where he hoped to be fed. The lord being absent and the lady being tired of songs about battles, the

minstrel came upon the idea of entertaining the lady with a song of praise for her beauty and virtue. The trick worked, and the minstrel shared the idea with his colleagues.

25. Georges Duby, *Medieval Marriage*, pp. 108, 109; see also Duby, *The Chivalrous Society*, trans. Cynthia Postan (Berkeley, CA: University of California Press, 1977).

26. All English quotations are from *The Art of Courtly Love*, trans. John J. Parry (New York: Columbia University Press, 1941).

27. Felix Schlösser, *Andreas Capellanus: Seine Minnelehre und das Christliche Weltbild des 12. Jahrhunderts*, 2nd ed. (Bonn: H. Bouvier & Co., 1962), reads the *de arte* as a *summa amatoria*.

28. Peter Abelard, *Theologia Christiana*, PL 178, col. 1165–1202.

29. Peter Abelard, *Historia Calamitatum*, 2nd ed., ed. J. Monfrin, (Paris: Librairie Philosophique J. Vrin, 1962). English quotes are from J. T. Muckle, *The Story of Abelard's Adversities* (Toronto: Pontifical Institute, 1964).

30. Muckle feels that the letters are too sensual and too sinful to be true, while the other two major doubters of the correspondence's authenticity, Robertson and P. von Moos, maintain that the letters are too exemplary to be genuine. Robertson and von Moos see the correspondence as a literary *exemplum* meant to show a story of conversion. Peter Dronke, who is the last to take a stance on the issue, however, argues, "The fact that there can be even a meaningful discussion about whether or not the Heloise of the letters ever assented inwardly to religious life, for me rules out the possibility that the letters belong to the literary genre of conversion stories." Peter Dronke, *Abelard and Heloise in Medieval Testimonies* (Glasgow: University of Glasgow Press, 1976), p. 11.

31. Dronke, *Abelard and Heloise*, pp. 11–14.

32. Ibid., p. 26. Regarding Robertson's second charge, Dronke musters Abelard's own evidence from the poem to Astrolabe, their son, in which he shows Heloise as still essentially unrepentant.

33. Ibid., p. 30.

34. *Epistolae Duorum Amantium, Briefe Abelards und Heloises?*, ed. Ewald Könsgen (Leiden: E. J. Brill, 1974).

35. Richard W. Southern, *Medieval Humanism* (New York: Harper Torchbook, 1970), p. 91.

36. Robert W. Hanning, *The Individual in Twelfth Century Romance* (New Haven, CT: Yale University Press, 1977), p. 25.

37. Philippe Delhaye, "Le Dossier Anti-Matrimonial de l'*Adversus Jovinianum* et son Influence Sur Quelques Ecrits Latins du XIIe Siècle, *Mediaeval Studies*, 13 (1951), p. 74.

38. Leif Grave, *Peter Abelard; Philosophy and Christianity in the Middle Ages*, trans. F. and C. Crowley (New York: Harcourt, Brace & World, 1970), pp. 55ff; Henry C. Lea, in *Sacerdotal Celibacy*, p. 283, similarly remarks:

> Heloise recognized that while the fact of his openly keeping a mistress and acknowledging Astrolabius as his illegitimate son, would be no bar to his preferment, and would leave open to him a career equal to his ambition, yet to admit that he had sanctified their love by marriage, and had repaired, as far as possible, the wrong which he had committed, would ruin his prospects forever. From a worldly point of view it was better for him, as a churchman, to have the reputation of shameless immorality than that of a loving and pious husband; such was the standard of morals created by the Church and such were the conclusions inevitably drawn from them.

39. See Dronke, *Abelard and Heloise*, p. 29.

40. Hans Liebeschütz, *Medieval Humanism in the Life and Writings of John of Salisbury* (London: The Warburg Institute, 1950), p. 1.

41. *Joannis Sarisberensis Episcopi Carnotensis Policratici sive de nugis curialium et vestigiis philosophorum libri VIII*, Vol. II, ed. C. Webb (Oxford: Clarendon Press, 1909). All English quotes are from *Frivolities of Courtiers and Footprints of Philosophers*, trans. J. B. Pike (Minneapolis: The University of Minneapolis Press, 1938).

42. Delhaye, "Le Dossier," p. 78.

43. Ibid., p. 77.

44. *Gualteri Mapes de nugis curialium distinctiones quinque*, ed. Thomas Wright (London: Camden Society, 1850). English quotes are from *Master Walter Map's Book De nugis curialium*, trans. F. Tupper and M. B. Ogle (New York: Macmillan, 1924).

45. Robert A. Pratt, "Jankyn's Book of Wicked Wives," *Annuale Medievale*, 3 (1962), p. 13. The earliest MS, according to Pratt, is a

late twelfth- early thirteenth-century compilation now MS number 550 in the Library of Lambeth palace.

46. As Pratt explains, p. 14–15,

> His learned, literary tour de force needed annotation and exposition; generous to a fault, commentators supplied both in abundance.... The commentators offer information on the nature and methods of the university instruction, on medieval attitudes toward mythology and the pagan gods, toward sacred and profane history, toward woman and her evil wiles, and toward the sensual weakness of man.

47. *The Latin Poems Commonly Attributed to Walter Map*, ed. Thomas Wright (Hildesheim: Georg Olms, 1841, rpt. 1968).

48. Ibid., p. viii.

49. Pratt, "Jankyn's Book," p. 9; Claus Uhlig, *Hofkritik im England des Mittelalters und der Renaissance* (Berlin: Walter de Gruyter, 1973), p. 105. In the *De nugiis* "wird das Leben bei Hofe zum ersten Mal nicht aus der moralistischen Sicht eines Klerikers, sondern aus der unbefangenen Perspektive eines mitten darin stehenden Höflings beschrieben."

50. Delhaye, "Le Dossier," p. 80.

51. Quintilian suggests that a *persuasio* or a *dissuasio* ought to begin with a short introduction saying something about the author (*Inst.*, Book III, ch. viii, para. 11–12). This should be followed by a statement of the case:

> ... it is generally necessary to give a circumstantial detail of the affair so as to move their passions which is the great point to be considered in such assemblies. In order to do this, we are frequently to rouse and to calm their resentments; we are to work upon their fears, their wishes, their hatred and to touch every spring of their passion.

Map does precisely that.

52. See Joan Crow, "A Little Known Manuscript of the *Quinze Joyes de Mariage*," *Studies in Medieval French*, ed. E. A. Frances (Oxford: Clarendon Press, 1961), p. 1.

53. Because Europa is not an active seductive force in the story, clearly there must be what R. Krautheimer calls a "tertium comparationis" at work here: a base of comparison which is not formal but

iconographic and refers not to likeness of narrative detail but to a common meaning or function.

54. Valerius' *exempla* are ambiguous because of the obvious erudition and playful tone of the work and not necessarily because of the subject matter. Churchmen have been noted for describing women who were the innocent victims of men's lust as seducers. Jacob's daughter, Dinah, for instance, is often blamed for the tragedy of her family because she "allowed" herself to be raped, and sometimes a wife or sister is invented for Judas to account for his treachery.

55. Paul Lehmann, *Die Parodie im Mittelalter,* 2nd ed. (Stuttgart: Anton Hiersemann, 1963), p. 122.

56. *Gallic Salt,* ed. and trans. Robert Harrison (Berkeley, CA: University of California Press, 1974).

57. Hugh of Folietto, *De nuptiis libri duo, PL* 176, col. 1212. Felix Bock, *Aristoteles Theophrastus Seneca de matrimonio,* Leipziger Studien XIX (1899), pp. 1ff., had proposed that Hugh used a now lost intermediary for his quotes from Theophrastus' *Liber aureolus* and not Jerome's *Adversus Jovinianum.* This would make Hugh's treatise extremely important. His theory, however, has been refuted by Ernst Bickel, *Diatribe in Senecae philosophi fragmenta,* Vol. 1, *Fragmenta de Matrimonio* (Leipzig: B. G. Teubner, 1915), pp. 26ff.

58. Delhaye, "Le Dossier," p. 83.

59. Particularly popular were the *Dolopathos,* a collection of *exempla* illustrating female perfidy and lasciviousness, told by seven sages and the *Disciplina Clericalis,* a collection of Oriental *exempla* by the converted Spanish Jew Petrus Alphonsus. Several of these *exempla* found their way into sermons and examples-collections.

60. Even though Hugh's treatise is by far less known than the other twelfth century misogamous tracts, it was included in one of the earliest manuscripts of misogamous compilations. Pratt comments ("Jankyn's Book," p. 13):

> [in MS. no. 550 in Lambeth Palace] under the title "De periculo coniu-
> gis," after a brief preface are found Theophrastus, excerpts from Jerome,
> passages from the Book of Proverbs ... this compilation [which precedes
> the *Valerius*] is actually a little known treatise, De nuptiis, by Hugh of
> Folietto.

61. Peter of Blois, *Epistola LXXIX ad R. amicum suum*, PL 207, col. 243–246.

62. Pio Rajna, "Tre studi per la storia del libro di Andrea Capellano," *Studi di Filologia Romanza*, 5 (1891), pp. 266–272.

63. Rajna argues that both the *De arte honeste amandi* and the *De dissuasione uxorationis* are the works of Andreas Fieschi.

64. The longevity of philosophic misogamy is observed, among others, by Nietzsche. Nietzsche, himself unmarried, comments on the continuous tradition of philosophic celibacy in his *Genealogy of Morals*. He numbers Heraclitus, Plato, Descartes, Spinoza, Leibniz, Kant and Schopenhauer among the unmarried.

65. See Henry C. Lea, *Sacerdotal Celibacy*, pp. 164ff.; J. Gilchrist, *The Church*, pp. 98ff.

66. Henry C. Lea, *Sacerdotal Celibacy*, p. 209.

Chapter 4

1. Henry C. Lea, *Sacerdotal Celibacy in the Christian Church* (Philadelphia: J. B. Lippincott, 1967), p. 209, notes that the many students who streamed to twelfth- and thirteenth-century universities could not all be absorbed by the Church, and many of them remained unbeneficed; for many, their learning (i.e., their "philosophy") was the only marketable commodity and means of livelihood. The statistics of the situation are significant: by the end of the twelfth century, approximately one out of every twelve adult males was a cleric. The enormous growth in the number of secular clergy and monks is evident in English records: 850 in 1066, but 5,000 in 1154.

2. See, for example, Martha C. Howell, "Citizenship and Gender: Women's Political Status in Northern Medieval Cities" in *Women and Power in the Middle Ages*, ed. Mary Erler and Maryanne Kowaleski (Athens, GA: University of Georgia Press, 1988).

3. Vern L. Bullough, *The Subordinate Sex* (Urbana, IL: University of Illinois Press, 1973), p. 173; see also Carolyn Walker Bynum, *Jesus as Mother* (Berkeley, CA: University of California Press, 1982) which cautions against seeing in the popularity of maternal and feminine imagery, any increase in respect for actual women, lay or religious.

4. Eleanor McLaughlin, "Equality of Souls, Inequality of Sexes: Woman in Medieval Theology" in Rosemary Ruether, *Religion and Sexism: Images of Women in the Jewish and Christian Tradition* (New York: Simon and Schuster, 1974), p. 254.

5. Janice Raymond, *A Passion for Friends* (Boston: Beacon Press, 1986), pp. 99–105; Brenda M. Bolten, "Mulieres Sanctae," in *Medieval Women*, ed. Derek Baker (Oxford: Basil Blackwell, 1978); R. W. Southern, *Western Society and the Church in the Middle Ages* (Harmondsworth: Penguin Books, 1970), pp. 309–31; Bynum, *Holy Feast and Holy Fast: the Religious Significance of Food to Medieval Women* (Berkeley: University of California Press, 1987), p. 193, on the barriers to female mendicancy.

6. Thomas Aquinas, *Summa Theologiae: The Basic Writings of Saint Thomas Aquinas*, Vol. 1, ed. A. C. Pegis (New York: Random House, 1945).

7. David Herlihy, "Land, Family, and Women in Continental Europe, 701–1200," *Women in Medieval Society*, ed. Susan Mosher Stuard, p. 17.

8. Ibid., p. 30.

9. Innocent III, *De misera conditionis humane*, ed. Robert E. Lewis (Athens, GA: University of Georgia Press, 1978), p. 170.

10. See Augustine, *Doctrina de bonis matrimonii quam colligit et exposuit Amandus Reuter* (Rome: Universitatis Gregorianae, 1942), especially pp. 41–62, 172–80.

11. Augustine, *De bono coniugali, The Fathers of the Church*, Vol. 27, ed. R. J. Deferrari, trans. C. T. Wilcox (Washington: Catholic University of America Press, 1955), ch. 11, p. 25.

12. Augustine, *De bono coniugali*, ch. 6, pp. 16–17.

13. John T. Noonan, *Contraception* (Cambridge: Harvard University Press, 1966), p. 151.

14. The emergence of scientific jurisprudence was just another facet of the widespread cultural revival of the twelfth-century renaissance. The rediscovery of Roman law in the late eleventh century led to the founding of a school of civil law glossators at Bologna. Growth of interest in the civil law was soon paralleled by canonical developments. For a concise account of early canon law developments and the importance of Gratian and his successors, see Walter Ullmann,

Law and Politics in the Middle Ages (London: Sources of History Limited, 1975), ch. 4, 5.

15. See Elizabeth M. Makowski, "The Conjugal Debt and Medieval Canon Law," *Journal of Medieval History*, 3 (1977), pp. 99–114.

16. Huguccio, *Summa* C. 32 q. 2 c. 2 ad v. *quod enim*, as cited in Rudolf Weigand, "Die Lehre der Kanonisten des 12. and 13. Jahrhunderts von den Ehezwecken," *Studia Gratiana*, Vol. 12, p. 471.

17. Huguccio, *Summa* C. 32 q. 2 c. 4 ad v. *set et elia*, p. 472.

18. Ibid., D. 13, p. 472.

19. Innocent III, *On the Seven Penitential Psalms: 4*, as cited in Noonan, *Contraception*, p. 197.

20. *Glossa ordinaria* to the *Decretum* in *Corpus iuris canonici* (Rine 1584), C. 33 q. 4 c. 7, p. 1691.

21. Ibid., C. 33 q. 4 c. 1, p. 1689; C. 33 q. 5 c. 21, p. 1693.

22. Ibid., C. 32 q. 2 c. 3, p. 1497; C. 27 q. 1 c. 21, p. 1401.

23. Noonan, *Contraception*, pp. 316–20.

24. *Digest* 24.1.32.13; 50.17.30, in *Corpus iuris civilis*, ed. Krueger, Mommsen, Schoell & Kroll, 3 vols (Berlin: Weidmann, 1872–95); see also P. Corbett, *The Roman Law of Marriage* (Oxford: Claredon Press, 1930), pp. 56, 57, 68; G. E. Howard, *A History of Matrimonial Institutions* (Chicago: University of Chicago Press, 1904), p. 291; for an idea of the way in which the Roman law was modified by the canonists, see, J. T. Noonan, "Power to Choose," *Viator*, 4 (1973), pp. 419–34; James A. Brundage, "Concubinage and Marriage in Medieval Canon Law," *Journal of Medieval History*, I, no. 1 (1975), pp. 6–7.

25. Derrick Sherwin Bailey, *Sexual Relation in Christian Thought* (New York: Harper & Brothers, 1959), p. 138.

26. See, for instance, *Decretum Gratiani* in *Corpus iuris canonici*, ed. Emil Friedberg, Vol. I (Leipzig: B. Tauchnitz, 1879; rpt. Graz: Akademische druck-u verlagsanstalt, 1959), C. 27 q. 2 c. 2, 3 and 9; Rolandus Bandinelli, *Summa*, ed. F. Thaner (Innsbruck: Wagner, 1874; rp. Aalen Scientia Verlag, 1962), C. 27 q. 2, p. 128; Rufinus of Bologna, *Summa decretorum*, ed. Heinrich Singer (Paderborn, West Germany: F. Schonigh, 1902; rp. Aalen Scientia Verlag, 1963),

C. 27 q. 2, p. 445; *Glossa ordinaria* to the *Decretum,* C. 27 q. 2 c. 10, p. 1415; Gerard Fransen, "La formation du lien matrimonial au moyenâge," *Revue de droit canonique,* Vol. 21, 1971, p. 108.

27. See C. 32 q. 7 c. 25; Rolandus, *Summa* C. 33 q. 1, p. 189; *Summa Parisiensis,* C. 32 q. 5 c. 16, p. 246.

28. Bailey, *Sexual Relation,* pp. 129–41; G. H. Joyce, *Christian Marriage: An Historical and Doctrinal Study* (London: Sheed and Ward, 1948), pp. 150ff; *Dictionaire de théologie catholique,* Vol. 9, (Paris: Letouzey et Ane, 1903–1950 (i. e. 1899–1950)), ed. A. Vacant, E. Mangenot, E. Amann, pp. 2066–208; Seamus Heany, *The Development of the Sacramentality of Marriage from Anselm of Laon to Thomas Aquinas* (Washington: Catholic University of America Press, 1963); Rudolf Weigand, "Das Scheidungsproblem in der mittelalterlichen Kanonistik," *Theologische Quartalschrift,* 151, no. 1 (1971), pp. 52–60; Gabriel La Bras, "Le mariage dans la théologie et le droit de l'Eglise du XI au XIII siècle," *Cahiers de Civilisation Médiévale,* 2 (1968), pp. 193–94.

29. C. 27 q. 2 d. p. c. 34 and 39; see above as well.

30. Paucapalea, *Summa über das Decretum Gratiani,* ed. J. F. Schulte (Giessen: Emil Roth, 1890; rp. Aalen Scientia Verlag, 1965), C. 27 q. 2 c. 10, p. 115.

31. Rolandus, *Summa* C. 27 q. 2 d. p. c. 17, p. 129.

32. Rufinus, *Summa* C. 27 q. 2, p. 441.

33. Huguccio, *Summa* C. 27 q. 2, pp. 764, 793; Heany, *The Development,* p. 18.

34. *Glossa ordinaria* to the *Decretum* C. 1 q. 1 c. 1, p. 517 and C. 32 q. 2 c. 13, p. 1502.

35. Rufinus, *Summa* C. 32 q. 2, p. 481.

36. Joannes Andreae, *Novella commentaria in libros decretalium* 3.32.1 (Venice: F. Franciscum, 1581; rpt. Turin: Bottega d'Erasmo, 1963), 1.*de sac unctione*.1, no. 15, pp. 170–71; see also, Hostiensis, *Lectura in quinque libros decretalium commentaria* (Venice: Iuntas, 1581; rpt. Turin: Bottega d'Erasmo, 1965), 1.*de sac unctione*.1, p. 111a; Hostiensis, *Summa aurea* (Lyons: n. p., 1537), 1.*de sac unctione,* p. 35 and 1.*de sac. non iterandis* no. 7, p. 36 ra.

37. Gerald Owst, *Literature and Pulpit in Medieval England,* 2nd ed. (New York: Barnes and Noble, 1961).

38. Ibid., p. 386.

39. Ibid., p. 384.

40. Ibid., p. 385.

41. Arthur Moore, *Studies in a Medieval Prejudice, Antifeminism* (Diss., Vanderbilt University, 1943).

42. Ibid., p. 22.

43. Ibid., p. 23.

44. August Wulff, *Die Frauenfeindlichen Dichtungen in den Romanischen Literaturen des Mittelalters* (Halle a. S.: Druck von E. Karras, 1914).

45. *Gallic Salt,* ed. and trans. Robert Harrison (Berkeley CA: University of California Press, 1974).

46. The two conveniently available editions of the poem are *Latin Poems Commonly Attributed to Walter Map,* ed. Thomas Wright, 1841 (Hildesheim, 1968), pp. 77–85; and *Poésies populaires Latines du Moyen Âge,* ed. Edélstand Du Méril (Geneva: Slatkine Reprints, 1977), pp. 179–86. Moore, *Studies,* p. 29, says, "If there is one distinguishing point between the 'Dissuasio Valerii' and the 'Golias de conjuge non ducenda,' it is the sparkling wit of the former as contrasted with the heavy and malicious crudeness of the latter." [I see no heavy crudeness nor lack of wit in the *De conjuge,* but rather, a great deal of sophisticated subtlety. —K. W.]

47. Wright, *Latin Poems,* p. 78.

48. *Reliquiae Antiquae,* ed. Thomas Wright and James Orchard (London: W. Pickering, 1841–43), p. 168.

49. *Miracles de Notre Dame par Personages,* Vol. 3, no. 19, ed. G. Paris and V. Robert (Paris: F. Didot, 1848–1900).

50. The connection, as stated above, occurs already in Aristotle's *Parva Naturalia;* i.e., that too much work and too frequent intercourse shorten the lifespan of the male.

51. *Die Disciplina Clericalis des Petrus Alfonsi,* ed. Alfons Hilke and Warner Soderhjelm (Heidelberg: C. Winter, 1911).

52. Golias in the Latin of the Vulgate refers to Goliath, a giant, with whom the Israelites struggled for forty days. It was in this sense of wickedness, as an Antichrist, that Bernard of Clairvaux referred to Abelard as a Golias. Eventually, Golias became a kind of anti-hero associated with peripatetic, often rapacious, clerks. This certainly is the sense in which Giraldus Cambrensis refers to a certain "parasite named Golias" whose lechery and calumnious poems Giraldus is eager to castigate. Twenty poems are ascribed to Golias, but they do not show consistency of authorship. Most of them were written in England and are satires directed against the corruptions of the clergy.

53. Not all translations, of course, make this case patent. The thirteenth-century French translation of the *De conjuge* appears under the title *Diatribe contre le mariage* in company with miscellaneous misogynistic texts in the MS Harleian 2253 (reprinted in *Latin Poems*, pp. 292–94). It is a free translation of the Latin original into 178 octosyllabic lines addressed not to Golias but to a certain Gawein. The translator follows the original quite closely and records faithfully the speeches of the three angels. Johannes' speech (p. 294), however, is interpolated with a string of woeful apostrophes:

> Allas! fet-il, ge unge fu mary!
> Allas! fet-ele, qu unque vus vy!
> Allas! fet-yl, que su vyfs!
> Allas! fet-ele, qu unge vus pris!
> Allas! de su, allas! de la, etc.

Another interpolation occurs at the end of the poem where the translator gives profuse thanks for his escape from the pain and suffering of matrimony.

The English version of the poem, which Wright places in the fifteenth century, but Wolff in the fourteenth century, is substantially different enough from the original to warrant discussion. The poem appears under the title "The payne an sorowe of evyll maryage," and one of the versions is written, as Wright observes, "very much in the style of John Lydgate," who, incidentally, is the author of several misogynistic tracts according to F. Utley's compilation of such titles as the *Crooked Rib* (Columbus: Ohio State University Press, 1944), p. 63). The English version consists of sixteen stanzas of seven lines each while the printed edition of Wynkyn de Worde has seven extra stanzas.

The first part of the translation follows the original closely until the end of Petrus' speech. From there until the end of the poem the speeches of the other two angels are summarized. The famous Solomonic allusion is repeated and (unlike the original) the quote is identified: "Solomon saith ther be thyngis thre, / shrewed wyfes, rayne, and smokes blake, / Makith husbands there howses to forsake." The translator also includes a moral to the story and concludes with an exhortation to young men to eschew marriage. The didactic intent is even further emphasized in the Wynkyn de Worde edition, which begins (p.295) with the stanza exhorting young people to learn and profit from the lesson of the *De conjuge*:

> Take hede and lerne thou lytell chylde, and se
> That tyme passed wyl no agayne retourne
> And in they youthe unto vertues use the.
> Lette in thy brest no manner vyce sojourne,
> That in thyne age thou have no cause to mourne
> For tyme lost, not for defaute of wytte:
> Thynke on this lesson, and in thy mynde it shytte

Both translations omit the setting in the valley of Mambre and substitute a bland *locus amoenus* setting. Thus, the irony of the poem is greatly downplayed, while (by means of the exhortatory introduction and conclusion) and didacticism and applicability are emphasized.

54. Jean de Meung, *Le Roman de la Rose*, ed. Daniel Poirion (Paris: Garnier-Flammarion, 1974). References to lines in this work appear parenthetically in the text. Translations from: *The Roman of the Rose*, trans. Harry W. Robbins (New York: Dutton, 1962).

55. On the fragments of Chaucer's translation of the *Roman* and the controversy surrounding it, see *The Romaunt of the Rose and the Roman de la Rose, a Parallel Text Edition*, ed. Ronald Southerland (Berkeley, CA: University of California Press, 1968).

56. On Christine and the *Querelle*, see L. McDowell Richardson, *The Forerunners of Feminism in French Literature of the Renaissance from Christine of Pizan to Marie de Gournay* (Baltimore: Johns Hopkins University Press, 1979); C. C. Willard, "A Fifteenth-Century View of Women's Role in Medieval Society: Christine de Pizan's Livre e des Trois Vertus," *The Role of Women*, ed. Rosemarie Morewedge, (Albany: SUNY Press, 1975) pp. 90–120; Enid McLeod, *The Order*

of the Rose: The Life and Ideas of Christine de Pizan (London: Chatto and Windus, 1976). Willard says (pp. 95–96):

> This poem [the *Epitre au Dieu d'Amour,* 1399] and possibly the *Dit de la Rose* (1403) certainly belong logically with the series of letters which she [Christine] exchanged with Gontier Col and Jean de Montreuil over the literary and moral values represented by the *Romance of the Rose,* even though we have no way of knowing whether the connection was intended or fortuitous. It was perhaps inevitable that the question of the slanderous attitude towards women expressed by Jean de Meung should arise, although it is less certain that this is the basic premise of the letter. . . . Christine was at most merely pointing out flaws in Jean de Meung's logic in his censure of women. . . .

57. Lionel Friedman, "Jean de Meung, Antifeminism and Bourgeois Realism," *Modern Philology, 57* (1959–60), p. 1323.

58. The amplification of this Theophrastian topos in most medieval works of general satire is not surprising in view of the insolubility of Christian matrimony. Both Deschamps and Chaucer enlarge on the topos in a similar way and Matheolus even suggests a "trial period."

59. Henry A. Kelly, *Love and Marriage in the Age of Chaucer* (Ithaca, NY: Cornell University Press, 1975), p. 41.

60. A favorite saying of churchmen; quoted by G. Rattray Taylor, *Sex in History* (New York: The Vanguard Press, 1954), p. 20.

61. *Les Lamentations de Matheolus et le Livre de leesce de Jehan Le Fevre de Resson,* édition critique, edited by A. G. van Hamel (Paris: E. Bouillon, 1892–1905). Referred to in text as *Matheoli Lamentationes.* Translations provided by authors.

62. *Les Quinze Joyes de Mariage,* ed. Joan Crow (Oxford: Basil Blackwell, 1969), p.1; *Les Quinze Joies de Mariage,* ed. Jean Rychner (Geneva: Libraire Droz; Paris: Libraire Minard, 1963). References to this work will appear parenthetically in the text.

63. Ibid., pp. ix ff.

64. Joan Crow, "A Little Known Manuscript of the *Quinze Joyes de Mariage,*" *Studies in Medieval French,* ed. E. A. Frances (Oxford: Clarendon Press, 1961), pp. 139ff.

65. Ibid., p. 139.

66. Crow, *Les Quinze Joyes* pp. viii ff.

67. Christine de Pisan, "Les Joyes de Notre Dame," *Ouvres Poétiques*, Vol. III, ed. M. Roy (Paris: Firmin Didot, 1896), pp. 11–14. Jean Rychner, pp. viii, ix says, "Si donc les joies de mariage sont au nombre de quinze, c'est que, sans révérence, l'auteur a parodié le titre d'une prière à la Vierge, les Quinze joies de Notre Dame dont on connaît plusieurs versions dès le XIIIe siècle.

68. Cf. Crow, *Les Quinze Joyes* pp. viii ff.

69. Eustach Deschamps, *Ouvres Complétes,* ed. Gaston Raynaud; (Paris: Firmin Didot, 1894).

70. *Le Miroir de Mariage,* Ouvres Complètes d'Eustache Deschamps, Vol. IX: ed. Gaston Raynaud (Société des Anciens Textes Français.)

71. John L. Lowes, "Chaucer and the *Miroir de Mariage,*" *Modern Philology*, VIII (1910–ll) pp. 165–86, 305–334.

72. John C. McGalliard, "Chaucer's Merchant's Tale and Deschamps' *Miroir de Mariage,*" *Philological Quarterly*, XXV (1946), p. 200.

73. Geoffrey Chaucer, *Riverside Chaucer,* 3rd ed., ed. Larry D. Benson (Boston: Houghton Mifflin, 1987).

74. George Lyman Kittredge, *Chaucer and His Poetry* (Cambridge MA: Harvard University Press, 1915), pp. 185–210.

75. Henry Barrett Hinckley, "The Debate on Marriage in the *Canterbury Tales,*" *PMLA*, 32 (1917), pp. 292–305; Marie Neville, "The Function of the Squire's Tale in the Canterbury Scheme," *JEGP,* 50 (1951), pp. 167–79; William Laurence, "The Marriage Group in the *Canterbury Tales,*" *Modern Philology*, 11 (1913), pp. 247–58.

76. Laurence, "The Marriage Group," pp. 248 ff.

77. See, for example, Clifford P. Lyons, "The Marriage Debate in the *Canterbury Tales,*" *ELH* 2 (1935), 252–62; and Steven Axelrod, "The Wife of Bath and the Clerk." *Annuale Mediaevale,* 15 (1974) pp. 109–24, says that, actually, the Wife has her eye on the Clerk as Husband Number Six.

78. D. W. Robertson *A Preface to Chaucer, Studies in Medieval Perspective* (Princeton, NJ Princeton University Press, 1962), p. 320.

79. Ibid., p. 322.

80. See, for example, Lowes, "Chaucer and the Miroir."

81. Ritamary Bradley, "The Wife of Bath's Tale and the Mirror Tradition" *JEGP,* 55 (1956) pp. 624–30.

Conclusion

1. Christine de Pisan, "The Debate over the Romance of the Rose" in Katharina M. Wilson, *Medieval Women Writers,* (Athens, GA: University of Georgia Press, 1984), p. 344.

INDEX